PIANO

PIANO

PIENO

Susan McKenna Grant

PIANO

PIANO

PIENO

Authentic Food from a Tuscan Farm

Photographs by Michael Grant

HarperCollins*PublishersLtd*

Piano, Piano, Pieno
© 2006 by Susan McKenna Grant,
photography © 2006 Michael Grant. All rights reserved.

Published by HarperCollins Publishers Ltd

First Edition

No part of this book may be used or reproduced in any manner
whatsoever without the prior written permission of the publisher,
except in the case of brief quotations embodied in reviews.

The following individuals and publishers have generously given
permission to use quotations from copyrighted works. Excerpt
on page x from *La Stampa*, by Carlo Petrini. Copyright 2005.
Reprinted by permission of Slow Food®. Excerpt on page 7
from *Honey from a Weed* by Patience Gray. Copyright 2004.
Reprinted by permission of the estate of Patience Gray and the
publisher, Prospect Books. Excerpt on page 8 from a sundial
in Liguria, source unknown. Excerpt on page 9 from *The Art
of Eating* newsletter (Spring 1992) by Ed Behr. Copyright 1992.
Reprinted by permission of the author.

Every effort has been made to trace ownership of quotations
used in this book. In the event of an inadvertent omission or
error, please contact the publisher.

HarperCollins books may be purchased for educational,
business, or sales promotional use through our Special
Markets Department.

HarperCollins Publishers Ltd
2 Bloor Street East, 20th Floor
Toronto, Ontario, Canada
M4W 1A8

www.harpercollins.ca

Library and Archives Canada Cataloguing in Publication

Grant, Susan McKenna
Piano, piano, pieno : authentic food from a Tuscan farm /
Susan McKenna Grant. — 1st ed.

ISBN-13: 978-0-00-639552-2
ISBN-10: 0-00-639552-X

1. Cookery, Italian. 2. Tuscany—Description and travel.
I. Title.

TX723.2.N65G72 2006   641.5945
C2005-905539-1

RRD 9 8 7 6 5 4 3 2 1

Printed and bound in the United States
Design by Sharon Kish • Set in Jenson and Opsmarckt

Project
benefactor
Slow Food Foundation
for Biodiversity
2006

The Slow Food Foundation for Biodiversity was created by
the Slow Food movement in partnership with the Region of
Tuscany, recognizing that the appreciation of gastronomy must
include the additional step of safeguarding our gastronomic
resources. The author's advance royalties have been used to
adopt the Slow Food Presidium for Polish Mead.

In memory of
Evelyn Susan and
William Thomas McKenna

Contents

Preface

It was at the beginning of the millennium, with half my life spent and the other half yet to go, that I decided to throw my lot in with the Italians and move my household, including myself, two dogs and a husband (who would become somewhat of a commuter), to Italy. In the heart of Tuscany, halfway between Florence and Siena, we discovered La Petraia, an ancient property set proudly on top of the Chianti Mountains. Its 165 acres had been abandoned as a working farm more than fifty years earlier, but the property was a beauty. It offered us the promise of grapes, olives and the restoration of a large chestnut forest. Wild game roamed freely, including mouflon, boar, deer, hare, pheasant and fox. Petraia's distinction of being one of the highest farms in the Chianti Classico zone allowed us to see Siena's *campanile* and *duomo* on the southern horizon. The twenty miles of undulating hills in between we found dotted with just a few ancient towers, a view that has remained unchanged for several centuries. We decided we wanted her and she agreed to have us, which

is how I began a new adventure as an *imprenditrice agricola*—in other words, a farmer.

Tuscany is a place where people can, and do, look a long way back before taking a step forward. The wisdom that comes from this I find reassuring and often lacking in our North American culture. When we became owners of La Petraia, we discovered we had inherited an Etruscan archeological site named Piazza di Siena, buried on a thickly wooded peak just above our house. It's not hard to see why the Etruscans picked such a magical spot to settle. From here, looking south, you can see halfway to Rome. To the east are breathtaking views of the famous Arno Valley, beyond which rises a series of mountain ranges, first the Pratomagno, then the often snow-covered Casentino, and finally the majestic Apennine range that forms Italy's spinal column. To the south-west is the same mythical view of Siena we have from the house. Perhaps it was Etruscans from Piazza di Siena who first cleared our fields millennia ago. Maybe they were the ones to name this place Petraia, suggesting a stony land, or a quarry. Today you don't walk far here without stumbling over remnants of their history. The property is littered with stones, many of which show the signs of ancient handiwork. It's hard sometimes, on summer evenings, not to imagine an Etruscan whisper in the breeze as the mountain air sweeps down from Piazza di Siena, refreshing us after a long day spent restoring Petraia's proud heritage.

Most Italians don't believe me when I tell them I came here to farm. The first assumption is that I've come for love, to marry an Italian. The second is that I don't really live here, I just play at it, being one of the throngs of *stranieri* who own holiday homes in Tuscany. Lastly there is a suspicion I am *in pensione*, an odd concept to me, being nowhere near retirement age by North American standards. When I am able to convince someone I came to Italy to live and work as a farmer, I am prepared for a skeptical headshake, a chuckle or even an outburst of hysterical laughter. But the longer I stay, the more I detect an ounce or two of respect in the laughter. Is it possible they are laughing *with* me now, not *at* me?

By local standards, La Petraia is considered a rather lonely and remote place. Its location, about fifteen minutes' drive outside Radda in Chianti, on top of a mountain and a mile up a rather steep dirt road, is a bit off the beaten track. But many people have heard the rumor of her existence. I've met people as far away as Florence and Siena, each an hour's drive, who know of Petraia, yet someone born and raised two miles away is apt never to have set foot here. To someone with a Canadian psyche (such a big, empty country), living on a property like this doesn't feel the least bit absurd, but it certainly seems curious to many Italians. Everyone knows Italy is a challenging place to carry on a life. The idea that a female *straniera* would volunteer for this punishment, particularly in a place so *isolato*, is hard to buy. Especially when Canada is not just *bellissimo* but a perfectly organized country, home to the world's finest peacekeeping forces and some of its most progressive politicians. For Italians, who seem so much more visually cognitive than the average human, it is the travelogues on the *ti-vu* that account for this adoration of my homeland. There is the Great Canadian Wilderness, Niagara Falls, the Rocky Mountains and the picturesque fishing villages of the Maritime provinces. Why would anyone leave, particularly to come here?

In reality, starting a business here is full of trial and tribulation. Not a healthy place for the meek or the weak of heart. The bureaucracy is even more horrific than its infamous reputation, and accomplishing the simplest task takes ridiculous amounts of time and energy. Here you learn to add a year or two to all estimates given. So unusual did my request for a visa to live and work the land I own seem to the Italian immigration officials, it took me two years to obtain the necessary permissions to live

on my own farm as a self-employed person. I was repeatedly told that my case was *molto particolare*, very unique. I was a "reverse immigrant," a type they had little experience dealing with.

In Italy there is a long tradition of foreign writers whose perspective is that of the traveler who's been seduced, stayed awhile and maybe bought a vacation or retirement home. Their real lives are anchored firmly elsewhere, and the pictures they paint, while true, lack the depth that comes from putting roots down in a place. Then there are writers like Luigi Barzini, Charles Richards and Tobias Jones who by birth, for love or for work are firmly planted in this soil. Their Italy is a gloomier, more sinister place, with, as Tobias Jones suggests, "a dark heart." I have glimpsed that dark heart and I remain seduced.

I've heard it said that there are virtually no Italians alive today who are more than one generation from the land. After a decade spent traveling and living in Italy, I believe this is true. Most people I know own a bit of land somewhere, even if they are hardcore city dwellers. If not, there is usually a *zia*, a *nonna* or a *cugina* they depend on for their annual supply of wine, oil, vegetables and fruit. With a bit of land you are *ricca*. You are rich because you have the ability to supply yourself with a better quality of life than your money can buy, and you are rich because you have a connection with the life your ancestors led and with *la natura*. Therein lies the promise of a true *dolce vita*.

There is, among Italian "foodies," which is to say Italians, great knowledge of and respect for traditional and homegrown foods. Preserving, for example, is something many people do. Tomatoes are faithfully made into sauce, fruit into *marmellata*. Other vegetables, like eggplant, peppers, beans, mushrooms and cucumbers are preserved in oil (*sott'olio*) or vinegar (*sott'aceto*). Food bought in stores is inevitably suspect, purchased only after much consideration, examination and discussion. The owner of the fruit and vegetable shop wears white surgical gloves and picks out your tomatoes for you to ensure they are not bruised or mauled. She's a skilled matchmaker, a seasoned professional whose job is to pair you with the perfect produce. She wants to know what your intentions are for these tomatoes and when you plan to serve them. You are expected to play your role in the operation, standing vigilantly and suspiciously by her side, ready to pounce if anything less than perfect lands in your bag.

Our nearest market town, a small city of about 23,000 people, is a forty-minute drive but just fifteen miles of hairpin curves away. I travel there every so often to replenish my larder at our nearest shopping center. The main attraction is a huge supermarket that would not be out of place in any large North American suburb. Next door to this development, in an *anni sessanta*, or sixties-style, townhouse, lives a woman who keeps a flock of chickens in her modern garage. The hens are often out free-ranging on the pavement near the entrance to the supermarket. Shoppers arriving and departing from the mall must keep their wits about them in order not to run over one of them. This sort of individual determination and enterprise has managed to keep such superstores at bay in Italy for years. Like everywhere else, this is changing fast, but it has been touching images like this, refusing the future's plea, that inspired me to come here to live, to work and then to write this book.

Susan McKenna Grant
La Petraia, 2005

Introduction

The idea of moving to Italy to farm was not much of a stretch for me. Both of my parents had farmed, and so farming was, as they say, in my blood. My husband and I had long shared a dream of finding a rural property where we might become self-sufficient. A good part of our first decade together was spent travelling through Europe and North America in search of an earthly paradise where we could plant some roots. The discovery of La Petraia, the property we now own, turned this dream into a reality.

Along with farming, I was intent on turning La Petraia into an *agriturismo*, giving me the opportunity to open a small, intimate dining room and offer meals to overnight guests. A farm shop would provide the outlet for our production of wine, honey, oil, preserves and breads.

I started to record the most successful menus I put together for our visitors. Many of the recipes in this book are based on those meals, which in turn came from the traditional foods of north and central Italy.

The recipes in these pages, with the exception of a few of my own dishes inspired by our farm, are based on authentic regional foods. But since it is almost impossible to find two Italians who agree on the right way to make anything, they are a far cry from definitive. More often than not, these are dishes I have eaten repeatedly in the regions they come from over more than a decade. The majority are traditional interpretations, but there are also some modern ones. These were added to give readers a glimpse into one of the most essential and often overlooked elements of the Italian food experience. Italian food today is not all governed by *la cucina povera,* the rustic and delicious foods that made famous the country's kitchen. It is also influenced by countless inventive chefs who take their inspiration from time-honored customs and an astounding selection of high-quality local ingredients. These chefs are using their legacy to create ingenious new dishes that bring to light the harmony, so fundamentally Italian, in the pairing of elegance and rusticity.

I use the order of the classic Italian meal composed of many small courses as my format. It is a way of eating I've adopted and come to appreciate. For the cook, several courses of equal importance provide endless scope for expression and exploration. A greater variety of food can be introduced at each meal, and we are encouraged to linger longer at the table, enjoying our company. Our digestion and sense of well-being are enhanced, and we feel truly satisfied. Carlo Petrini, founder of the Slow Food movement, perhaps sums all of this up best when he talks about his concept of "conviviality," something that lies at the heart of his incredible organization. The same sympathies are expressed in the terms "soul food" and "comfort food," opposites of "junk food" and "fast food." This food slows us down and fills us up. It inspired the title of this book, *Piano, Piano, Pieno,* or "Slowly, Slowly, Full."

In Italy, meals are such important events that they often possess a theatrical quality, first in the planning and anticipation, then in the production and presentation, and finally in the reception and endless deliberating by the audience. No matter where you are—at the market, the hairdresser, on the local bus or waiting in line at the post office— men and women alike are discussing what they had for dinner last night or what they plan on eating today. Even a *panino* taken standing up in a bar can be pretty heady stuff once it gets dissected like this. You may find the *rucola* grows wild; the *lardo* is made in a small village just above the quarries of Carrara and preserved in marble caskets; the cheese is Maccagno, made only with milk from a certain few cows still allowed to graze all summer long on the Alpine pastures of Monte Rosa, Europe's second-highest peak; or the bread, a *pane Toscano,* currently applying for Italy's second *denominazione di origine protetta* (DOP) bread designation, is baked only in wood-burning ovens, never contains salt and is made using a sourdough starter with wheat grown exclusively in Tuscany.

This fascination with food, found not just in Italy but all over Europe, is a reflection of the importance placed on culinary heritage and tradition. Each dish, every ingredient, has a story to be told and a reason to be celebrated. For a North American of European descent, these stories form an important part of the legacy my ancestors left to me. Coming to Europe to live and work has given me a way to explore this history and attempt to reclaim some of it as my own. Knowing the story of the food we make for ourselves helps us place it in context, to better respect and appreciate it. In the end this knowledge helps it taste better and do more for us. This is what we mean when we say we have "acquired a taste" for something. What we have really acquired is knowledge, context, history and culture. The good taste is the payoff.

Piano, Piano, Pieno is not so much an Italian cookbook as it is a book written by a Canadian who happens to live and work in Italy. The recipes are Italian. But food we eat today has traveled far and has resonance in many different cultures. I don't know how many times I have eaten something in Italy and said to my husband, "My mother used to make this!" She even said this herself on her visits to us in Italy. She raised her family not on Italian food but on the food she learned how to cook from her mother, a woman whose descendants came to Canada from the British Isles. Six degrees of separation. Maybe less. It is indeed a small planet that we all share.

In general, at La Petraia I cook what I grow or raise myself, along with what I source locally. Over the years I've discovered three principles that guide me in the kitchen. I believe they can be found behind good food everywhere:

- **Quality food: simple, seasonal and local**
- **Time to spend**
- **The most important ingredients**

QUALITY FOOD: SIMPLE, SEASONAL AND LOCAL

This principle I expect you've heard before. Thirty years ago and more, a few inspired cooks and writers, Alice Waters, Richard Olney, Elizabeth David, M.F.K. Fisher, Patience Gray and a host of others, began to change the way we think about what and how we eat. Today many of the world's most revered chefs are religious about presenting seasonal and local food inspired by what nearby farmers have to offer. This notion translates easily to the French concept of *terroir*, which is based on the idea that true appreciation of food and wine is the result of an intimate understanding of place.

Farmers' markets are now springing up in city centers all over the map, providing a wide array of high-quality seasonal products to choose from—fresh game, farmhouse cheeses, rare heirloom vegetables, grass-fed free-range meats and poultry, beautiful hearth-oven breads. Buying what is produced locally is no longer an impractical philosophy, and using these ingredients often brings the reward of better taste. Cooks who follow the seasons can pick from the best-looking local produce harvested at the perfect stage of ripeness. Food like this is best appreciated in its simplest and most unadulterated form—a style of cooking Italians have mastered. Simplicity is the most important ingredient in this book. It is the thing most great cooks have either an intuitive or a hard-earned understanding of and where, more often than not, their brilliance lies.

The cost of seasonal and locally raised food, especially in urban areas, can put it out of reach of many people. But for those who can afford it, spending a bit more now can be considered a good investment in the planet, in our own health and in that of future generations.

"Once we lose touch with the spendthrift aspect of nature's provisions epitomized in the raising of a crop, we are in danger of losing touch with life itself."
Patience Gray,
Honey from a Weed

Time to Spend

A trip to any big supermarket today reveals aisles of hot tables, salad bars, snack foods, breakfast food and other time-saving convenience items. A glance at the average shopping cart going through the checkout tells the story. It appears we must all be saving a great deal of time. Why is it, then, living in this world with every modern convenience imaginable, we seem to be left with less time than our parents had to spend on one of the basic rituals of family life, dinner?

Over the years I have tried to shift my focus away from how I *save* my time to how I *spend* it. It is, after all, a nonrenewable resource. We can't take it with us, so what's the point in saving it? I've gradually increased the time I spend raising, cooking and preserving our food. I make a trip to the supermarket once a month rather than at the end of every busy week. My family is eating healthful, better-tasting and locally raised food. The time I "spend" gardening, foraging, preserving and cooking I find much more enjoyable than the time I used to "save" driving to crowded supermarkets, fighting for a parking spot and competing with every other harried shopper to fill my basket with processed foods and sorry-looking produce from some faraway place.

Living on a farm where I can grow and raise most of my own food affords me a degree of self-sufficiency. I realize this isn't a viable option for most people today, but I think a gradual shift of focus has begun. More and more people are finding it rewarding to spend some time seeking out local farmers' markets or a supermarket that carries the most local produce. Some are even trying to preserve a bit of the harvest. It is also encouraging to see that organic food is one of the fastest-growing sectors of the food business.

THE MOST IMPORTANT INGREDIENTS

The most important ingredients are never found in cookbooks. These are things like passion, respect, culture and love. I have enjoyed more meals in simple *osterie* than in starred restaurants simply because the people doing the cooking understood this basic truth. They believed passionately in what they were doing and eagerly shared their knowledge. They were respectful of their raw materials. The dishes they prepared were local, reflecting their particular culture, climate, heritage and landscape. The recipes they used were ones handed down to them, often with accompanying stories. These were cooks concerned with preserving the "culture" in one of the most endangered words in our vocabulary: *agriculture*. Theirs was the quest for authenticity.

Good food does not have to be fancy or complicated, but it does need to be made with love. Love is one ingredient we have that is free and abundant. In my experience, it gets results in the kitchen. I was fortunate to learn this secret from a mother who was incapable of cooking without it. I can easily tell when it is missing from a meal. It is that certain *je ne sais quoi* that transforms the ordinary into the sublime.

"Most great food has its origins in the family: It either is or it comes from the dishes prepared by grandmothers and mothers and taught to daughters and granddaughters."
Edward Behr,
The Art of Eating,
Spring 1992

A Note on Measurements

For the sake of simplicity, most of the recipes in this book use the imperial system of volume measurement.

Where ingredients can be purchased (and are best added) by weight, and where volume measure is not appropriate (such as for meats, dried mushrooms, sometimes cheese), I give weights first in metric (grams) and next in imperial (ounces), since I am most comfortable working with metric and find it the most accurate.

In the bread chapter and in certain other recipes throughout the book, where weighing ingredients is of critical importance to both the authenticity and the consistency of the result, I list ingredients first in metric and imperial weights (grams and ounces) but have also included imperial volume measures (teaspoons, cups) for readers who are not accustomed to working with a kitchen scale.

Chapter 1 Il Pane ✤ Bread

For me, planning a meal starts here. First I decide what kind of bread to make, and from there I gather the momentum and inspiration for the meal it should accompany. I suppose the intrigue relates to the fact that I am working with a living thing. Creating life to sustain life.

In North America, the first half of the last century saw bread go from a staple many people made at home once or twice a week to something sold in a plastic bag and purchased at a convenience store, a supermarket or even a gas station. Fortunately, a sea change has begun and a booming industry of artisanal bakeries now produces European hearth-style breads. This, in turn, seems to have sparked a renaissance in home baking.

Bread making is part of my daily routine, something quite unusual in the Italian farm community I live in. In Europe this activity has been the reserve of the professional for generations. Home baking is rare and considered somewhat of a lost art. When I talk about bread baking with

my Italian friends, even those of my mother's generation, they wave their hands backwards and say, *"Prima, prima, ricordo mia nonna ha fatto questo"*—"I remember my grandmother doing this a long, long time ago."

I like to keep the bread I make simple and limit the ingredients. Breads containing superfluous ingredients often are a meal in themselves, and the range of foods they complement is limited. On the other hand, a plain white or whole wheat loaf goes with almost anything. The best bread, and the one that disappears the quickest at the table, is made simply using flour, water, a leavening agent and salt. If you use a natural dough starter, you can limit the ingredients to three—flour, water and salt. And it is even possible to eliminate the salt. Tuscan bread contains no salt, and I usually have a loaf on hand at La Petraia. This bread makes wonderful *crostini, fett'unta* and *bruschetta* and goes well with the hearty Tuscan soups and *affettati*, or cured meats, that form an essential part of the local menu. Because salt attracts moisture, its absence in bread prevents the growth of mold and promotes a longer shelf life.

To add a touch of elegance to a special meal, I sometimes do add an ingredient or two to produce a seed bread or walnut loaf. These breads go well with cheese and cured meats; leftovers are good to have on hand for breakfast the next day.

Bread baking is surprisingly simple and extremely forgiving. You can fit it into almost any schedule—it demands but a few meditative moments of your attention a day and equally few pennies from your pocketbook. In return you can keep a supply of tasty and nutritious bread on the table for your family. Throw in a hunk of cheese, some olive oil and a tomato and you have a meal. Add a glass of wine and a salad and you've got a feast. Bread truly is the staff of life, and learning to make it well can easily become a lifelong vocation. I know of few greater joys than waking in the morning to the knowledge that today is a bread-baking day.

Before You Get Started

Pre-ferments

I use organic flour and, for leavening, favor the use of long, slow and easy starters, what the professional baker calls a "pre-ferment." This bread takes time, but like most good things it is worth waiting for. While making a starter may sound like a lot of trouble, it is actually very simple. Once you see the results, you will understand why a pre-ferment is a way to get the most out of your ingredients, to develop flavor and texture and to extend shelf life. All the formulas in this chapter, with the exception of the *focaccia* and the pizza dough, are made using a pre-ferment.

The nomenclature of pre-ferments is complex and can be confusing. Bakers work with sponge-type, stiff starters (*levain-levure* to the French) that use a small amount of commercial yeast and more flour than water. Sometimes a more liquid starter that contains equal parts flour and water with a bit of yeast is preferred, what the French call a *poolish*. Other times  some old dough is used (*pâte fermentée*) to get things under way. The Italian term, which seems to include all kinds of pre-ferments, is *biga*, but bakers in Italy often simply refer to their starter as the *primo impasto* (first mix). For the purposes of this book, I use the term *biga* for the yeasted pre-ferment I prefer, which, like the French *poolish*, is composed of equal parts flour and water by weight.

For a different texture, more complex flavor and more of a challenge, try working with an entirely natural starter requiring no commercial yeast—known by many different names: sourdough in North America, *levain* in France and *lievito madre* or *lievito naturale* in Italy. This approach allows you to make beautiful, hearty loaves with as few as two ingredients: flour and water.

Like a fine wine or a mature cheese, good bread requires time to develop its maximum potential. This doesn't mean it requires slavery—leavening times can be adjusted to accommodate the most frenetic schedules. The tactility of the task makes it a natural activity in which to engage children. They love to help when it comes to bread making, and indeed it is something even a toddler can enjoy. As a beginner you may feel intimidated by the idea of baking a true artisanal loaf at home, but I'm sure you will be surprised by the ease and agreeable nature of the task. You may even find yourself musing when you begin to plan a meal, "So what will I serve for bread?" The true feast starts here. Everything else is just company for the bread, a *companatico*.

INGREDIENTS

MEASURING YOUR INGREDIENTS

Most professional bakers adhere to the metric system of measurement for baking bread, as it is the easiest. In this book measurements are given in metric (grams, liters, etc.) and imperial (ounces, cups, tablespoons, etc.). Ideally, your ingredients should be weighed, not measured. This is true in many aspects of food preparation, but nowhere is it more important than in baking. I encourage you to avoid volume measure. It is nowhere near as accurate as weighing things. Your cup will be a little more rounded than mine, your flour a bit heavier if you live in a humid climate. You can test this easily for yourself. Take a 1-cup measure and fill it with flour. Weigh it. Do this several times. You'll be astonished at the difference in each cup's weight. Now multiply this difference by the several cups of flour called for in a bread recipe. You see what I mean?

Weighing ingredients provides more accurate measure, and your results will be much more authentic and consistent. Once you get used to working with kitchen scales, you will likely discover how much easier things are and how quickly you can mix up a batch of bread.

Flour

Be careful with the flour you choose. It is your most important ingredient. White flour should be unbleached. Ideally, the protein content of flour used for artisanal breads should be around 11 to 11.5 percent. Flour sold as "bread flour" in many parts of North America has a high protein content and is not suitable for making most of the breads in this book. Depending on where you live, the protein content of your flour can vary dramatically. Canadian all-purpose flour, for example, generally contains a higher protein content than most U.S. all-purpose flour, making it closer to some U.S. bread flours. To reduce the protein content, when baking in Canada I use equal parts all-purpose and cake-and-pastry flour. To find out the approximate protein content of the flour you use, check the nutritional information on the side of the flour package. (Divide the grams of protein by the grams in a serving and multiply by 100.) Alternatively, you can ask a local artisanal baker what kind or brand of flour they recommend. If you bake a lot, it may be worth seeking out a local flour mill to buy your flour in larger quantities.

In natural starters, flour is the principal source of the wild yeast and bacteria cells required to get the fermentation under way. These elements are most plentiful in a good-quality, unbleached flour. If you intend to make a lot of whole grain bread, it is important to locate a source of fresh flour, as the germ in the whole grain contains oil that oxidizes very quickly. Buy your whole grain flour in small quantities from a reliable supplier and keep it in the refrigerator or freezer. If you bake enough to justify the expense, you can acquire a good-quality small grain mill for your home.

Flour absorbs different amounts of moisture depending on its strength, or protein content, and the environment, so sometimes you need to adjust the amount of water called for in a formula. If you live in a dry place, your flour will be dry, and you will need to add a bit more water to your dough. The opposite will be true if your weather is humid. If you are using a hard winter wheat, you may need to increase the amount of water, because this flour contains more protein and is more absorbent than softer wheat. Canadian hard winter wheat has a very high protein content. In Italy this wheat is highly regarded amongst bread bakers and millers and is referred to as "Manitoba" flour, after the Canadian province of the same name. It is usually added to the softer European flour to create a stronger blend suitable for bread making. When I bake with this flour in Canada, I always have to add a lot more water than is called for in recipes I find in U.S. and British cookbooks.

Yeast

I use instant dry yeast or fresh yeast (sometimes referred to as compressed cake yeast). Instant dry yeast goes by different names according to the manufacturer, but its distinguishing features are two: it does not need to be activated in water, and its granules are smaller than those of active dry yeast. These yeasts do not require proofing in warm water. Just toss them into the bowl with the other ingredients. All of the recipes in this chapter call for instant dry yeast. If you use fresh yeast, you should use roughly three times as much by weight.

Active dry yeast is another form of yeast, perhaps the one most familiar to home bakers. Its granules are larger than those of instant dry yeast and it must be proofed first in warm water to activate it. If you use this kind of yeast, you'll need to use roughly 30 percent more by weight and follow the manufacturer's instructions for proofing.

Salt

Why is salt important? Salt adds flavor. Because artisanal bakers coax flavor out of their bread by careful choice of flours, under-mixing the dough and allowing it a long, cool first rise (fermentation), they are not as dependent on salt as a flavor agent. Artisanal loaves generally contain less salt than industrial-produced breads made with intensive mixing techniques, short fermentation times and no pre-ferment.

Salt also reinforces the gluten developed in the dough and slows down the oxidation that occurs as the dough is mixed. This keeps the crumb from becoming bleached white. Sea salt is preferred over iodized table salt.

Water

It is advisable to use spring water if you live in an area where your water is chlorinated. Although the amount of chlorine in the water is unlikely to inhibit the fermentation of your dough, it can affect the flavor and the smell of bread.

The temperature of the water you add should be determined by the temperature of the room you are working in, the temperature of your flour and the length of your mix. For optimum dough development and flavor, professional bakers aim for the temperature of their final, mixed dough to be around 76°F/25°C. They measure the temperature of the flour and the room. Consideration is given to the fact that the dough will heat up in the mixer (3°F to 6°F, or 2°C to 3°C, per minute of mixing, depending on the speed). Taking all of these factors into account, they calculate the precise temperature of the water they need to add. This is important in a commercial bakery, where mixes are large and consistency is critical.

For the home baker, however, this kind of precision can be a bit tedious. In summer, when my kitchen is hot, I use water that is 66°F to 68°F/19°C to 20°C. In winter I use lukewarm water, around 73°F/23°C. If you want to be exact and own an instant-read thermometer, you can take the temperature of your room and flour and adjust the water temperature accordingly.

Most important, shocks of hot or cold should be avoided, as they will hamper yeast development. Always remember that your dough is alive, and like you it prefers a comfortable climate.

Equipment

Most people already own all the equipment required to make bread. A cookie sheet, a bowl and strong arms are all you need to get started. For the novice baker, the minimalist approach to equipment and ingredients is best. There is no sense investing in a lot of gadgetry and special equipment until you know you will be incorporating bread making into your life on a regular basis. It is good to learn how to make bread as simply as possible in the beginning. Knead the dough by hand and you will develop an excellent feel for it. As you hone your craft, and if your budget allows, there are tools you can invest in to make the task easier. I have outlined a few of my own indispensables below, most of which I have acquired gradually, over the years.

Kitchen Scale

Your most important piece of equipment when it comes to baking bread, a kitchen scale should be your first investment if you don't already own one. Look for a digital model accurate from 1 gram to at least 2 kilograms, and try to test it out before you buy it. Accuracy at the low end of the scale is important for weighing ingredients used in small amounts such as yeast and salt.

Scrapers

A square-edged metal bench scraper is used for cleaning your kneading surface and dividing your dough, and a rounded plastic one is handy for cleaning out your mixing bowl.

Pizza Paddle or Peel

For easy transfer of your loaves into and out of the oven.

Lame or Razor Blade

For slashing the loaves before you bake so they can expand in the oven without tearing the crust. If the idea of working with a razor makes you nervous, you can experiment with using scissors to cut fanciful patterns in your dough (see page 30).

Mister

For spraying water into the oven to create steam in the first few moments of baking. This slows the formation of the crust and allows the bread to rise to its maximum potential (see page 33).

Bannetons

These are European bakers' baskets made of willow. They help loaves keep their shape during the final fermentation and create a pretty, floury pattern on the bread. After shaping, the loaves are left to proof in well-floured baskets and then turned out onto a parchment-lined peel or baking sheet ready for the oven. These baskets are expensive but they will last a lifetime if properly cared for. If there is an artisanal bakery in your area, you can inquire to see if they will sell you some of their used ones. They are available new at most restaurant supply stores. You can improvise by placing a well-floured tea towel in a breadbasket or bowl. After shaping the loaf, place it in the basket for its final proof, and when ready to bake simply turn it out onto a parchment-lined peel, score and bake.

Baking Stones

Baking stones help to create a hearth-like atmosphere in a home oven. They are easily found in most department and kitchenware stores. Placed on a rack in the bottom third of your oven, they can be left in place most of the time—even while you are baking roasts, casseroles or pizza. I never take mine out. A baking stone will give your bread a wonderful crust and ensure a more evenly baked crumb.

Parchment Paper

Parchment paper prevents the dough from sticking to your peel, baking stone and baking sheets, which makes for easy cleanup. If you have a baking stone, you can place your loaf on a peel lined with parchment paper, and then transfer both the loaf and the paper directly onto the stone. If you don't use a stone, baking your bread on a sheet of parchment on a cookie sheet will do. Ecological recycled parchment paper is now widely available.

Stand Mixer

This is a significant investment, but if you have some experience making bread and can afford the luxury it will prove to be a great asset. A mixer allows you to work with wetter dough and is necessary to produce a decent *ciabatta* (page 34) and *Genzano* (page 58) bread. It is also excellent for making cakes and pastries.

Grain Mill

If you do a lot of baking using whole grain flour, you might consider a home grain mill. The first time I used mine I couldn't believe the difference the fresh flour made to the taste of my whole wheat bread. Electric and hand-cranked grain mills are generally available in health food stores and come in all shapes and sizes to fit every budget and family size. Look for one that uses a stone and not a steel blade to grind the grain.

GETTING STARTED

THE MIX

"Mixing" is the term professional bakers use to describe the kneading process. For the artisanal baker it is a more accurate term, depicting a gentler practice. Many of the doughs in this chapter are intentionally under-mixed. An under-mixed dough does not look "as smooth as a baby's bottom," a description frequently used to explain the look of a properly kneaded bread dough. Instead, these doughs develop this aspect only after a long fermentation (or first rise). The result is a light, tasty loaf with more complex flavor and a longer shelf life.

Many recipes for bread made using a mixer advise that the dough is mixed enough when it cleans the sides of the bowl. This is usually not what you want when you are making an artisanal loaf. Dough that comes together in a ball at the mixing stage is often over-mixed, and has developed too much strength too soon. Your dough needs time to gain strength and develop flavor. It should gain some strength in the mix and the rest from a long first fermentation (or first rise) that includes several gentle turns (see pages 24 to 26).

Since most of the doughs in this chapter are mixed for a short time and contain a fairly high percentage of water, you will find they are sticky to work with. The secret to working with wet, sticky dough is to use wet rather than floured hands. Dough doesn't stick to wet hands, and you won't be adding unworked flour to the mass. After the dough has been given a couple of turns during the fermentation (first rise), it will gain strength and become less sticky and easier to work with. All of the breads in this chapter, with the exception of the *ciabatta* (page 34) and the *Genzano* (page 58), can be made by hand. Working by hand often produces superior results and, contrary to popular belief, for home bakers working in small batches it takes no more time. Because I prefer a short, slow mix and a long fermentation, kneading times by hand should be more or less the same as they are in a mixer. (When we were testing the formulas in this chapter, I was surprised when the bread my tester, Robin Young, mixed by hand came out of the oven looking better than the identical dough she made in the mixer.)

To mix dough by hand, try using the technique Robin used. It comes from France, where it predates the invention of the mechanical mixer. This technique was brought to the United States and popularized amongst artisanal bakers by Didier Rosada. Didier has taught artisanal baking at the National Baking Center and the San Francisco Baking Institute and coached Team USA, the team of artisanal bakers sponsored by the Bread Bakers Guild of America, to two World Cup championships at the Coupe du Monde de la Boulangerie, held every three years in Paris.

To mix dough by hand using this method, combine all the ingredients in a bowl and mix together. Turn the dough out onto your work surface and pick up the mass from the end closest to you. Throw the dough in front of you onto the work surface—your goal is to stretch the dough out as far as you can.

  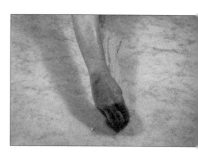

Fold the dough into thirds like an envelope by bringing the bottom third up just past the middle and the top third down, just past the middle. Take hold of the dough from the side instead of the front. In this way you are going to be stretching the dough, and developing gluten, in the other direction. Throw the mass as before, stretching it out as far as you can. Fold and pick it up again from the side, and repeat the procedure.

For home bakers working with small amounts of dough, this is a wonderful technique. After a few throws, you will notice the dough has developed considerable strength, and you are done.

Autolyse

I have had success using a method invented by the French bread-baking professor Raymond Calvel, called *autolyse*. An *autolyse* is a rest period given to the dough after a brief pre-mix. During the *autolyse*, the gluten strands start to form and the water begins to be absorbed by the mass. This method allows a considerable reduction in overall mixing time, and helps prevent the oxidation and flavor loss that result from over-working the dough.

If you use a mixer, the flour, water and sometimes the pre-ferment (*biga* or liquid *levain*) are combined and mixed very briefly before a short rest period, usually 20 minutes. If you are working with a dough that contains a lot of water, like *ciabatta* (page 34) or *Genzano* (page 58), or if you are working with a stiffer *levain* (page 43), you don't need to add the pre-ferment until the final mix. After the *autolyse*, the remaining ingredients (yeast, salt and the pre-ferment, if it has not already been incorporated) are added and the dough is given the final mix.

If you are mixing by hand, it is best to combine all the ingredients (flour, water, pre-ferment, salt and yeast) at the start of the *autolyse* to ensure their proper dissolution and distribution. The dough is mixed briefly and then given a shorter 10-minute *autolyse*.

Most of the recipes in this chapter suggest the use of an *autolyse*, and instructions are provided within each one for working by hand and with a mixer.

Fermentation and Giving the Dough a Turn

After the dough is mixed, it must be left to ferment. Fermentation is the process whereby the yeast acts on the sugar and starch naturally present in dough and converts them to alcohol and carbon dioxide gas. Contrary to popular belief, a long, cool fermentation, a minimal amount of commercial yeast, and dough that is slightly under-mixed are what the baker wants to develop the best-tasting loaf. These three factors will help slow down the entire process, giving flavor and texture time to develop properly. The result is a tasty, long-lasting loaf with good volume and cell structure. Typically the bread-making cycle should involve (1) a primary fermentation or first rise, (2) a pre-shaping followed by a short rest period, (3) a final shaping and (4) a final fermentation, sometimes called the proof or the final rise.

Professional artisanal bakers know that it is better not to over-mix bread dough. A dough that has been mixed or kneaded for too long risks oxidation, resulting in color loss (a bleached-looking, whiter dough) and a loaf that will not develop its full complexity of flavor and texture. It is better to let the dough develop some of its strength slowly in the bowl after you've kneaded it—that is, during the first rise or fermentation. A gentle turn or two will help to strengthen the dough. Turning the dough means that you are moving the yeast cells to a new location so that they can find fresh food.

You never want to "punch down" your dough. To give the dough a turn, sieve a light veil of flour onto your work surface. You want to avoid adding too much extra flour to the dough at this stage. Using wet hands, remove the dough from the bowl and gently place it on the floured surface. With two outstretched hands, gently but firmly press down on the mass, stretching it out into a rectangle. Be gentle, and don't deflate the dough too much. Some of the carbon dioxide gas being produced in the dough will be released, which is important, as too much can hinder yeast development.

Fold the dough back up, like you might fold a letter to fit into an envelope, and gently place it back into your bowl. At the end of each turn you should see your dough gaining strength. (The recipes state how long the fermentation should last and how many turns to do during that time.)

Making Great Bread on Your Schedule

Bread baking should fit into your schedule, not vice versa. When you think about the things bread needs to become great—minimal interference, coolness and slowness—it is easy to see how making it can fit easily into a busy schedule. Coolness you have in your refrigerator, interference you don't have time for, and slowness you can schedule. You can follow the fermentation times given in the recipes, or you can adjust the process to fit your own timetable. For example, you can mix the dough and leave it to ferment when you come home from work in the evening. Before going to bed, you can shape it and let it proof overnight in the refrigerator. It will be ready for the oven in the morning. The refrigerator is your ally—don't hesitate to use it if you have to. In the winter an unheated room or garage will also work. Professional bakeries have special temperature-controlled rooms for this purpose. Slowing down the fermentation to suit your schedule is called "retarding."

A lot of books recommend that you bring the dough back to room temperature after retarding, but my own experience suggests that this step is unnecessary. I have posed the question to professional bakers, who have agreed with me, and I have watched in busy bakeries as dough is taken out of the retarder and popped straight into the oven.

SHAPING THE BREAD

For me, the easiest and the best shapes are the simple ones: a round (*pagnotta* in Italian and *boule* in French) or the thick, oval log called a *filone* (or *bâtard* by the French). Your goal is to get these shapes as tight as you can (so that they keep their shape in the oven) without handling the dough too much. You want to try to preserve as many as possible of the gas bubbles you have worked so hard to create. This takes time to master, and experience. Above all, it takes a light touch. While first attempts may be badly shaped, don't despair; these loaves will still be delicious, probably better than anything you can buy. Soon you will be shaping perfect loaves. If you are lucky enough to live near an artisanal bakery, try to watch a pro at work. You can learn a lot by observing a professional. It is increasingly common for bakeries to have a glass wall or window through which you can observe the process.

In all of the formulas that follow, you will have enough dough for more than one loaf. My guidelines for the amount of dough to use per shape are:

Log: 300 to 400 g (10 to 14 oz)
Round: 400 to 500 g (14 oz to 1 lb)

Forming a Log

Place the piece of dough on a lightly floured surface. Gently pat the dough into a rectangle about 4 inches by 6 inches. With the shorter side facing you, bring the bottom half of the dough up to just past the middle and then fold the top half down to form an envelope.

Fold the top half of the envelope over onto the bottom half. You will now have a rough log shape, about 4 to 5 inches long. Seal the seam by pressing down on it firmly with the heel of your hand and be sure not

to leave any opening. Roll the log seam side down and, starting at the middle of the loaf, use both hands to gently stretch the dough by rolling it back and forth and extending your hands outwards at the same time. Your goal is to eliminate the bottom seam while simultaneously stretching out the log. You want to try for a log that is 8 to 10 inches long. Gently taper the ends of the dough.

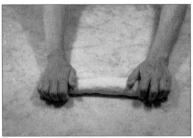

Gently transfer the log, seam side up, to a log-shaped *banneton* or to an oval or log-shaped wicker basket lined with a floured linen or tea towel for its final rise.

Forming a Round

Place the piece of dough on a lightly floured surface and gently flatten the mass. Fold the outside edges into the center to make a loose ball shape.

Turn the ball over and gently tighten the loaf by cupping it in your outstretched hand and turning it towards you against the table. Your goal, again, is to eliminate the seam on the bottom without deflating the loaf.

Transfer the round, seam side up, to a *banneton*, a wicker bread basket or a bowl lined with a floured tea towel for its final rise.

To bake, transfer, seam side down, onto your parchment-lined peel or cookie sheet and score (see below).

Scoring the Bread

Many of the loaves in this chapter need to be scored before they go into the oven. Scoring opens the crust so your loaves will be able to expand in the oven, reaching their full potential without tearing open the crust and distorting the shape of the loaf. You can use a razor blade or a pair of scissors. Professional bakers use an instrument called a *lame*, which

is available in some kitchenware and restaurant supply stores. Scissors are used to make pretty patterns and are recommended if you're not comfortable working with a sharp blade.

If you use a razor blade or a *lame*, slash at a very shallow angle, 30 to 45 degrees to the loaf. I usually make a cross or tic-tac-toe pattern on a round loaf, and a single slash down the center on a log.

Several shallow cuts with scissors down the center of a log create an *epi* or wheat sheaf effect, while cutting around the outside of a round with scissors results in an attractive sunflower shape.

 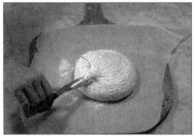 

Several shallow angled slashes down the center of a slender log will give you a baguette style (not shown).

A *Biga* Starter

Mixing up a *biga* for the next day's baking is often the last thing I do in the evening before I go to bed. It takes next to no time, and it is ready to use first thing in the morning.

INGREDIENTS	GRAMS	OUNCES	VOLUME
Unbleached all-purpose flour	200 g	7 oz	1½ cups
Water	200 g	7 oz	¾ cup+2 tbsp
Instant dry yeast	⅛ tsp	⅛ tsp	⅛ tsp

Mix everything together with a spatula for a minute or two. Let sit, covered, at room temperature for 6 hours or overnight. When it is ready to use, it should have risen to three times its volume, and its surface should be full of bubbles.

A Crusty Loaf (Using a *Biga* Starter)

This is a versatile, light, airy loaf packed with flavor. It is the bread I make most frequently at Petraia because it goes with almost everything. It becomes a Tuscan-style bread if you omit the salt. A saltless loaf is perfect for the Tuscan recipes in this book, including the *crostini* recipes on pages 88, 92 and 93, *acquacotta* on page 135 and *pappa al pomodoro* on page 137.

INGREDIENTS	GRAMS	OUNCES	VOLUME
Unbleached all-purpose flour	500 g	17.5 oz	3½ cups
Water	280 g	10 oz	1¼ cups
Biga (1 recipe)			
Sea salt (optional)	10 g	2 tsp	2 tsp
Instant dry yeast	2 g	½ tsp	½ tsp

Bread should be left to cool completely before it is sliced and eaten. When you take bread from the oven, it continues to bake as it cools. Slicing into hot bread is slicing into an unfinished loaf.

Pre-mix and Autolyse

BY HAND:

Combine all of the ingredients. Mix briefly by hand for 1 to 2 minutes as described on page 22. Place the dough in a bowl, cover and let rest for 10 minutes.

USING A MIXER:

Add the flour, water and *biga* to the work bowl of a stand mixer fitted with the dough hook and mix on low for about 1 minute. Cover the bowl and let rest for 20 minutes. Add the salt (if using) and yeast.

The Mix

Mix for 6 minutes on the lowest speed of a stand mixer fitted with the dough hook, or by hand using the technique described on page 22.

Fermentation

Place the dough in a bowl and cover with a clean kitchen towel (or plastic wrap if your kitchen is dry). Leave in a cool place until doubled in bulk. This should take 3 to 4 hours. Give the dough 2 turns during this time (see pages 24 to 26).

Pre-shape and Rest

Cut and weigh the dough according to the shape you want to make (see page 27). Shape each piece into a tight round and let it rest for 20 minutes. Like the *autolyse*, this rest period is important. It will help you achieve a tight shape in the final shaping without overworking the dough.

Final Shaping and Proof

Shape each piece once again into a tight round or a log and place it seam side up either in a *banneton* or in a bowl lined with a floured tea towel.

Cover with a clean tea towel and leave to proof until the dough slowly returns when pressed with a finger, about 1 hour and 15 minutes.

Bake

Preheat the oven to 500°F/260°C.

Turn the dough out onto a parchment-lined peel or cookie sheet. Score the loaves (see page 29) and slide the parchment and loaf onto the baking stone, or place the cookie sheet in the oven. Immediately turn the heat down to 450°F/230°C. Bake for 45 to 50 minutes.

When the bread is done, it will be a lovely deep golden brown color on top and dark brown on the sides and the bottom. It should sound hollow when you tap on it on the bottom. It should also tell you it's done—a properly cooked loaf will crackle and pop for the first few minutes after it comes out of the oven.

A lot of people get worried when they look in the oven and see how dark their loaves are getting. Don't be tempted to take your bread out early—you want to let the sugars in the dough caramelize just enough to create a beautiful crust on a loaf that looks like it has been pulled from the embers of a wood-burning oven.

Creating Steam in a Home Oven

Professional bakers have steam-injected ovens that inject steam early in the baking process, creating a moist atmosphere. This allows the dough to rise to its maximum potential before a crust is formed. You can create steam in a home oven in a couple of ways. One way is to use a plant mister filled with water. When you are ready to bake and have slashed your loaf, mist it once or twice before you put it into the oven. Two or three more sprays on the oven walls in the first 10 minutes of baking will keep the crust moist. If you do this you must be careful not to spray the water directly onto your baking sheet (it can buckle) or stone (it can break) and be very careful not to spray the oven light, as it can explode. Always stay attentive when you open an oven that has been sprayed. Stand well back to make sure you are not exposed to the hot steam that will escape when you open the door. Use heavy-duty oven gloves that come up to the elbow.

Another way to create steam is to place a heavy ovenproof pan (cast iron is perfect) in the oven while it preheats and then pour about a cup of hot water into it when you put your bread in to bake. Be careful to stand well back from the oven, wear heavy-duty oven gloves and shut the oven door quickly. Steam or no steam, always keep your head well back from the oven door when you open it.

Ciabatta (Using a *Biga* Starter)

Ciabatta is probably the best-known Italian bread in North America. Along with the French baguette, it is one of the breads an artisanal baker learns to make well in order to earn his or her stripes. The reasons for *ciabatta*'s popularity are obvious once you taste it. This bread is delicious. Its dough contains a large percentage of water, which gives the finished loaf a chewy, light crumb full of large air bubbles. It has an unforgettable sweet wheaty taste, and it goes with everything.

Ciabatta dough is stunning. It starts off the mix almost a batter, then gradually comes together, gaining most of its strength during the first rise. After a couple of turns it has morphed from wet, sticky dough into one with a shiny elastic surface rippled with voluminous gas bubbles. Delicate yet resilient at the same time, this airy dough should be handled carefully and minimally. It is more accurate to say it is cut rather than shaped. A mixer is necessary to make *ciabatta*, as the dough is too wet to work by hand.

INGREDIENTS	GRAMS	OUNCES	VOLUME
Unbleached all-purpose flour	500 g	17.5 oz	3½ cups
Water	360 g	12.75 oz	1⅔ cups
Biga (1 recipe, p. 31)			
Sea salt	10 g	2 tsp	2 tsp
Instant dry yeast	2 g	½ tsp	½ tsp

Pre-mix and Autolyse

Add the flour and water to the work bowl of a stand mixer fitted with the dough hook and mix on low for a minute. Cover the bowl and let it rest for 20 minutes. Add the remaining ingredients.

The Mix

Mix on low speed for 3 minutes. Switch to the paddle attachment and mix at medium speed for another 6 to 7 minutes. The dough will be moist and gluey. It will gain strength during the fermentation.

Fermentation

Let the dough rise for 4½ hours, giving it a turn (see pages 24 to 26) every 90 minutes (2 turns). You will notice a substantial development during this time—the dough will become noticeably stronger and will develop a pattern of gas bubbles on its surface. It should feel very light and full of air.

Final Shaping and Proof

This dough needs almost no shaping. Gently transfer it to a lightly floured work surface. Sprinkle a bit of flour on top and very slightly pat it into a loose square. Be very careful not to deflate it. Using your bench scraper, cut the dough into 2 rectangles or 4 squares. Transfer the loaves to a parchment-lined peel or baking sheet and let them rest until the dough almost returns when pressed with a finger, leaving only a small dent. This will take between 1 and 1½ hours.

Bake

Preheat the oven to 500°F/260°C.

Using your fingertips, gently dimple the loaves before sliding them into the oven. Immediately turn the oven down to 450°F/230°C and bake for 45 to 50 minutes. When the bread is done, it will be a lovely deep golden brown color on top and dark brown on the bottom. It will sound hollow when tapped on the bottom.

A Whole Grain Loaf (Using a *Biga* Starter)

This formula produces a light whole grain loaf that goes with most foods and keeps for several days. If you prefer a darker loaf, see the recipes for whole grain breads using natural starters on pages 48 to 53.

INGREDIENTS	GRAMS	OUNCES	VOLUME
Unbleached all-purpose flour	200 g	7 oz	1½ cups
100% whole wheat flour	300 g	10.5 oz	2⅓ cups
Water	280 g	10 oz	1¼ cups
Biga (1 recipe, p. 31)			
Sea salt	12 g	2½ tsp	2½ tsp
Instant dry yeast	2 g	½ tsp	½ tsp
Olive oil or butter	1 tbsp	1 tbsp	1 tbsp
Liquid honey	1 tbsp	1 tbsp	1 tbsp

Pre-mix and Autolyse

BY HAND:

Combine all of the ingredients. Mix briefly by hand for 1 to 2 minutes as described on page 22. Place the dough in a bowl, cover and let rest for 10 minutes.

USING A MIXER:

Add the flours, water and *biga* to the work bowl of a stand mixer fitted with the dough hook and mix on low for about a minute. Cover the bowl and let rest for 20 minutes. Add the remaining ingredients.

The Mix

Mix for 6 minutes on the lowest speed of a stand mixer fitted with the dough hook, or by hand using the technique described on page 22.

Fermentation

Place the dough in a bowl and cover with a clean kitchen towel (or plastic wrap if your kitchen is dry). Let it sit in a cool place until doubled in bulk. This should take 3 hours. Each hour, give the dough a turn (2 turns in all). (See pages 24 to 26.)

Pre-shape and Rest

Cut and weigh the dough according to the shape you want to make (see page 27). Shape each piece into a tight round and let it rest for 15 minutes. Like the *autolyse*, this rest period is important. It will help you achieve a tight shape in the final shaping without overworking the dough.

Final Shaping and Proof

Shape each piece once again into a tight round or a log and place it seam side up either in a *banneton* or in a bowl lined with a floured tea towel.

Cover with a clean tea towel and leave to proof until the dough slowly returns a finger imprint, 45 minutes to 1 hour.

Bake

Preheat the oven to 500°F/260°C.

Turn the dough out onto a parchment-lined peel or cookie sheet. Score the loaves (see page 29) and slide the parchment and loaf onto the baking stone, or place the cookie sheet in the oven. Immediately turn the heat down to 450°F/230°C. Bake for 10 minutes.

Turn the oven down to 400°F/200°C and bake for another 30 minutes or until done. When the bread is done, it will be dark brown and will sound hollow when you tap on it on the bottom.

The La Petraia Variations

Four Whole Grain Loaves with a *Biga* Starter

The preceding recipe for a whole grain loaf lends itself to many variations. Here are four of the most popular ones at Petraia.

Fruit and Nut Loaf

This bread is excellent toasted for breakfast, and goes nicely with a cheese plate. You can also shape it into dinner rolls.

During the last minute of mixing, add 100 g (3.5 oz) of dried fruits and/or nuts. You can also add ½ tsp of allspice. Here are some examples of combinations to use:

50 g (1.75 oz) (⅓ to ½ cup) nuts, such as walnuts, pecans or hazelnuts, plus

50 g (1.75 oz) (⅓ to ½ cup) dried fruit, such as raisins, apricots,
cherries, peaches or apples

Five-seed Bread

During the last 2 minutes of mixing, add:

56 g (2 oz) (⅓ cup) seeds (I like a combination of sunflower, poppy,
sesame, linseed and pumpkin seeds)

A nice addition to this bread is ½ tsp Chinese five-spice powder. If you
like you can coat the crust with poppy or sesame seeds before you bake
it. To do this, when the dough is ready to bake, spray the top with water.
Place ½ cup of seeds on a piece of wax paper and gently turn the dough
out onto the seeds. Gently roll the dough so that its top is covered with
the seeds. Invert onto your parchment-lined peel, score and bake.

Alpine Whole Grain Bread

Some breads in the Alpine regions of Europe use milk for the liquid
ingredient. Makes sense with all those cows. Simply substitute milk for
the water in the whole grain loaf. The result will be a beautiful loaf with
a long shelf life and a tighter crumb.

Olive Bread

During the last 2 minutes of mixing, add:

112 g (4 oz) pitted black olives

The ones I like best are the shriveled black olives preserved in oil. These
are called *al forno* in Italy because they are dried in the oven or in the
embers of the fire. They have a strong flavor, well suited to baking.

Making Your Own Natural Starter

Liquid *Levain*

Creating your own natural starter or sourdough culture will take a few seconds of your time each day for a week. Once you have achieved a healthy, bubbling mass of starter, you are ready to bake. If you look after your starter properly once it is made, it will last a lifetime. This formula is based on one I learned at the San Francisco Baking Institute. It's really the simplest, most foolproof and sensible method I've found, after trying many. When working with natural starters, I like to use unbleached, organic flour, as it is apt to contain more wild yeast than bleached flour. This starter should have a batter-like consistency, something the French term a "liquid *levain*." Ideally, feedings should be 12 hours apart from Day 1 to Day 4.

Day 1 Evening:

    28 g (1 oz) (¼ cup) rye flour
    28 g (1 oz) (2 tbsp) water
    ⅛ tsp liquid honey

Stir well, cover and allow to ferment in a warm area.

Day 2 Morning: First Feeding

    28 g (1 oz) (2 tbsp) of the mixture from above (discard the rest)
    28 g (1 oz) (¼ cup) rye flour
    28 g (1 oz) (2 tbsp) water

Stir well, cover and allow to ferment in a warm area.

Day 2 Evening: Second Feeding

    28 g (1 oz) (2 tbsp) of the mixture from above (discard the rest)

28 g (1 oz) (3 tbsp) unbleached all-purpose flour

28 g (1 oz) (2 tbsp) water

Stir well, cover and allow to ferment in a warm area.

Day 3 Morning Through Day 4 Evening: Feeding

Continue feeding as above, twice a day, using unbleached all-purpose flour.

Day 5: Final Refreshments and Build-up Day

You should have an active, bubbling mass of goop that smells yeasty. (If not, keep up the twice-daily feedings until you have a powerful, active starter. It may take another day or two. I find that hot, humid weather is the best for getting a starter going; in the winter it tends to take a little longer.)

Today is the build-up day, a day you will always need before your baking day to reactivate your starter with three refreshments and to build up its volume. Feedings ideally should be 8 hours apart.

MORNING:

28 g (1 oz) (2 tbsp) starter

28 g (1 oz) (3 tbsp) unbleached all-purpose flour

28 g (1 oz) (2 tbsp) water

Stir well, cover and allow to ferment in a warm area.

MIDDAY:

28 g (1 oz) (2 tbsp) starter from above (discard the rest or save to make the crackers on page 51)

28 g (1 oz) (3 tbsp) unbleached all-purpose flour

28 g (1 oz) (2 tbsp) water

Stir well, cover and allow to ferment in a warm area.

To the above add:

> **85 g (3 oz) (⅔ cup) unbleached all-purpose flour**
> **85 g (3 oz) (⅓ cup) water**

Stir well, cover and allow to ferment in a warm area.

Day 6: Baking Day

At this point you are ready to bake. It's best to start with the Master Formula on page 45 before trying any of the variations. But the first and most important thing to do today is to reserve and feed some starter for your next bake.

Take:

> **28 g (1 oz) (2 tbsp) starter (reserve the rest)**

Add:

> **28 g (1 oz) (3 tbsp) unbleached all-purpose flour**
> **28 g (1 oz) (2 tbsp) water**

Stir to mix, put in a jar and let sit at room temperature for 2 hours, then refrigerate. In the meantime, proceed to bake, using one of the recipes that follow.

How to Use and Maintain Your Refrigerated Starter

If you are not baking regularly, you need to keep your starter alive by feeding it every 3 to 4 days. To do this, take 28 g (1 oz) (2 tbsp) of the starter you have saved in the refrigerator (discard the rest) and an equal amount of flour and water. Stir, leave at room temperature for 2 hours, then return to the refrigerator.

To make bread with your refrigerated starter, begin at "Day 5" on page 41. You need a day to refresh and build up your starter, and then you can bake the next day.

If you are going to be away for an extended time, there are a few ways to keep your starter alive:

1. For a short absence of a week to 10 days, give your starter a final refreshment, using twice as much flour as you normally do. Essentially, you're giving it a lot to eat at once so it will keep longer without being fed.

2. You can make an even drier starter in your mixer or food processor by mixing in enough flour to make a powder. This dry starter will keep for several weeks in the fridge. You will need a few days when you return home to revive it—use equal parts flour and water, twice a day, to return it to an active liquid *levain*.

3. Some bakers freeze their starter, but I find it just as easy to make a new one. If you do freeze it, you'll need to thaw it and give it two or three refreshments a day for several days until you see that it is very active again. It should be kept at room temperature during this time.

Acidity and Sourness in Naturally Leavened Bread

The natural-starter formula on page 40 is for a liquid *levain*, which, if maintained properly, should perform consistently over time. This starter will be fairly active and will produce a dough that is strong, is easy to handle and ferments fairly rapidly. The bread you make with it should have a mild taste and an airy, light crumb. It will not have a very pronounced sour flavor.

Many bakers prefer a more sour-tasting loaf. You can achieve this by maintaining a stiffer starter. My formula uses an equal amount of flour and water in the *levain* build-up and maintenance. To get more sourness in your dough, try reducing the water by up to 50 percent at each of the three refreshments on your build-up day. This produces a more sour-tasting loaf with a denser, chewier crumb and a thick, blistery crust—something akin to a classic San Francisco sourdough. It will take longer to ferment, will have a longer shelf life and will develop stronger flavor than bread made with a liquid *levain*.

Technically, a stiffer starter produces a dough that has more acetic acid, and there is a fine line between enough and too much of this type of acidity. An excess hampers yeast development and can cause the proteins in the dough to toughen and possibly break down. This leads to a gluey, smelly dough that can be hard to work with. Excessive acidity in a starter can yield a dense, heavy loaf that doesn't rise well in the oven. Experimentation on your part is the best way to understand your starter and know the best density of *levain* to use to produce the loaf you prefer. A stiff starter is used for the Italian holiday breads *pandoro* and *panettone* (see pages 377 to 388). The stiffer, more acidic starter gives a complex flavor and long-lasting quality to these rich, sweet breads. I also work with a stiff starter in the summer, because the heat and humidity in my kitchen cause my liquid *levain* to ferment too rapidly (see page 45), but my preference for bread making is always cool weather and a liquid *levain*.

The science of sourdough cultures and how they work is quite evolved, and a complex combination of factors affects how acidity develops. Temperature, the amount of time between feedings, the amount of starter used in the final dough and the protein content of the flour all play a role. For anyone interested in learning more about this subject, I have included several excellent sources on page 417.

The Master Formula

A Country-style Hearth Bread (Using a Natural Starter)

It is helpful if you have worked first with a *biga* before you move on to a natural starter. Natural starters can be temperamental, and it is better to have experience making bread using commercial yeast before diving in to the world of sourdough. Having said that, this is my favorite bread to make. It is so rewarding to create your own wild yeast and to be able to produce a loaf that needs nothing but flour, water and salt. Once you have mastered working with a natural starter, you might want to try the final challenge—making one of the Italian celebratory breads *pandoro, panettone or colomba* (see pages 377 to 388).

The following is my basic recipe for a country-style hearth bread. Once you have it down, you can experiment to come up with your own favorite breads or try one of the variations of the master formula.

A dough made with a natural *levain* ferments at a different pace than one containing commercial yeast and prefers a warmer temperature—around 77°F to 78°F/25°C to 26°C is ideal. I live in a place where the summers are hot and not air-conditioned. The winters are drafty and cool. On winter baking days, I keep my kitchen warm by turning on the oven and stoking up our woodstove. In summer, I reduce the amount of *levain* in the dough; otherwise, fermentation is too rapid. A sourdough loaf that has fermented too quickly will not have cultivated enough acidity, nor will it have had enough time to develop good flavor and texture. The formula below is my standard one, with a summer adjustment included if you find your dough ferments too rapidly in warmer weather.

You will notice that the commercial yeast is optional. Professional bakers sometimes add a bit of yeast to their sourdough bread to help

THE SUMMER ADJUSTMENT

In the height of summer, when my kitchen is very hot and humid, my liquid *levain* ferments too rapidly. To tame it, I convert it to a stiff starter and use half as much in the recipe. To make a stiff starter out of your liquid *levain* on the build-up day (see page 41), refresh it three times, using half the amount of water called for. This means each refreshment requires 1 part *levain*, 1 part flour and ½ part water. After each refreshment, the starter will be stiffer. This variation will produce slightly less dough, but still enough to form into two loaves.

guarantee consistent results, and doing so at home can be a good idea, especially if you are a first-time bread baker.

INGREDIENTS	GRAMS	OUNCES	VOLUME
Unbleached all-purpose flour	500 g	17.5 oz	3½ cups
Water	310 g	11 oz	1⅓ cups
Liquid *levain* (p. 40)	185 g	6.5 oz	¾ cup
Sea salt	12 g	2½ tsp	2½ tsp
Instant dry yeast (optional)*	⅛ tsp	⅛ tsp	⅛ tsp

* If you choose to add yeast, be sure you have reserved and refreshed some of your starter for your next bake before you begin the mix.

Pre-mix and Autolyse

BY HAND:

Combine all of the ingredients. Mix briefly by hand for 1 to 2 minutes as described on page 22. Place the dough in a bowl, cover and let rest for 10 minutes.

USING A MIXER:

Add the flour, water and *levain* to the work bowl of a stand mixer fitted with the dough hook and mix on low for about a minute. Cover the bowl and let rest for 20 minutes. Add the salt and yeast (if using).

The Mix

Mix for 6 minutes on the lowest speed of a stand mixer fitted with the dough hook, or by hand using the technique described on page 22.

When the mix is complete, the dough will not clean the sides of your bowl, and it will seem sticky and wet. This is correct. It will gain strength after each turn during the fermentation.

Fermentation

With a natural *levain*, fermentation times depend on a variety of factors, including how well your starter has been maintained, the temperature, your flour, the humidity and so on. The ideal room temperature is 78°F/26°C. The dough should be ready in 4 to 4½ hours; give it a turn (see pages 24 to 26) every 90 minutes (2 turns). If you've added a pinch of yeast, you may need less time. After each turn you will notice the dough gaining strength. At the end of the fermentation it should have increased in volume by 75 percent, and air pockets should be visible on the surface.

Pre-shape and Rest

Cut the dough in half, shape it into two rounds and let it rest for 30 minutes.

Final Shaping and Proof

Shape again into two tight rounds or logs and let rise in *bannetons* or bowls lined with floured tea towels. Cover with a clean tea towel or plastic wrap. If conditions are very humid, you can leave the dough uncovered. Leave to proof until the loaves have increased in size by about 75 percent. The time will depend on the temperature of your kitchen and how active your starter is, but generally will be between 1½ and 2 hours. Don't be afraid to leave it for longer if it does not look ready. You should see the surface of the dough lightly rippled with gas bubbles, and it should spring back when you touch it, leaving only a small dent.

The shaped loaves are also perfectly suited for proofing overnight in the refrigerator if you don't have time to bake the same day you make the dough. To do this, cover the bannetons with a clean tea towel or plastic wrap and refrigerate.

Baking

Preheat the oven to 450°F/230°C.

Turn the dough out onto a parchment-lined peel or cookie sheet. Score the loaves (see page 29) and slide the parchment and loaf onto the baking stone, or place the cookie sheet in the oven. Bake for 10 minutes.

Reduce the heat to 400°F/200°C. Bake for another 35 to 40 minutes, until done. When the bread is done, it will be a lovely deep golden brown color on top and dark brown on the sides and the bottom. It will sound hollow when tapped on the bottom.

THE LA PETRAIA VARIATIONS

FOUR WHOLE GRAIN BREADS WITH A NATURAL STARTER

Once you have mastered the art of making a sourdough loaf, you can begin to get creative with the breads you make. I have several standards here at Petraia. I'm sure you will be able to come up with your own variations. Remember not to get too carried away with ingredients. Whole grain loaves tend to ferment a little faster, so you may find fermentation times slightly shorter with these breads.

A Plain Whole Grain Loaf

This is a versatile, light and healthful bread that, unlike a lot of whole grain bread made with sourdough, is neither dense nor sour. It has a nutty, slightly sweet wheaty flavor adored by young and old alike. This is a bread capable of accompanying a broad range of foods. I serve it alongside hearty soups or with cheese and cured meats. It also makes great sandwiches and toast.

INGREDIENTS	GRAMS	OUNCES	VOLUME
Unbleached all-purpose flour	150 g	5.3 oz	1 cup + 1 tbsp
Organic whole wheat flour	350 g	12.5 oz	2⅔ cups
Water	325 g	11.5 oz	1½ cups
Liquid *levain* (p. 40)	185 g	6.5 oz	¾ cup
Sea salt	12 g	2 ½ tsp	2½ tsp
Liquid honey	2 tsp	2 tsp	2 tsp
Olive oil or butter	2 tsp	2 tsp	2 tsp
Instant dry yeast (optional)	⅛ tsp	⅛ tsp	⅛ tsp

A little fat (oil or butter) is good to add when you are working with whole grain flour, as it lubricates the bran and prevents it from tearing the gluten. This ensures the development of a loaf that is not too heavy or dense, as whole grain breads can sometimes be.

Follow the instructions in the master formula, adding the honey and oil with the salt.

Variations

See the variations for the whole grain loaf with a *biga* starter on pages 38 to 39. They will all work with the above loaf.

Rye Sourdough Bread

This tasty dark rye bread is delicious thinly sliced and topped with a thin slice of *speck* or perhaps a dab of mascarpone (or cream cheese) and a slice of smoked salmon. While I generally advise against the use of bread flour, this recipe is the exception to the rule. Because this bread contains a lot of rye flour, which does not develop gluten, the use of high-protein wheat flour will give your loaves good structure.

Look for unbleached, organic bread flour with around 13 percent protein content.

INGREDIENTS	GRAMS	OUNCES	VOLUME
Bread flour	250 g	9 oz	1⅔ cups
Whole rye flour	250 g	9 oz	2 cups
Water	300 g	10.5 oz	⅓ cups
Liquid *levain* (p. 40)	185 g	6.5 oz	¾ cup
Sea salt	12 g	2½ tsp	2½ tsp
Olive oil or butter	2 tsp	2 tsp	2 tsp
Caraway seeds (optional)	1 tsp	1 tsp	1 tsp
Instant dry yeast (optional)	⅛ tsp	⅛ tsp	⅛ tsp

Rye flour tends to yield a better bread when you use a sourdough starter. This will be a sticky dough, and as with any sticky dough it is advisable to work with wet, rather than floured, hands to avoid the unnecessary addition of flour. Rye flour lacks gluten-forming potential, so this bread will not rise as much as a wheat loaf, and it will have a denser crumb.

Add the caraway seeds, if using, during the last 2 minutes of your mix.

Rye bread is best shaped into a log. To score, a series of short angled slashes down the middle of the loaf are best, like this: / / / / / / / /

Variation

If you prefer a dense rye with a tight crumb, use 10 percent less water. The dough will be very stiff and it will not double in volume. Shaped into a tight, slender log, this stiff dough will not need a *banneton* during its final rise. Leave the shaped loaf on a sheet of parchment for the final rise or proof. It can be scored immediately after it is shaped rather than just before it goes into the oven.

La Petraia Chestnut Bread

Because chestnut flour does not have the ability to develop gluten like wheat flour, this bread is denser than the whole wheat loaf. Chestnut flour also has a rich, smoky taste, which, in combination with the sweetness of the currants, gives this bread an intriguing and very special flavor. It is a good bread to make in the cooler months of the year, wonderful sliced thinly and served with a cheese course. It feels especially at home partnered with a plate of mixed Tuscan pecorino cheese and a drizzle of chestnut honey.

INGREDIENTS	GRAMS	OUNCES	VOLUME
Unbleached all-purpose flour	320 g	11.3 oz	2⅓ cups
Whole wheat flour	100 g	3.5 oz	¾ cup
Chestnut flour	85 g	3 oz	⅔ cup
Water	300 g	10.5 oz	1⅓ cups
Liquid *levain* (p. 40)	185 g	6.5 oz	¾ cup
Sea salt	12 g	2½ tsp	2½ tsp
Olive oil or butter	2 tsp	2 tsp	2 tsp
Fennel seed (optional)*	1 tsp	1 tsp	1 tsp
Currants (optional)*	100 g	3.5 oz	¾ cup
Instant dry yeast (optional)	⅛ tsp	⅛ tsp	⅛ tsp

Add in the last minute of your mix.

Whole Grain Seed Flatbread or Crackers

I sometimes find myself with a bit of leftover starter and, rather than throw it out, I invented this easy flatbread. Broken up into crackers, it keeps for at least 2 weeks in a cookie tin, although it never lasts that long here. The secret to getting a crispy, flavorful cracker is the extra virgin olive oil you brush on before the bread goes into the oven. Use your best oil and be generous.

For every 185 g (6.5 oz) (¾ cup) of liquid *levain*, add enough flour to make a stiff dough, about 1 cup. I use ¾ cup of white bread flour and ¼ cup of whole wheat or whole rye flour. To this add ¼ cup of seeds and ¼ cup of olive oil. You can use sesame seeds, poppy seeds or flax seeds. A combination of all three is also nice. (For a spicier flatbread, add some coarsely ground black pepper along with the seeds.)

Mix this dough until it comes together in a ball, as you would for a pastry dough. I do this step in my stand mixer using the dough hook. The dough should be dense with seeds. Let it rest, covered with plastic, in the refrigerator for an hour, and then roll it out as thin as you can between two sheets of parchment paper. Peel away the top sheet of parchment and, using the tines of a fork, puncture holes all over the dough. To make bite-sized crackers, use a pastry cutter to trace a grid of squares or rectangles on the dough so it can be broken into pieces after it comes out of the oven. If you omit this step, you will produce one large and dramatic-looking flatbread to be broken off in random bits.

If you like a puffy cracker, leave the dough at room temperature, uncovered, until it has developed a skin—about 45 minutes. If you omit this step (which I usually do), you will have a thinner, crispier cracker.

Brush the dough very generously with olive oil, let it sit for a few minutes and then brush it again. Sprinkle some sea salt on the top and bake in a 450°F/230°C oven until golden brown and crispy, 15 to 20 minutes. Watch carefully in the last few minutes of baking, as these thin crackers burn easily.

The dough can be mixed and then frozen for several weeks before being rolled out and baked. To use it, thaw it overnight in the fridge. I make these crackers in large quantities at Christmas and then package them in pretty cellophane packages as gifts. They are always a huge hit.

Variations

1. If you substitute white flour for the whole wheat and leave out the seeds, you will produce a very tasty saltine-type cracker.

2. To make a delicious snack, or to serve with an *aperitivo*, make deep-fried crackers. Proceed as directed above, but don't add any oil or salt to the top of the dough after you roll it out. Cut the dough into squares or circles and leave it to rest for half an hour. Deep-fry in extra virgin olive oil. The crackers will puff up in the hot oil. Drain on paper towels and sprinkle with sea salt before serving.

3. If you own a crank-style pasta machine, you can use it to roll out thin crackers. Roll to the second-to-last setting.

SOME SPECIAL ITALIAN BREADS AND THEIR STORIES

Years ago I overheard a successful artisanal baker from North America say that there was no good bread in Italy. I was shocked by this remark, but sadly it was not the first time I'd heard it. The artisanal baking industry in North America is a fairly recent development and, like the restaurant business used to be, its first wave was heavily influenced by the French. Terminology, techniques and production methods were largely borrowed from France. Fortunately, attitudes have changed as more bakers have come to understand and appreciate traditional Italian bread. Unlike France, Italy is a country where it is rare to see someone walking down the street tearing off pieces of a fresh loaf of bread. It is almost as rare to see Italians drink a glass of wine without food. Both bread and wine are designed to go with food, to be complementary to a meal.

Since the first course in an Italian meal is usually pasta, bread often doesn't appear at the table until after the starchy first course is cleared away. In Tuscany the bread is saltless, a bit dreary on its own perhaps, but it makes a fine marriage with the food of the region, a cuisine that tends to be salty. The taste and texture of a Tuscan loaf make it the preferred bread to use when making *crostini* and a necessary ingredient in a proper *zuppa di pane* or *panzanella*. In Emilia-Romagna one might find the breads dry, with an almost cardboard-like texture. To a French-educated bread palate this might seem unappealing, but combined with the rich food of the region, this bread is perfect. What better than a piece of the famous *Coppia Ferrarese* to wrap a beautiful rosy-colored slice of *prosciutto di Parma* around or to sop up the remnants of a rich *ragù?* In the area around Genoa, the *focaccia* melts in your mouth, recalling the lightness of the Ligurian Sea. In the Alto Adige the *bretzel* and the wonderful flat rye breads marry beautifully with the hearty mountain fare.

Sadly, bread, like wine, is increasingly falling prey to a homogeneity that sees mixes sold to bakers and identical loaves produced in *forni* all over the country. It is my hope that the bold streaks of anarchy and pride that run so deep in the Italian consciousness will prevent this banality from taking too much hold here.

In my experience, regional breads (or foods) are hard to reproduce in an exact fashion away from their place of origin. The pizza of Naples is a world apart from any other pizza. It is worth a trip to Naples. The same can be said for the bread from Altamura, Casola, Castelvetrano, Genoa, Genzano, Casola, Ferrara and Triora, to name just a few Italian towns famous for their bread. Ask why this is so and you are likely to be told it has to do with differences in the air and the water, the mozzarella cheese and tomatoes in the pizza or the olive oil in the *focaccia*.

What follows are a few stories of wonderful Italian breads and the places they come from. The formulas do not attempt to replicate the breads, merely to pay tribute to them. To taste the real thing, you simply have to go there, breathe the air, drink the water and taste the food. Then you will really come to appreciate the bread in its full glory.

Pane Casereccio Siciliano
✦ Semolina Bread from Sicily (Using a *Biga* Starter)

One of my first visits to Italy was to Sicily, and its special semolina breads are still some of my favorites. As one ventures into the *mezzogiorno*, or southern Italy, bread takes on a golden aspect, as if it has spent more time in the sun than its northern cousins. This is especially true in the wheat-growing regions of Apulia and Sicily, where most of Italy's hard durum wheat is grown. Milled into a sunny-colored yellow flour called semolina, durum wheat is used to make the dried pasta for which Italy is famous. When mixed into bread dough, it produces a beautiful yellow loaf with a sweet, nutty flavor that has wonderful keeping qualities.

In Sicily, yellow bread dough is shaped into fanciful snails and reptilian forms, sprinkled with sesame seeds and baked in wood-burning ovens. In the town of Lecce, in Puglia, I ran into other delicious semolina breads called *puccie* that are made with semolina flour and studded with whole black olives. Sometimes they contained hot pepper flakes and chopped onions. To make these, see the variation on page 58.

Durum wheat is strong, and it is easy to over-develop dough made with it. It is best to under-mix and let your dough gain strength during the fermentation. You can find Italian durum flour, called semolina, in most specialty Italian grocers and some supermarkets.

There are two kinds of Italian durum semolina flour: a coarse-grain one (similar to cream of wheat) used for pasta and desserts, and a finer-grain one that has been *rimacinata*, or "reground," for bread. Look for the Italian finely ground durum flour usually called semolina (but just to make things confusing, it is also sometimes called *semola di grano duro*). It should have the consistency of all-purpose flour, with a pale buttery color.

INGREDIENTS	GRAMS	OUNCES	VOLUME
Durum semolina flour*	500 g	17.5 oz	3⅓ cups
Water	325 g	11.5 oz	1½ cups
Biga (1 recipe, p. 31)			
Sea salt	10 g	2 tsp	2 tsp
Instant dry yeast	2 g	½ tsp	½ tsp
Sesame seeds (optional)	¼ cup	¼ cup	¼ cup

*See note at left

Pre-mix and Autolyse

BY HAND:

Combine all of the ingredients. Mix briefly by hand for 1 to 2 minutes as described on page 22. Place the dough in a bowl, cover and let rest for 10 minutes.

USING A MIXER:

Add the flour and water to the work bowl of a stand mixer fitted with the dough hook and mix on low for about a minute. Cover the bowl and let rest for 20 minutes. Add the remaining ingredients.

The Mix

To mix the dough by hand, use the technique described on page 22. If using a stand mixer, fit it with the dough hook and mix on the lowest speed for 3 minutes, then increase the speed to medium for 2 minutes. The dough will be sticky.

Fermentation

Cover the bowl with a clean kitchen towel (or plastic wrap if your kitchen is dry), and let it sit in a cool place until doubled in bulk. This should take 2½ to 3 hours. Give the dough 2 turns during this time (see pages 24 to 26).

Pre-shape and Rest

For a Sicilian-style loaf, you will need two pieces of dough. Shape each piece into a tight round and let them rest for 15 minutes.

Final Shaping and Proof

For a Sicilian-style loaf, shape each piece of dough into a skinny log about 18 inches long. You may find it easiest to work with wet hands when shaping this sticky dough.

Roll the log up into a snail or a double snail shape (see photos) and place on a sheet of parchment paper. Spray the loaves with water and sprinkle a thick layer of sesame seeds over them. Cover with a clean tea towel and leave to proof until the dough slowly returns when pressed with a finger. The final fermentation takes about 45 minutes.

Bake

Preheat the oven to 500°F/260°C.

Slide the parchment onto your peel. If you use a baking stone, slide the parchment directly onto it in the oven. Otherwise, use a baking sheet.

Make bread crumbs with any leftover bread and use them to make the Cart Driver's Spaghetti on page 209.

Once the loaves are in the oven, immediately turn the heat down to 450°F/230°C. Bake for 45 to 50 minutes.

When the bread is done, it will be a deep golden brown and should sound hollow when you tap on it on the bottom. It should also tell you it's done—a properly cooked loaf will crackle and pop for the first few minutes after it comes out of the oven.

Variation

In Puglia, *puccie* are usually made using unpitted olives, but it may be advisable to pit them if you fear biting into one of the pits by accident! The smell that will fill up your kitchen when these delicious *panini* are baking is heavenly.

You can make *puccie* by adding 1 cup of olives to the dough. If you pit them, chop them very roughly—the olive pieces should be fairly large. You can also add ½ tsp of paprika or hot chili powder and ½ cup of minced onions; add to the dough at the end of the kneading time and mix briefly to combine the ingredients. Follow the instructions for the main recipe until the pre-shape. Turn the dough out onto a lightly floured surface and gently press it into a 12-inch square. Using your bench scraper or a chef's knife, cut 9 pieces of dough, each 4 inches square. To shape, pick up each piece of dough and let half of it fall onto a sheet of parchment, while folding the remaining half over top of it. Proof as directed above (omitting the sesame seeds). The *puccie* will need 25 minutes to bake.

Pane Casereccio di Genzano
◆ Bread from Genzano (Using a Natural Starter)

The region of Lazio, which lies in central Italy and boasts Rome as its capital, is one of Italy's richest bread regions. There is wonderful bread from Salisano and the famous *pizza bianca* of Rome. From the area around the Colli Albani come three spectacular breads—those of Lari, Velletri and Genzano.

I stumbled upon the bread of Genzano one day several years ago quite by accident. I had dropped my husband off at the Rome airport one morning and decided to take a drive into the Colli Albani to visit a local organic growers' cooperative. Around lunchtime I stopped in the town of Genzano, home to the Pope's summer residence and the Vatican's astronomical research facility, and I grabbed a sandwich in a small bakery that had caught my eye earlier in the day. The bread was sliced from a thick, crusty loaf with a black crust and an airy interior that was irresistible. I took a walk around the town to see if I had lucked out and found one special bakery or if this was the standard Genzano fare. Every bakery I visited had the same loaf for sale, the *pane comunale,* and I later came to discover that it is one of Italy's proudest. Bread from Genzano is shipped daily to Rome, where it is found in the finest restaurants and best *gastronomie.* It was awarded an *Indicazione geografrica protetta,* or IGP, in 1997, the first bread in Europe to achieve this status.

Pane di Genzano is made using a natural leaven. It has a long mix and a short fermentation, and it is baked in a very hot oven. It forms a thick, hard, caramel-tasting crust, which protects a moist, light and airy crumb. The crust is almost jet black, the crumb pure white, a stark contrast seldom seen in any kind of bread and one that endows it with an appealing minimalist aspect. *Pane di Genzano* has a sweet, sophisticated flavor, and it is unbelievably light. Like its sweeter and richer northern cousins, *panettone* and *pandoro,* this bread shows off the Italian genius for making the most of the many attributes of a natural starter, doing away with the standard assumption that sourdough bread must always be heavy, dense and sour.

I have come up with a loaf that recalls this wonderful bread. Most of the dough's strength is derived from the long mixing period. It has a short fermentation, and it will not double in volume on its last rise. Most of its volume comes from the oven spring, which is the expansion that occurs— usually within the first 10 minutes—after you place a loaf in the oven.

Because of the length of time this dough is mixed, it is easiest to make with a stand mixer. Since it has a short fermentation time, it is important to let the dough rest in a warm environment. At Petraia I make this bread only in the summer, when my kitchen is very warm.

INGREDIENTS	GRAMS	OUNCES	VOLUME
Unbleached all-purpose flour	500 g	17.5 oz	3½ cups
Water	350 g	12.5 oz	1½ cups
Liquid *levain* (p. 40)	75 g	2.7 oz	⅓ cup
Sea salt	10 g	2 tsp	2 tsp
Instant dry yeast	2 g	½ tsp	½ tsp
Bran for sprinkling			

The Mix and Autolyse

Mix the flour and water together and knead for 1 minute by hand or on the lowest speed of a stand mixer, just to moisten all the flour. Put the dough into a bowl and let rest for 20 minutes.

Add the *levain*. Mix on low speed for 10 minutes in a stand mixer fitted with the dough hook. Switch to the paddle attachment and add the salt and yeast. Mix on medium speed for another 10 minutes.

Fermentation

Cover the mixing bowl and let the dough rest for 2 hours at 80°F/27°C, giving it a turn after the first hour.

Pre-shape and Rest

Gently place the dough on a wet or lightly floured work surface and cut it in half. Using wet hands, shape each piece into a tight round. Let rest for 20 minutes.

Final Shaping and Proof

Using wet hands, shape each round into the tightest round you can manage. Place in well-floured round *bannetons*, or in bowls lined with floured tea towels. Cover with clean tea towels and let rise for 1 hour. The bread will not double in bulk, but it will rise a bit. The more dramatic increase in volume occurs after it goes into the oven.

Bake

Preheat the oven to its highest temperature, 500°F to 550°F/260°C to 290°C.

Turn the loaves out onto a peel lined with parchment. Sprinkle each loaf with some of the bran and score the loaves to make a cross (see page 29). Bake for 35 to 40 minutes.

When the bread is done, the loaves will sound hollow when tapped on the bottom and a very, very dark crust will have formed.

Pane di Patate ✦ Potato Bread

In Italy, potato breads are found in the mountain regions of Tuscany and Emilia-Romagna and in Puglia and Calabria. Traditionally, potatoes were added to bread dough as a way to stretch out the wheat flour. Bread that contains potatoes has wonderful flavor and keeps for several days. Potato starch acts on the crust, browning it quickly, and so this bread is baked at a lower temperature than the other breads in this chapter.

INGREDIENTS	GRAMS	OUNCES	VOLUME
Unbleached all-purpose flour	500 g	17.5 oz	3½ cups
Potato	400 g	14 oz	3 to 4 medium
Potato water	200 g	7 oz	¾ cup + 2 tbsp
Biga (1 recipe, p. 31)			
Sea salt	8 g	1½ tsp	1½ tsp
Instant dry yeast	1 g	¼ tsp	¼ tsp

For the Potatoes

Boil the potatoes in abundant salted water (you will be using the water as the liquid ingredient in the dough, so make sure you have enough). Reserve the cooking water and let cool. Rice the potatoes (or peel and mash them).

The Mix

This bread has no *autolyse*. Mix all the ingredients together and knead for 6 minutes, by hand or in a stand mixer fitted with the dough hook.

Fermentation

Place the dough in a bowl (or leave it in the bowl of your stand mixer) and cover it. Let it rest for 2½ hours, giving it a turn at the halfway point.

Pre-shape and Rest

Gently place the dough on a wet or lightly floured work surface and cut it in half. Using wet hands, shape each piece into a tight round. Let rest for 20 minutes.

Final Shaping and Proof

Shape each round into a tight round or log. Place in well-floured *bannetons,* or in bread baskets or bowls lined with floured tea towels. Cover with clean tea towels and let rise for 45 minutes to 1 hour, until doubled in bulk.

Bake

Preheat the oven to 450°F/230°C.

Turn the loaves out onto a parchment-lined peel or cookie sheet. Score the loaves to make a cross (see page 29) and slide the parchment and loaf onto the baking stone, or place the cookie sheet in the oven. Bake for 10 minutes. Turn the heat down to 400°F/200°C and bake for another 30 minutes or until the loaves sound hollow when tapped on the bottom and the crust is a dark caramel color.

Focaccia Classica di Genova
♦ Classic Focaccia from Genoa

Before my husband and I moved to Chianti, we rented an apartment in the Ligurian coastal town of Santa Margherita Ligure for a year. When we decided to buy an Italian home, it was in Liguria that we wanted to live. For my husband, who is an old sea dog, it was the proximity of the sea and the prospect of a sailboat that lured him to the coast. For me it was the Ligurian *entroterra*, or backcountry, and its fascinating cuisine. For both of us the warm climate and the promise of a long growing season held appeal. We were disappointed when we realized we couldn't afford this part of Italy. The fashionable seaside resorts that line the Italian Riviera have driven real estate prices sky high. We could buy a small condo in Santa Margherita, but that same money would get us our 165-acre farm in central Tuscany. There wasn't much of a choice. We are not condo dwellers. We still hold the Ligurian region close to our hearts and consider it our second Italian home.

Liguria is one of Italy's wealthiest regions, and people there live longer than they do anywhere else in the country. Not a hard thing to fathom when you consider the climate (mild), the landscape (rugged) and the diet (vegetables, seafood, olive oil). The ancient capital, the city of Genoa, sits near the middle of this slender region, overlooking the Ligurian Sea. It is the point where Liguria divides itself into two distinct parts. The Riviera di Ponente, or Western Riviera, stretches up towards the French border, and the Riviera di Levante, or Eastern Riviera, down to Tuscany. Both parts are dominated by the Sea of Liguria on one side and mountains on the other.

Despite the region's rugged terrain and small size, it is a fertile and abundant place. The small coastal plains are densely cultivated, and the mountains are heavily terraced. Liguria produces a wealth of produce, including some of the world's best olive oil, a vast assortment of fruit and vegetables, mountain cheeses, chestnuts, berries, grapes for wine and, in the Riviera di Ponente, flowers. The region is one of the largest flower producers in the world.

Genoa is a dramatic city, spilling down from the mountains to the old port that was once one of the world's most important trading centers. On a clear day in winter the views from the aptly named Gulf of Paradise to the east can take your breath away. There are snow-covered Alps on the horizon to the north, a glistening sea in front of you and the rugged Apennine range behind. On the surrounding terraces grow oranges, lemons, olives, grapes, loquats and cherries. Flowers bloom year-round and life here is good.

Delicious *focaccia*, or *fugassa* as it is called in the local dialect, is found everywhere in Liguria, but now it is too often made using olive oil or lard in place of the extra virgin olive oil called for in the classic preparation. Fermentation times are often shortened, and the result is a less flavorful, less digestible bread that does not keep well for more than a few hours. In and around the city of Genoa, however, there are still a few bakeries that make *focaccia* according to the classic formula. Over the past several years they have organized themselves and seen to it that Genoa's famous snack was included in the Slow Food Movement's Presidia of endangered products. *Presidiare* means "to guard," and it is the aim of Slow Food to protect and promote endangered foods and foodways.

I met several of the bakers who belong to the *Focaccia Classica di Genova* Presidium. They all had slight variations in their formulas and mixing times, but all agreed on two fundamental principles: only extra virgin olive oil is allowed as the fat component and a minimum production time of seven hours is required. All of them stressed that the time is often longer, depending on the local weather conditions. This *focaccia* has a light, pillow-like, ivory-colored crumb and a chewy crust. The fragrant oil and the sea salt topping add wonderful flavor. It seems to melt in your mouth. In a word, it is irresistible.

The Genovese, rightfully, take enormous pride in their *focaccia*. Here it is considered food of the gods, and it is one of the first solid foods a baby is given to teethe on. It is the treat children rush to buy from their local baker after a long day at school (a special discount often applies to those not yet tall enough to see over countertops or old enough to count), and it graces the tables of the simplest *osterie* and the finest restaurants.

Focaccia-type flatbreads are made in other regions of Italy, to be sure, as they are in North America and other parts of the world, but the city of Genoa is this bread's native home and nowhere else does it taste as good. Genovese baker Marcello Tumioli, of Panificio Tumioli, whose formula I include below, told me that, while there are a few bakers who make the bread using a *biga*, normally, *focaccia* is made using a straight dough.

DIASTATIC MALT POWDER

The bakers of Genoa, like many professional bakers, add malt to their *focaccia* dough. Diastatic malt powder can assist the fermentation of the dough and the caramelization of the crust, but this ingredient may be difficult to find for home bakers. I have excellent results with this formula, even when I do not include malt.

INGREDIENTS	GRAMS	OUNCES	VOLUME
Unbleached all-purpose flour	500 g	17.5 oz	3½ cups
Water	280 g	10 oz	1¼ cups
Extra virgin olive oil	28 g	1 oz	2½ tbsp
Sea salt	12 g	2½ tsp	2½ tsp
Instant dry yeast	12 g	1 tbsp	1 tbsp
Diastatic malt powder (optional)	pinch	pinch	pinch

To sprinkle on top of the dough after you have shaped it:

2 tbsp olive oil

2 tbsp water or white wine

Sea salt or *fleur de sel*

The Mix

Mix all of the ingredients by hand as described on page 22 or on the lowest speed of a stand mixer fitted with the dough hook for 6 minutes and then on the second speed for 2 minutes.

Fermentation

Place the dough in a bowl and cover with a clean kitchen towel or a plate. The first fermentation takes 3 hours and 20 minutes in a kitchen that is 68°F/20°C. The cooler and slower the rise, the better. The dough should double in bulk.

Pre-shape and Rest

Measure a sheet of parchment paper large enough to hold a piece of dough 12 by 18 inches, and place it on a baking sheet. Oil the parchment and turn the dough out onto it. Using your fingertips, gently stretch the dough out as much as you can. It will resist you, which is correct. Give the dough a 30-minute rest, covered with a clean kitchen towel. After the rest it will be easier to stretch.

Shaping

Wet the dough by splashing a bit of the oil and water (or wine) over it and stretch it out evenly, using the tips of your fingers. Your goal is to create deep wells in the dough that will trap the olive oil and withstand the long proof ahead, emerging from the oven with *focaccia*'s characteristic dimpled crust.

Once you have extended the dough, drizzle the remaining extra virgin olive oil on top and then sprinkle with the sea salt or *fleur de sel*. Splash the remaining water, wine or a combination of the two on top and, using your fingers again, gently spread the oil, water and salt evenly over the dough.

Proof

The final proof is about 3 hours, or until the dough is very well risen. Leave the dough uncovered; some of the water you've sprinkled on will evaporate during this time. If you notice the surface getting too dry, spray it with a little room-temperature water.

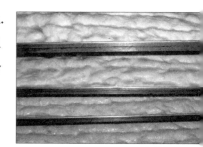

Bake

Preheat the oven to 450°F/230°C. Bake for 20 minutes or until golden brown.

Variations

In Liguria focaccia is usually available plain or with any number of different toppings. Marcello Tumioli told me the authentic ones are sage, white onion or pitted green olives. However, in Liguria today there are lots of other variations. Here are a few of the more popular toppings I have come across. The toppings should be added before the oil and the salt, with the exception of the sage, which is mixed into the dough itself. Amongst the bakers I talked to, it was generally agreed that, after plain focaccia, onion was the most popular flavor. In terms of quantity, there is no hard-and-fast rule. Use enough to generously cover the dough.

Finely chopped sage (mixed into the dough)
Thinly sliced white onions
Thinly sliced pitted green olives
Thinly sliced potatoes
Thinly sliced tomatoes

Pizza Dough

This chapter would not be complete without a recipe for pizza dough of the kind found in Naples—the most famous pizza in Italy. Unlike a lot of modern pizzas, the authentic pizza from Naples does not have a thin crust (that would be a Roman-style pizza); it has a thick, airy crust that is featherlight and chewy at the same time. Neapolitan-style pizza is not easy to find in other Italian regions (I've yet to find one), and the trouble is, once you've tasted the real thing, you will never think about pizza in the same way. Of course, for that you need to go to Naples.

The following formula is based on that of my favorite food writer, Ed Behr, in his article "Pizza in Naples," which appeared in the Spring 1992 issue of his excellent publication *The Art of Eating*. It produces a light, airy dough that is very close to that found in Naples.

The two important factors involved in producing a successful dough are to use a flour with a low protein content (around 9 to 10 percent), and to use a small amount of yeast. The dough will require several hours to proof, and can be made the night before if left to proof in a cool place. I use Italian 00 flour or Canadian cake-and-pastry flour. All-purpose flour, I find, is too strong.

This dough is also used to make the potato, cabbage and cheese pie on page 271 and forms the basis of the Florentine Carnival Flat Cake on page 375.

THE RECIPE MAKES ENOUGH FOR 1 PIZZA, 12 INCHES IN DIAMETER

200 g (7 oz) (1⅔ cups) cake-and-pastry flour
120 g (4.25 oz) (scant ½ cup) water
½ tsp sea salt
½ tsp instant dry yeast

Combine all the ingredients and mix by hand as described on page 22 or in a stand mixer at the lowest speed for 5 minutes. Cover and let rise in a cool place for several hours. The dough should have doubled in bulk.

An hour or more before you are ready to bake, place a baking stone on the middle rack of your oven and preheat the oven to its highest temperature.

Place the dough on a lightly floured surface and shape into a tight ball, and then pat into a disk 4 inches wide. Cover with a clean tea towel and let rest for at least an hour.

To stretch the pizza dough, lift the disk on top of your two clenched fists held at eye level a couple of inches apart. Gently stretch the dough out by moving your fists apart as far as you can without tearing the dough. Rotate the dough slightly (about 30 degrees) and repeat the stretching operation. You will notice a thicker rim forming around the edge of the dough. Continue rotating and stretching the dough until you have an evenly stretched and rimmed circle that resists when you try to stretch it any more. The disk should be close to 12 inches wide and about ⅛ inch thick.

If you want to add a bit of drama to the operation, like the Italian *pizzaiolo* (pizza maker) does, try gently tossing the disk upwards while giving it a slight spin and catching it again on your fists. If you start with a very small toss, as you gain confidence you will find you can send the dough a bit higher each time.

Ideally, pizza dough should not be flattened with a rolling pin, although I have to admit that I have seen this done even in Italy.

If you are making pizza and not one of the other recipes in this book that uses this dough, place your dough on a parchment-lined peel or baking sheet and proceed to cover with your favorite toppings (see below for examples). Bake in your preheated oven until the crust is golden, about 15 minutes, more or less, depending on how hot your oven is.

Pizza Toppings

The best pizza is limited to tomato, mozzarella and no more than one or two other things. My favorite is the classic *pizza margherita*. It includes a handful of chopped fresh tomatoes over which is sprinkled 100 g (3.5 oz) of thinly sliced mozzarella cheese. Extra virgin olive oil is drizzled on top, and when it comes out of the oven it is garnished either with a sprig of fresh basil placed in the center of the pizza or with a few leaves of basil strewn over the top.

Otherwise, let your imagination be your guide, but generally pizza should always include some tomato (chopped fresh or sauce) and fresh mozzarella cheese. After that, choose one or two other ingredients: onions, mushrooms, ham, bacon, salami, thinly sliced carrots or eggplant, capers, anchovies, arugula, Parmesan cheese, and so on. Have fun and don't forget that the final flourish should always be that drizzle of extra virgin olive oil.

Fruit Pizza for Breakfast, Brunch or Dessert

Thinly slice a peeled and cored Golden Delicious apple (or 2, depending on the size) and arrange the slices in attractive rings of concentric circles on top of the pizza dough. Top with a generous sprinkle of sugar (about ¼ cup) and a dash of cinnamon.

Chapter 2 Antipasti ✽ Starters

Giuliano Bugialli points out in *The Fine Art of Italian Cooking* that the word *antipasto* was used in Florence as early as 1546, long before the pasta course found its way to the Italian table. The word means before the meal, *pasto*, not before the pasta, as many people assume. It is curious that the concept seems to have disappeared centuries later when, in 1891, the Florentine silk merchant Pellegrino Artusi published his seminal work, *La Scienza in Cucina e l'Arte di Mangiar Bene*. He doesn't mention the word *antipasto*, but he does describe how tidbits he calls *tramessi*, or starters, were offered after a first course in Tuscany, while in other parts of the peninsula they were served before the meal proper. It is almost certain that, until very recently, an antipasto course would have been reserved for the tables of the wealthy. Even today an antipasto is usually prepared only for special occasions, such as Sunday lunch or one of the many feast days that fill the Italian culinary calendar.

The antipasti on offer change from region to region in Italy. In Tuscany they generally include a large platter of cured meats accompanied by a plate of *crostini misti*. In Liguria it is a slice of *torta salata*, a wedge of *testaroli* with pesto and maybe a warm seafood salad. In Emilia-Romagna some fried bread, pickled vegetables and a platter of gorgeous prosciutto di Parma and Parmesan cheese are likely to appear. In the Val d'Aosta you might be served a platter of fried polenta topped with melting *lardo d'Arnad*, or a bit of *fonduta* made with the local fontina cheese. In Piedmont stuffed peppers, *bagna caoda* and *vitello tonnato* take pride of place, and a whole meal can be made out of the antipasto course alone.

Often the actors who appear on the antipasto stage are stolen from other courses and offered up in smaller amounts. *Testaroli*, for example, are also eaten as a first course, and *vitello tonnato* as a second. Sometimes I serve a tiny portion of soup in an espresso cup, a soft-boiled egg fresh from our hens topped with a little truffle butter, or a slice of *frittata*.

The antipasto and the dessert courses are the playful bookends to the more substantial and serious parts of an Italian meal. I often find them the most memorable. I like to offer guests at least two or three different things to start, accompanied by an *aperitivo*, usually a glass of *spumante*. It is a pleasant way to begin a meal, to show off a bit and set the bar for what is to follow. I keep starter portions small, just enough to whet the appetite. Too much of a good thing is no longer a good thing, and more people today are appreciative of a light touch.

Salvia e Fiori di Zucca Fritti
⋆ Deep-fried Sage Leaves and Squash Blossoms
Deep-fried sage leaves and squash blossoms are standard early-summer appetizers in Tuscany. Huge baskets of blossoms are available in the

markets simply for frying, while a special kind of sage with extra-large leaves is cultivated *da friggere* (for frying). Members of the squash family such as zucchini and pumpkin are grown as much for their flowers as for the vegetable itself. These prolific plants fruit abundantly, and their bounty rapidly tires the palate. More often than not I leave them to grow very large for fodder for my pigs and courtyard animals. But never the precious blossoms. They are a fleeting seasonal delicacy. Zucchini blossoms can be found in Italian markets in early summer. If you grow your own, the blossoms to pick are the male ones—those that don't bear fruit.

Italians have mastered the delicate art of deep-frying. If you are on the coast, it will be seafood; if you are inland, you will be served vegetables or meat. The key to a good *fritto* is a light batter, the best-quality oil you can afford (olive oil is ideal) and, as always, the freshest ingredients.

Sage leaves and squash blossoms should be used as soon as possible after you pick or buy them. Ideally, they should have about ½ inch or so of their stems left to serve as a handle, making it easy to pick them up off the platter after they've been fried.

For the pastella (batter)
   ¾ cup all-purpose flour
   ¼ tsp salt
   A pinch of freshly grated nutmeg
   1 cup water

For the fritti
   3 or 4 squash blossoms (zucchini, pumpkin, summer squash, etc.)
      per person
   Several large leaves of fresh sage per person

If you don't like anchovies, the sage leaves are delicious on their own, lightly floured, dipped in batter and fried.

Flour for dusting

1 anchovy fillet for every 4 sage leaves, cut in half crosswise (optional).

Olive oil for frying

Sea salt to taste

For the pastella

Whisk together all of the ingredients for the batter and let sit at room temperature for at least 30 minutes before using.

For the fritti

Preheat the oven to 200°F/95°C.

Wash the blossoms and remove the pistils inside, being careful to check for bugs. Drain on a clean kitchen towel.

Gently wash the sage leaves and pass them through the dusting flour, shaking afterward so a very fine coating of flour remains. Place half an anchovy fillet on one floured sage leaf and top with another leaf, pressing gently together to form a secure sandwich.

Use enough olive oil to cover the bottom of your sauté pan by about an inch. Heat the oil over high heat until it is very hot but not smoking. You can test the oil for readiness by dropping a cube of bread into it; the bread should brown in about 1 minute.

Dip the squash blossoms and sage-anchovy sandwiches in the batter and then fry a batch at a time in the hot oil, without crowding the pan, and turning once they are golden on one side to cook the other. Transfer to a plate lined with a paper towel to drain. Keep warm in the oven while you fry the remainder.

Sprinkle with the sea salt just before serving.

Variations

Squash blossoms are sometimes stuffed (especially in Campania, where Italy's best mozzarella is produced) with a small cube of fresh mozzarella and a fillet of anchovy before being battered and fried.

Other young garden vegetables can be added to the mix to make a *fritto misto dell'orto*. I use thinly sliced baby zucchini and spring onions, baby carrots, tiny new potatoes and green beans, but let your imagination be your guide. In early spring in Tuscany the blossoms of the acacia tree are fried, a rare treat marking the start of the frying season.

A Word of Advice for Those with a Fear of Frying

Many people avoid deep-frying because it's a messy business producing food that is ideally consumed *à la minute*. The way around this is to forget about impressing anybody with fried foods. Instead, serve a course of *fritti* for those near and dear to you. This is not food easily prepared for an elegant dinner party, but it's marvelous in the most intimate of company. Frying in small quantities means you can use a small pan and a small amount of oil and work fast, controlling the mess and the time involved. More importantly, you can be sure this heavenly food is eaten just as it should be—hot, right out of the pan, with a sprinkle of sea salt. The bonus is that a once formidable task becomes drop-dead easy.

Polpettine ✦ Mediterranean Spinach Meatballs

These small meatballs, at least a third greens, are a healthy and delicious treat. They are one of my standards at La Petraia, always receiving raves. Meatballs containing a large percentage of vegetables are common throughout the Mediterranean. Mashed potatoes are sometimes used instead of greens, but I prefer this version.

You can use any kind of greens—spinach, kale, beet tops and chard all work well. The seasoning can be adapted to suit your tastes. Use any kind of meat you like—I have made these meatballs successfully with chicken, lamb, pork, beef, venison and wild boar. I usually incorporate a couple of different kinds of meat—whatever I have on hand. *Polpettine* are often fried in olive oil, but my preference is to bake them.

The raw mixture freezes well, and I usually double the recipe and freeze half. In the *Secondi* chapter there is a main course based on these: Spinach Meatballs Served in a *Frico* Basket with a Cucumber and a Tomato Sauce (see page 245).

SERVES 6 TO 8

For the polpettine

    500 g (18 oz) boneless meat or poultry, cut into cubes of about
        1 inch
    280 g (10 oz) steamed greens* (or an equivalent amount of
        thawed frozen spinach), squeezed very dry
    1 egg
    70 g (2.5 oz) (⅔ cup) fresh bread crumbs (preferably homemade)
    70 g (2.5 oz) (¾ cup) finely grated Parmesan cheese
    1 large garlic clove, roughly chopped
    2 tbsp chopped mixed fresh herbs, such as oregano, basil,
        marjoram and rosemary
    1 tbsp chopped fresh parsley
   See note on page 165 for cooking greens.

¾ tsp Chinese five-spice powder

A pinch of freshly grated nutmeg

A few flakes of hot chili pepper

Salt and pepper to taste

For the coating

1 egg, lightly beaten

¾ cup fresh bread crumbs or coarsely ground cornmeal

For the polpettine

Put all the ingredients for the *polpettine* into the work bowl of a food processor and process very briefly to get the consistency of ground meat. Form into meatballs 1 to 1½ inches in diameter.

For the coating

Dip each meatball first in the egg and then in the bread crumbs or cornmeal. Place on a parchment-lined baking sheet. The meatballs can be refrigerated at this point until you are ready to bake them.

Bake in a 350°F/175°C oven for 25 minutes.

Serve on a platter. Break several sticks of spaghetti into small pieces and stick one in each meatball to act as a toothpick for serving.

Frico Croccante ✦ Crunchy Fried Cheese from Friuli

The region of Friuli-Venezia Giulia is one of Italy's most exotic. Bordering on Slovenia and the Istrian peninsula of Croatia, Austria and the Veneto, it has a rich culture and history. The dramatic snow-capped Julian Alps and those of the Carnia fall away to gently rolling hills around Udine, where much of Italy's best white wine is produced. The gracious old city of Trieste and the Adriatic coast provide the region with a hint of urban sophistication and a maritime flavor. A visit to the main square of Udine reminds you that this was once part of the vast Venetian empire. Friuli is Italy's gateway to Eastern Europe, and Trieste and Udine are cities full of fashionable cafés that would not be out of place in Vienna or Budapest. Pastries are stuffed with cinnamon and poppy seeds, while *gulasch* and delicious dumplings called *cjarson* are found on almost every menu.

Frico uses the local montasio cheese. Montasio is a cow's milk cheese that has been awarded DOP (denomination of protected origin) designation by the European Union. The cheese is eaten at various ages and has wonderful cooking qualities. Fresh, it is lovely in melting dishes. Aged a bit, it can be used for recipes like *frico*. Older still, it takes on spicy notes and makes an excellent grating cheese or a crunchier *frico*.

Frico is standard fare in Friuli and comes in many varieties. These are usually specific to a mountain valley or local *comune*. It comes crunchy or melting. It is made with potatoes, onions, spinach, apples and countless other ingredients. There is *frico* as antipasto, first course, second course or dessert.

This recipe is the standard, most common type, called *frico croccante*, or crunchy *frico*. It is easy to make and can be prepared hours ahead of time. All you need is a hunk of cheese and a nonstick frying pan. If montasio is hard to come by, Parmesan or any dry, hard cheese will do for a substitute. It can be made as large disks and presented as an appetizer for people to break off a piece, or it can be shaped into a dish to hold risotto as a first course or meatballs as a main course (see Spinach Meatballs Served in a *Frico* Basket with a Cucumber and a Tomato Sauce, on page 245).

If you are serving *frico* as an appetizer, a glass of *spumante* or any other sparkling or slightly fizzy white wine goes nicely. If you can find a white wine from Friuli, even better.

450 g (1 lb) grated montasio, Grana Padana or Parmesan cheese

Heat a nonstick frying pan over moderate heat until it is hot. Add just enough of the cheese to just cover the bottom of your pan. You are aiming for crêpe-like thinness here, so don't overdo it with the cheese—it will spread as it melts.

Turn the heat down and use a fork to push down on the *frico* as it cooks to release the fat. Cook until it is golden on the bottom. Using a spatula, flip the cheese over and continue to cook until the bottom is golden. (There is no need to press it again.) Remove from the pan.

For a fanciful presentation, you can drape the still warm *frico* over an upside-down glass to mold it into a dish shape.

Frico con Patate ✦ Frico with Potatoes

After plain *frico*, the next most popular version has to be one made with potatoes. I've encountered countless recipes for it, but they all contain the same basic ingredients—cheese and potatoes. Thicker than a crunchy *frico*, this one has a melting consistency. The finished dish can be served in small portions as an antipasto. Otherwise, it makes a perfect winter lunch alongside a crisp green salad.

Serves 4 to 6

56 g (2 oz) pancetta, cut into small cubes
1 onion, thinly sliced
4 or 5 medium floury potatoes

Freshly ground black pepper to taste

225 g (8 oz) montasio cheese (ideally about 3 months old), cut
   into small cubes (you could also use Gruyère or Beaufort)

Heat a nonstick frying pan over moderate heat and add the pancetta.
Cook until it gives off its fat and begins to brown, about 5 minutes.
Lower the heat and add the onion. Cook until it begins to wilt, about
5 minutes.

In the meantime, wash any dirt off the potatoes, peel them and cut
them into small cubes or matchstick pieces. When the onion is wilted,
add the potatoes to the pan. Stir and season with the pepper. Add a
small ladle of water and cook, partially covered, over moderately low
heat until the potatoes are tender. This will take about 20 minutes. You
will need to stir the mixture from time to time and add more water if it
looks too dry.

At this point add the cheese and keep stirring until it melts. Increase
the heat to high and cook for 2 to 3 minutes, continuing to stir. Transfer
to warm serving dishes and serve immediately.

Variation

For a crispier frico, cook until the bottom is golden and slide the *frico* onto
a plate. Put the pan over the plate and turn the *frico* back into it. Return to
the heat and cook until the other side is golden. Cut and serve in wedges.

Acciughe Marinate ✦ Marinated Anchovies

Here at Petraia we don't eat much fish. With the nearby village of Radda
perched on top of the Chianti mountain range a good two and a half

hours from either the Mediterranean or the Adriatic, the prospects of finding fresh fish are limited to the mobile fishmonger who turns up in the main square every Friday morning. In this way, the largely Catholic community is provided with the requisite fish for Friday lunch.

Fresh fish is expensive in Italy, and anchovies are one of the cheapest kinds available, selling for just a few euros per kilo. I am always astonished when the fishmonger agrees to fillet the anchovies for me—it's such a messy job. "*Certo*," he says with his generous smile and then proceeds to painstakingly and beautifully prepare my fillets, more than eighty of them to a kilo.

SERVES 4 TO 6

450 g (1 lb) fresh anchovies, filleted

1 medium red onion, finely diced

Oregano leaves (fresh if you have them)

Extra virgin olive oil (about ½ cup)

2 tbsp wine vinegar

Juice of 1 lemon

Salt and pepper to taste

Finely chopped fresh parsley for garnish

Arrange half of the anchovy fillets in a serving dish. Sprinkle with half the onion, oregano, oil, vinegar and lemon juice. Season with salt and pepper. Repeat using the remaining ingredients.

Tightly cover the dish with plastic wrap and refrigerate overnight. Serve cold or at room temperature. Sprinkle with parsley just before serving.

Spiedini alla Bandiera
◆ Cherry Tomato, Mozzarella and Basil Skewers

Although everyone knows the tomato is not indigenous to Italy but arrived here from South America, I believe I've discovered the reason for its appeal. *It grows like a weed.* It is nearing the end of October as I write this, and the tomato plants in my garden are still bearing fruit. I harvested my first tomato in the middle of May. Five months and counting.

Out of the dozen or so plants I had this year, I managed to put away a freezerful of tomato sauce, and there are shelves of canned tomatoes in my *cantina.* Seedlings still spring up near the compost from fruit left to rot there last year. The tomato, like me and many foreigners who come to live here, may not be a native but it has taken to this country like a duck to water.

Our cherry tomatoes really do taste like cherries, they're so sweet. They are perfect for this simple summertime dish. I serve this dish—named after the red, white and green Italian *bandiera,* or flag—as a starter, but it also makes an elegant lunch with a green salad and some crusty bread. Make these only if your ingredients are fresh and of the best quality. If you are lucky enough to own a bottle of *aceto balsamico tradizionale* (see page 110), a few drops can be used to finish the dish.

> **Several spaghetti strands, each broken in two or three pieces to use as skewers**
> **Cherry tomatoes (whole or cut in half, depending on their size)**
> **Fresh basil leaves**
> **Mozzarella cheese, cut into small cubes**
> **Quality extra virgin olive oil for drizzling**
> **Sea salt to taste**
> *Aceto balsamico tradizionale* **(optional)**

Onto each spaghetti strand, thread a piece of tomato, followed by a basil leaf, followed by a piece of cheese.

Serve the *spiedini* arranged on a platter, drizzled with olive oil and sprinkled with sea salt. A few drops of *aceto balsamico tradizionale* add a nice color and flavor.

Crescentina col Lardo ♦ Fried Bread with *Lardo*

Deep-fried bread dough is served as antipasto in many parts of Italy, and it has several different names. *Crescentina*, or *gnocco fritto*, is the name given to these delicious morsels in the mountains of Emilia, and they are especially good when topped with a piece of *lardo*, which melts to delicious result over them. *Lardo* is pork fat that has been seasoned with herbs and cured in salt. It was traditionally made in the winter months, after the family pig was slaughtered, when it was cool enough to cure the meat without risking spoilage. Many people, myself included, still make their own *lardo* and pancetta at this time of year.

Lardo is popular all over Italy and is sometimes sliced thinly like bacon or sold in paste form in a jar. Do not use ordinary lard; it is quite a different thing. If you find the idea of eating raw cured pork fat off-putting, or you can't find *lardo*, these fried balls are fine by themselves with just a sprinkle of good sea salt, or with a dab of fresh cream cheese or goat's cheese.

In Emilia-Romagna a complete antipasto course is created around these puffs of fried dough. Serve them with a plate of *affettati misti*, or mixed cured meats, including some *prosciutto di Parma*, along with a few chunks of Parmesan cheese (topped with a drop of *aceto balsamico tradizionale* if you can afford it). Some pickled onions complete the picture. If you want to be really authentic, try to find a nice fizzy Lambrusco red wine to serve.

For the crescentina dough

280 g (10 oz) (2 cups) all-purpose flour

150 g (5.3 oz) (⅔ cup) tepid water

1 tsp instant dry yeast

¼ cup olive oil, plus extra for frying

A pinch of salt

A pinch of sugar

To finish

100 g (3.5 oz) thinly sliced *lardo* (optional)

Salt to taste

Mix all ingredients for the *crescentina* (except the oil for frying) and knead by hand or on low speed in a stand mixer for 6 minutes. Leave the dough in the bowl it was mixed in, cover and let rise until doubled, about an hour.

On a lightly floured surface, roll out the dough to about ⅛ inch thick. Use a cookie cutter or pastry wheel to cut out circles, squares or rectangles, whatever shape you like. Place the dough on a piece of parchment paper or a clean kitchen towel and cover. Let rise again for about an hour—the dough should puff up, doubling in bulk. Alternatively, you can leave the *crescentina* in the refrigerator to rise for several hours or overnight, until you are ready to fry them.

When you are ready to fry them, preheat the oven to 200°F/95°C.

Cover the bottom of a sauté pan with olive oil to a depth of 1 inch and heat until it is very hot but not smoking. You can test the temperature of the oil by dropping a bread cube in it; the bread should turn golden brown in about 1 minute. When the oil is ready, add enough pieces of dough to half fill the pan—you need to leave ample space between each piece because they will expand. They will take 2 to 3 minutes to cook. Once they have puffed up and turned golden on the bottom, flip them over to cook the other side until golden. Remove to a plate lined with a paper towel. If you are using *lardo*, top each puff with a piece now. Keep the fritters warm in the oven while you finish frying. The *lardo* will melt to delicious effect on top of the hot fritters. Serve hot, sprinkled with salt.

Lardo di Colonnata

Perhaps the most famous Italian *lardo* is *lardo di Colonnata*, made in the breathtaking mountaintop village of the same name high above Carrara. This *lardo* was traditionally an important source of energy for the quarry workers, who would take a piece of it to work with them, along with a loaf of bread, a few tomatoes and a *fiasco* of wine. The *lardo* was, and still is, preserved in beautiful marble *conche*, or caskets. The marble comes from the same quarries as Michelangelo's David and it provides an ideal environment for the maturation of the lard.

Colonnata's *lardo* had become an almost forgotten food but has enjoyed a rebirth in recent years, having obtained an *indicazione geografica protetta* (protected geographical designation, or IGP) denomination from the EU. It can be found in all the best *gastronomie* and restaurants in Italy, and it commands a substantial price.

Crostini di Fegato di Pollo
◆ Tuscan Chicken Liver Spread

When my husband and I bought La Petraia, we spent months negotiating and closing the purchase. A whole team of experts was called in, and the sale took longer and cost several thousand dollars more than it would have in North America, where real estate transactions today seem almost as easy as buying your groceries. Our property, all 165 ancient acres of it, had been subdivided more than twenty times over the millennia. Each subdivision had a specific designation—pasture, wilderness, oak or chestnut forest. What's more, all the land that bordered on ours had been similarly divided, and there were endless bits whose owners, if they were registered farmers, we would have to track down to offer a right of first refusal, as is the law in Italy when an agricultural property changes hands.

When we finally finished, and held the deed in our hands, we hosted a celebratory dinner at La Petraia for everyone who had taken part in this onerous task. I decided to jump into the fire and attempt a traditional Tuscan meal, even though everybody knows a foreigner can't cook this way. As people arrived that evening, I could see the familiar look of trepidation on their faces that I translated as, "Who knows what we're in for tonight, but it'll soon be over." Imagine how delighted I was when our guest of honor, the assistant mayor of the town, exclaimed after tasting the chicken liver *crostini* I had passed around to start, "How does a girl from Canada know how to make these? They taste just like my grandmother's!" My secret, and his grandmother's too, it turned out, was the addition of Marsala rather than the traditional Tuscan Vin Santo.

In Tuscany you are hard pressed to find a restaurant that doesn't offer a plate of these delicious *crostini* as an antipasto. It is something not made at home much anymore. Instead, the paste is sold ready-made at the local *gastronomia*. Reminiscent of a French liver pâté, it is rumored that this is one of the dishes Caterina de' Medici introduced to the French kitchen in the sixteenth century, when she married Henry of Orleans, the future king of France. Traditionally it is made with a mixture of rabbit and chicken livers and served on grilled slices of Tuscan bread. For special occasions I like to add a twist by using the mixture as a filling for small puffs of *bignè*, or cream puff pastry (see page 90); they make perfect bite-sized treats to serve at a formal gathering of guests who stand mingling with a glass of wine.

As an aside, in Italian the word *crostino* also refers to someone who is a bit difficult, or hard to relate to—someone a bit crusty. This recipe has been adapted from Nancy Harmon Jenkins' wonderful book on Tuscan cooking, *Flavors of Tuscany*.

SERVES 8 TO 10

1 small onion, minced

A few flakes of hot chili pepper

¼ cup extra virgin olive oil

1 garlic clove, minced

280 g (10 oz) chicken livers (or a mix of rabbit and chicken livers)

4 anchovy fillets

¼ cup Vin Santo, Marsala or other sweet wine

1 tbsp salted capers, soaked to remove the salt, drained and
   finely chopped

1 tbsp finely chopped fresh parsley

A squeeze of lemon juice

Salt and pepper to taste

Grilled or toasted Tuscan bread

Cook the onions and chili flakes in the olive oil over moderate heat, stirring occasionally, for about 10 minutes or until the onions wilt and become transparent. Add the garlic and cook for another few minutes, until the garlic starts to give off its scent but does not brown.

Add the chicken livers and stir for a few minutes until lightly colored. Add the anchovies and begin to mash the mixture with a wooden spoon as it cooks. When the anchovies have dissolved, add the wine and continue to crush the livers. Alternatively, process the mixture briefly using a hand blender. Continue to cook for another few minutes, stirring occasionally, until the liquid has evaporated and the liver is cooked through completely, no longer pink. You should have a fairly smooth paste that is not too dry.

Remove from the heat and stir in the capers, parsley and a squeeze of lemon juice. Taste for salt and season with pepper if desired. Serve warm on top of toasted or grilled slices of Tuscan bread.

Bignè Salato ✦ Savory Cream Puffs

These are classic cream puff shells made with olive oil instead of butter. The cream puffs can be made ahead and frozen unfilled. How many eggs you need will depend on your flour and the humidity. The final dough should be almost but not quite thick enough to pick up with your hands and place in the piping bag. The cooked shells can be filled with the chicken liver mixture on page 88 or any other filling that strikes your fancy. To fill, slice the *bignè* in half and place a spoonful of the chicken liver paste inside. Replace the top and serve.

85 g (3 oz) (⅓ cup plus 1 tbsp) olive oil

225 g (8 oz) (1 cup) water

150 g (5.3 oz) (1 cup) bread flour

A pinch of salt

1 egg white

3 to 4 whole eggs

Preheat the oven to 325°F/165°C.

Place the olive oil and water in a pan and bring to a boil. Remove from the heat and add the flour and salt. Stir with a wooden spoon to mix well. Return to the heat, stirring constantly to dry the mixture out, 1 to 2 minutes. The mixture is ready when it is firm and the flour begins to leave a film on the bottom of the pan. Let cool for 5 minutes.

Add the egg white and then the whole eggs, one at a time, stirring rapidly until each egg is absorbed before you add the next. You are trying to get a thick paste-like dough, and 3 eggs could be sufficient.

Spoon the dough into a piping bag fitted with a #8 or #10 plain tip and pipe small balls of dough, 1 to 1½ inches wide and 2 inches apart, onto a parchment-lined baking sheet. If you don't have a piping bag, use a spoon.

Bake for 10 minutes, then reduce the heat to 300°F/150°C. The puffs need to bake until they are dried out completely on the inside or they will fall when you remove them from the oven. This should take another 30 minutes. They should have doubled or even tripled in size and will be golden brown when done. When you take them out, make a small slit along the side of each cream puff to let the steam escape. Cool on a rack.

Crostini con Cavolo Nero
◆ Crostini with Tuscan Black Kale

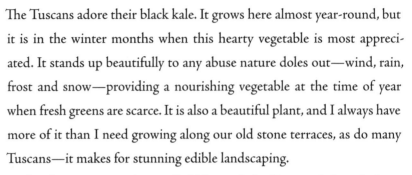

The Tuscans adore their black kale. It grows here almost year-round, but it is in the winter months when this hearty vegetable is most appreciated. It stands up beautifully to any abuse nature doles out—wind, rain, frost and snow—providing a nourishing vegetable at the time of year when fresh greens are scarce. It is also a beautiful plant, and I always have more of it than I need growing along our old stone terraces, as do many Tuscans—it makes for stunning edible landscaping.

Cavolo nero is sometimes called Tuscan kale, dinosaur kale or *lacinato* kale, but any type of kale will work for this recipe. You could also use spinach in a pinch. If you are using kale, cook it in an abundant amount of olive oil until it is very tender. You are looking not for a crunch here but for a vegetable that is luxuriously coated in good-quality oil and cooked long enough that it practically melts in your mouth.

Serves 4 to 6

1 bunch kale, stems and center ribs removed, leaves washed and
    finely chopped

Extra virgin olive oil

1 garlic clove, minced

A few flakes of hot chili pepper

4 to 6 rather thick slices of Tuscan bread*

½ garlic clove

Sea salt or fleur de sel

See page 31 or use an artisanal loaf.

Bring a pot of water to a rolling boil. Add the kale and wait until the water returns to the boil, about 30 seconds. Drain in a colander and run cold water over the kale to stop the cooking, but do not dry.

Over moderate heat, heat enough of the oil to cover the bottom of your sauté pan and add the minced garlic and the pepper flakes. Cook, stirring, until you can smell the garlic—a few minutes. Be careful not to let it burn. Add the kale and cook, stirring occasionally, for about 10 minutes or until very tender and any water left clinging to its leaves has evaporated. Cooking time will depend on the green you use.

In the meantime, prepare the bread. Grill the slices over a wood fire or gas or stovetop grill, or toast them. Rub each slice with the cut side of the garlic. Top with a generous pile of the greens. Drizzle with olive oil and sprinkle with sea salt.

Place one slice on each plate. This dish is generally eaten with a knife and fork rather than with the fingers.

Crostini con Burro di Sgombro
✦ Crostini with Mackerel Butter

This delicious fish paste uses mackerel, whose fat is valued because it contains a high percentage of heart-healthy omega-3 oils. It keeps well for several days in the fridge. Good-quality sun-dried tomatoes should be a bit soft—not dried out and shriveled up. If your sun-dried tomatoes are too dry, you can soak them in hot water for a few minutes to soften before processing with the other ingredients.

This recipe also works well using tuna preserved in olive oil.

112 g (4 oz) mackerel fillets preserved in olive oil

4 tbsp (½ stick) butter, softened

A few flakes of hot chili pepper

Several leaves of fresh Italian parsley and a few leaves of fresh basil

1 garlic clove

3 soft sun-dried tomatoes

Salt and pepper to taste

Tuscan bread,* sliced rather thick

*See page 31 or use an artisanal loaf.

Do not drain the mackerel. Place all ingredients except the bread in the work bowl of your food processor and process to a smooth paste. Refrigerate for 1 hour. When ready to serve, grill the bread over a wood fire or gas or stovetop grill. Spread the paste on the warm bread and serve.

Variation

I have also made this paste using smoked dried chipotle peppers in place of the tomatoes. The peppers will need to be soaked in hot water to soften before being used.

Torta Salata ◆ Ligurian Vegetable Tart

Liguria is famous for the quality of its olive oil, herbs and vegetables, and its most celebrated dishes are largely *di magro*, or vegetarian. The vegetable tart is found all over the region, and comes in many different versions. There is the famous Easter *torta Pasqualina*, traditionally composed of thirty-three layers—one for every year of the life of Christ—and stuffed with cheese, greens and eggs. There are tarts made with onions, *farro*, greens, artichokes, cheeses, asparagus, cardoons, rice, mushrooms and pumpkin.

Perhaps the most common, Ligurian *torta salata*, or savory tart, is filled with greens, traditionally a mixture of wild bitter greens called *preboggion*, or sometimes just *bietole* (Swiss chard), combined with the local ricotta-like fresh cheese called *prescinseua* or sometimes simply referred to as *cagliata*, or curds. But one also encounters two other green tarts in Liguria—one, commonly found in western Liguria, is filled with rice and greens, and another, found in and around the wealthy city of Genoa, incorporates pine nuts and raisins into the filling.

The pastry for these tarts is a simple one made of flour, olive oil and water. Although the tarts can be served warm, they are usually left to cool completely and served at room temperature in very small wedges as an antipasto. I sometimes cut them into bite-sized cubes to serve on a platter with some olives and salami or other cured meats. They make a perfect vegetarian main course or can be featured in a brunch or light lunch alongside a green salad.

Most bakeries and *gastronomie* in the region sell these tarts by the slice, and I suspect there aren't many Ligurians who can be bothered making them at home anymore.

MAKES 1 TART

For the dough
    280 g (10 oz) (2 cups) all-purpose flour
    150 g (5.3 oz) (⅔ cup) water
    3 tbsp extra virgin olive oil
    A pinch of salt

For the tart

1 filling of choice (recipes follow)
Olive oil for brushing

For the dough

Place the flour on your work surface and make a well in the middle. Combine the water, oil and salt and add it to the well bit by bit, mixing it into the flour with a finger as you go. Once all the liquid is incorporated, knead the dough for a minute or two until it is smooth. Alternatively, you can mix this dough in a stand mixer, using the dough hook and kneading it very briefly, just until you have a smooth dough.

Divide the dough into two balls, one slightly larger than the other, and cover with a clean towel. Let it rest at room temperature for 1 hour. Preheat the oven to 400°F/200°C.

For the tart

Roll out the larger piece of dough until it is very thin—about ⅛ inch thick—and place it in an oiled shallow round baking pan, 10 to 12 inches in diameter. Fill the shell with the chosen filling. Roll out the smaller piece of dough and cover the tart, pressing the edges to seal. Brush a little olive oil over the top and, using a knife, pierce a couple of steam vents in the crust.

Bake the tart for 10 minutes, then reduce the heat to 350°F/175°C. Bake for about another 25 minutes. The tart is done when the crust begins to turn golden and the delicious aroma fills your kitchen. Remove from the oven and turn the tart out onto a clean kitchen towel. Wrap the hot tart in the towel, invert it so that it is right side up again, and let it sit for 10 minutes. This will prevent the crust from becoming too hard. Remove the towel and place the tart on a rack to cool completely.

Ripieni per la Torta Salata
Ligurian Vegetable Tart Fillings

Mixed Greens Filling

In the town of Santa Margherita Ligure, where we once had an apartment, there was a daily farmers' market in the main square. The smaller stalls were occupied by local farmers, and they usually had a few spotted brown eggs, some seasonal vegetables from their *orto*, perhaps a few bottles of their own olive oil and, almost always, an abundant supply of *preboggion*, the wild herbs and greens used to make pasta fillings and savory tarts all over Liguria. Not the most attractive of plants—they are often hairy and inedible-looking, resembling weeds—they make a very tasty tart. It is unlikely you will come across *preboggion* in a North American market, but fortunately any dark, leafy green will work—chard, mustard, kale, spinach, beet or turnip. A mix of several different kinds works best.

750 g (1⅔ lb) mixed greens (see above), well washed

1 onion, finely chopped

¼ cup extra virgin olive oil

2 large eggs, lightly beaten

112 g (4 oz) (generous 1 cup) grated Parmesan cheese

112 g (4 oz) ricotta cheese, drained (see page 152)

Chopped fresh herbs, such as marjoram, oregano, parsley or
   savory, to taste

A pinch of nutmeg

Salt and pepper to taste

In a pot over moderate heat, steam the greens in the water left clinging to them after you have washed them until they wilt. Squeeze dry and finely chop.

Sauté the onion in the oil briefly, until it starts to wilt, then add the greens and cook for about 10 minutes or until tender. The cooking time will vary depending on the type of green you have chosen.

Place the greens in a bowl to cool, then add all of the remaining ingredients. Mix well and proceed to fill the prepared tart shell. Bake as directed on page 96.

Greens with Raisin and Pine Nut Filling

¼ cup raisins, soaked in grappa, brandy or warm water for
    several hours or overnight, and drained
450 g (1 lb) mixed greens (see introduction, page 97), well washed
1 small onion, finely chopped
¼ cup extra virgin olive oil
3 large eggs, lightly beaten
112 g (4 oz) ricotta cheese, drained (see page 152)
85 g (3 oz) (generous ¾ cup) grated Parmesan cheese
2 tbsp chopped fresh parsley
1 tbsp pine nuts
A pinch of freshly grated nutmeg
Salt and pepper to taste

Follow the instructions at the top of this page to steam and sauté the greens with the onion and olive oil. Combine the cooled greens with all of the remaining ingredients. Fill the prepared tart shell and bake as directed on page 96.

Greens with Rice Filling

1 cup rice

2½ cups milk

450 g (1 lb) mixed greens (see introduction, page 97), well washed

1 small onion, finely chopped

¼ cup extra virgin olive oil

1 large egg, lightly beaten

Finely chopped fresh marjoram to taste

Freshly grated nutmeg to taste

Salt and pepper to taste

Cook the rice in the milk until tender, about 20 minutes.

Follow the instructions on page 98 (top) to steam and sauté the greens with the onion and olive oil. Combine the cooled greens with all of the remaining ingredients. Fill the prepared tart shell and bake as directed on page 96.

Onion Filling

In this version, the greens are replaced with onions.

28 g (1 oz) dried porcini mushrooms

1 kg (2¼ lb) red onions, thinly sliced

2 tbsp olive oil

¼ tsp salt

1 tbsp balsamic vinegar

56 g (2 oz) (⅔ cup) grated Parmesan cheese

2 large eggs, lightly beaten

2 tbsp finely chopped fresh parsley

1 tsp finely chopped fresh rosemary

A pinch of freshly grated nutmeg

Pepper to taste

Soak the mushrooms in warm water for half an hour, then drain the mushrooms, reserving the soaking liquid. Strain the soaking liquid if it contains sand or grit from the mushrooms (see page 180).

Cook the onions in the olive oil in a large sauté pan over moderate heat until they begin to wilt, about 5 minutes. Reduce the heat to low and stir in the salt. Lightly cover the pan with a sheet of foil and continue to cook for another 10 minutes.

Add the mushrooms and ¼ cup of their soaking liquid to the onions. Continue to cook on low heat, covered lightly with the foil, for another 10 to 15 minutes, stirring from time to time, until the mushrooms are tender. Remove the foil and add the balsamic vinegar. Increase the heat to moderate and cook, uncovered, for about 10 minutes, stirring from time to time, until the onions begin to caramelize. Remove from the heat and let the mixture cool before adding the remaining ingredients. Stir well to combine. Fill the prepared tart shell and bake as directed on page 96.

Pumpkin Filling

1 kg (2¼ lb) pumpkin or squash, peeled and grated or cut into
    small julienne strips

Salt

28 g (1 oz) dried porcini mushrooms

1 cup rice

1 small onion, minced

¼ cup olive oil

5 eggs, lightly beaten

112 g (4 oz) (generous 1 cup) grated Parmesan cheese

Finely chopped fresh sage to taste

A pinch of freshly grated nutmeg

Salt and pepper to taste

Place the pumpkin in a colander and sprinkle generously with salt to cover. Leave to drain for 3 hours.

Meanwhile, soak the mushrooms in warm chicken broth or water for half an hour (see page 180). Drain the mushrooms, saving the soaking liquid for another use. Cook the rice in abundant boiling water for about 15 minutes, until tender. Drain the rice.

Sauté the onion and the drained mushrooms in the olive oil over moderate heat for about 5 minutes, until the onions are translucent and the mushrooms are tender. Remove from the heat and let cool.

Rinse the pumpkin in several changes of water. Drain and squeeze out any excess water. Combine the pumpkin with all of the remaining ingredients and stir well. Mound the filling into the prepared tart shell. (It will seem to be too much, but the pumpkin will shrink as it cooks.) Bake as directed on page 96.

Vitello Tonnato ✦ Veal in a Tuna Sauce

Vitello tonnato is a specialty of the Piedmont region, where it is usually served in very small portions as part of a series of appetizers. This preparation is actually a type of *bollito,* a boiled meat dish one often comes across in northern Italy. After the veal is boiled and cooled, it is cut into paper-thin slices and served with a tuna-based mayonnaise. I have eaten in dozens of *osterie* and restaurants in Piedmont. I don't recall once not having been offered this dish as an appetizer.

Tuna and olive oil, both used in abundance in *vitello tonnato*, may seem strange ingredients for a landlocked region dominated by the Alps, where the olive tree is not found. But preserved fish and olive oil are important staples in the Piedmont kitchen. They have been traded over Apennine passes with the neighboring region of Liguria for centuries.

The sauce traditionally contains raw egg yolks. In Italy, where many people keep a few hens and where the "drinking" of raw eggs is considered good for one's health, there is less concern over the use of raw eggs in mayonnaise. If you are nervous about using them you, can omit them.

This dish also makes a nice main course in the summer.

SERVES 6 TO 8

For the veal
   1 kg (2¼ lb) boneless veal loin
   2 cups white wine
   1 onion
   1 carrot
   1 celery stalk
   1 garlic clove
   A *bouquet garni* of 1 bay leaf and several sprigs of fresh parsley

For the tuna sauce
   2 egg yolks*
   2 anchovy fillets
   Juice of half a lemon
   If you do not wish to use raw egg yolks, you can omit them, but add another ½ cup of extra virgin olive oil.

1 cup extra virgin olive oil

112 g (4 oz) tuna preserved in olive oil, drained

2 tbsp salted capers, well rinsed

Salt to taste (you may not want any depending on the saltiness
    of the capers)

MAKE-AHEAD NOTE

This dish often improves
in flavor, so it can be
made a day ahead.

For the veal

Place the veal in a pot just large enough to hold it, then add the wine and
the remaining ingredients. Add enough cold water just to cover the veal.
Cover and bring to a bare simmer. The meat should cook for about 90
minutes. Remove from the heat and let the veal cool in the broth.

For the tuna sauce

Put all of the ingredients in a blender and process until you have a creamy
sauce.

To serve

When the veal is cooled, slice it thinly. Place a slice on each serving plate,
cover with a rather thin layer of the sauce and top with another slice of
veal and more sauce. Two or three slices per person are generally enough.
You can decorate the plate with a sliver of lemon rind and a few olives, if
you like, or a sprinkling of chopped parsley.

If you are planning to serve this dish as a main course for the warmer
season, a nice thing to do is to prepare a pancake-like stack of the veal
slices layered with the sauce on a large platter. Leave this to chill, covered
with plastic wrap, overnight. The platter can then be placed on the table
and everyone can help themselves.

Baccalà Mantecato ✦ "Pounded" Salt Cod

Baccalà mantecato is made in the Veneto region, and it bears a great resemblance to the Provençal specialty called *brandade de morue,* or creamed salt cod. Once a time-consuming dish that required two strong arms and a mortar and pestle, today a food processor makes light work of it. A white wine such as a Lessini Durello or a Soave from the Veneto are authentic accompaniments to this dish.

Serves 4 to 6

225 g (½ lb) salt cod
¾ cup white wine
1 bay leaf
¼ cup milk
2 tbsp chopped fresh parsley
1 small garlic clove
Pepper to taste
Scant ½ cup extra virgin olive oil

To finish
Extra virgin olive oil
Chopped fresh parsley
A selection of raw vegetables
Toast triangles

Soak the cod for 24 to 48 hours in several changes of water, or under a slow dripping tap, to remove the salt. The amount of time the cod needs to soak will vary. If you buy your salt cod from a reputable grocer, they should be able to give you a good estimate.

Put the salt cod into a pan with the white wine, bay leaf and ¾ cup water and simmer for 20 minutes. There should be sufficient liquid to cover the fish; add a little more water if necessary. Drain the fish and remove the skin and any bones. Cut the cod into several large pieces and place it in a food processor along with the milk, parsley, garlic and pepper. Turn on the machine and begin to slowly add the oil. Process until smooth.

Serve the *baccalà* in a small bowl with a drizzle of olive oil and some chopped parsley to garnish, along with a platter of raw vegetables and toast triangles.

Peperoni Ripieni con Tonno
◆ Cherry Peppers Stuffed with Tuna

Stuffed cherry peppers are one of my most popular appetizers and disappear at an astonishing rate. I grow the peppers in my garden. They are a hot variety, largish for a hot pepper, with a round shape. In Italy they are grown solely to be stuffed and are often referred to as *peperone da ripieno*, or stuffing peppers. In North America you can find them in specialty markets in the fall. They are usually called cherry peppers. All my Italian friends seem to have their own special recipe for filling these peppers, but tuna and anchovies are usually involved. This recipe is my favorite.

These peppers are simple to make and will keep well for at least 2 weeks in the refrigerator. I make them in large batches so that I always have some on hand. They are lovely as part of an antipasto platter that might also include some cured meats and olives. I also serve them for lunch along with some homemade bread, a few olives and a green salad. I think of it as a sort of deconstructed tuna salad sandwich.

Cherry peppers can vary quite a bit in size, so you may need more or less of the stuffing mixture for the number of peppers you have.

I often boil the peppers in water and vinegar as I harvest them from the garden, and then leave them in the fridge. One day last summer I glanced into my fridge to find a mountain of these cooked peppers. I had no time to stuff them, so I put them in my food processor, covered them with olive oil, added a pinch of salt and a couple of cloves of garlic and puréed them. The result was a beautiful spicy pink pepper pesto. I keep a supply of it in a jar in my fridge and add it to soups and pasta dishes. The mixture will keep for several weeks as long as you keep the contents covered in oil, and it can also be frozen.

Because the peppers are hot, they must first be boiled in vinegar and water, which cooks them slightly but removes a lot of their heat.

For the peppers

12 cherry peppers

2 cups white wine vinegar

The best extra virgin olive oil you can afford

For the stuffing

200 g (7 oz) tuna preserved in olive oil

1 medium carrot, peeled and cut into chunks

1 garlic clove

Leaves from a few sprigs of fresh parsley

2 or 3 anchovy fillets

2 tsp salted capers, rinsed

For the peppers

Slice the stem off the peppers. Put the vinegar and 2 cups of water in a pan and add the peppers. Bring to a boil and simmer for 15 to 20 minutes. The peppers should remain a little bit crunchy. Drain the peppers in a colander and run cold water over them to cool. Using a small sugar spoon, scoop out the pith and seeds of the pepper from the opening where you removed the stem. Pay attention here—it is important to remove all of the seeds. They contain most of the heat of the pepper, and if any remain they will spoil the subtle taste of this dish. Place the peppers upside down to dry on paper towels while you make the stuffing.

For the stuffing

Do not drain the tuna. Place all of the ingredients in a food processor and process until you have a fine paste.

Using a small spoon, stuff each pepper. Place the peppers, cut side up, in a jar. Push down a little as you add each new layer of peppers. Cover with the olive oil, seal tightly with a lid and refrigerate. The peppers are ready to eat now. As you remove the peppers, you may need to top up the oil in the jar so the peppers remain covered. When the peppers are all gone, I use the oil for cooking.

Sarde in Saor ✦ Smothered Sardines

This is a famous Venetian dish I sometimes make on Fridays if the fishmonger who visits Radda has fresh sardines. The sardines are deep-fried and then marinated in a sweet-and-sour sauce made with caramelized onions and raisins. It can be served as an antipasto or a light lunch. You can even make it a one-course meal if you add a slice of grilled polenta on the side. The dish is made at least one day before it is served, and will keep for several days in the fridge.

SERVES 4 TO 6

450 g (1 lb) fresh sardine fillets (have your fishmonger clean and
    fillet the fish and remove the heads)
Flour for dredging
Olive oil (you will need about 2 cups for the sardines and ⅓ cup
    for the onions)

Salt

450 g (1 lb) white onions, thinly sliced

½ cup white wine or water

½ cup white wine vinegar

1 tbsp pine nuts

1 tbsp raisins

½ tsp ground coriander

Wash the sardine fillets and dry them. Dredge in flour and place them in a sieve. Shake to remove the excess flour. Cover the bottom of a large sauté pan with olive oil up to about 1½ inches. Heat the oil over moderately high heat until it is very hot but not smoking. You can test the oil for readiness by frying a cube of fresh bread in it; the bread should turn golden brown in about 1 minute. Fry the sardines in batches, turning once after about a minute and a half, until they are golden, 3 to 4 minutes total. Drain on paper towels and sprinkle with salt.

Wipe the sauté pan and add enough olive oil to generously cover the bottom—about ⅓ cup. Heat the oil over low heat, then add the sliced onions along with a scant teaspoon of salt. Cover the pan and cook over a very low heat for about half an hour. Stir from time to time and check the liquid level. If the onions look too dry, add a tablespoon of water. When the onions are very tender and have begun to caramelize, add the wine, vinegar, pine nuts, raisins and coriander. Increase the heat to moderate and cook until the liquid has reduced to about ¼ cup.

Spread a thin layer of the onion mixture on your serving platter. Cover with the sardines, and then top with the remaining onions. Cover with plastic wrap and refrigerate overnight. Serve cold or at room temperature.

Pera al Grana ✦ Pears and Grana Padano Cheese

Grana is the generic name given to the hard, grainy cow's milk cheese made in most regions of northern Italy. There are several different kinds of *grana*, including the one best known outside the country, Parmigiano-Reggiano.

Grana Padano (DOP) is the *grana* produced in the Padana, or Po, Valley, which stretches across a large part of northern Italy, including parts of Lombardy, the Veneto, Trento, Emilia-Romagna and Piedmont. It is made of raw milk and is one of the most popular cheeses in the country. A large part of Italy's milk goes towards its production, 15 liters being used to make 1 kilogram of the cheese.

In North America we usually think of this kind of cheese as a grating cheese, but in Italy there are countless uses for it. Since the cheese is the main protagonist of this dish, it is worth searching out quality. Buy it from a reputable vendor where it is cut in front of you from the wheel. Don't throw away the rinds! I save them in the freezer and add them to stews and bean soups to add a richness and depth of flavor.

This antipasto is lovely served with an Italian sparkling wine such as a Franciacorta or Prosecco.

SERVES 4

112-g (4-oz) wedge of Grana Padano or Parmigiano-Reggiano
2 or 3 mature fall pears
Several fresh mint leaves for garnish
Aceto balsamico tradizionale or a dark honey such as chestnut or
   buckwheat*
See note at right.

Most industrially made balsamic vinegars will be too acidic to complement the cheese, so if you don't own a bottle of authentic balsamic, a dark honey is a very good substitute.

Using the tip of a sharp knife, break the cheese into several small chunks and place a few in the center of each plate. Peel and core the pears and cut them into 6 or 8 wedges each. Place the pear wedges around the rim of each plate, with a mint leaf between each one. Drizzle a few drops of the vinegar or some honey on top of the cheese and serve.

Aceto Balsamico Tradizionale

Aceto balsamico tradizionale—traditional balsamic vinegar—is the name given to the thick, sweet condiment made by a few families using age-old artisanal methods in and around the provinces of Modena and Reggio Emilia. It is sold in small clear-glass bottles bearing the seal of one of the two provincial *consorzi,* or associations, that have been established to safeguard the product. If you don't own a bottle of this luxurious stuff and are willing to make a bit of an investment, it is sold at specialty grocers at prices so high it is frequently displayed behind locked glass doors.

If you do invest in a bottle of traditional balsamic vinegar, use it sparingly—just a few drops at a time. The bottle I currently own is almost empty after two years of regular use. A few drops are wonderful on roast or boiled meat, grilled vegetables, cheese, some fruit such as strawberries or pears, and even vanilla ice cream.

Industrially produced balsamic vinegar is available in a wide range of quality and prices, and it is possible to find some good ones. Good balsamic vinegar is thick, so select only from those sold in clear bottles so you can judge their viscosity. Thinner balsamic vinegar sold at very low prices is usually too acidic for use as a condiment, but is perfect used as you would use any other kind of vinegar, to dress a salad, for example.

Uova su Salsa Verde e Parmigiano-Reggiano
◆ Greens, Eggs and Parmesan Cheese

This dish is a showstopper. You won't need to tell anyone how easy it was to make. It is a very elegant and surprising antipasto, or it can stand on its own as a light lunch or brunch.

I adapted this recipe from the book *L'Italia a Tavola con il Re dei Formaggi* (Italy at the Table with the King of Cheeses), produced for the Consorzio Tutela Parmigiano Reggiano, the organization responsible for the control and production of Italy's undisputed King of Cheese—Parmigiano-Reggiano. The recipe is from a restaurant in Quistello, in the province of Mantova, called Ambasciata that boasts two Michelin stars.

After tasting it, I was so smitten with the wonderful flavor, elegance and simplicity that I made the pilgrimage to Ambasciata to have dinner in the restaurant. Needless to say, I was not disappointed.

SERVES 4

4 medium zucchini
½ cup (1 stick) butter
1 tbsp salt
1 tbsp baking soda
4 very fresh free-range eggs
Olive oil for frying
A wedge of Parmesan cheese

Wash the zucchini and slice them 1 inch thick. Cut the butter into small cubes. Put the zucchini slices in a saucepan and add enough cold water to cover them by about 1 inch. Remove the zucchini and bring the water to a rolling boil. Return the zucchini to the water, along with the butter, salt and baking soda. When the water returns to a boil, lower the heat and simmer for about 10 minutes, until the zucchini are very well cooked. Drain the zucchini. Pass through the fine disk of a food mill or purée in a blender.

Fry the eggs in the olive oil sunny side up. Using a vegetable peeler, shave the cheese into about 8 thin slices.

Ladle a spoonful of the green sauce into each of 4 soup plates. Top with a fried egg and a few slices of the cheese. Serve immediately.

Chapter 3 I Primi ✤ The First Course

A formal Italian meal is composed of a wonderful flow of small courses—antipasto, a first course (*primo*), a second course (*secondo*), a side dish or two (*contorni*), possibly a cheese course (*formaggi*) and dolce (sweet or dessert), followed by a *digestivo* or grappa. In reality, very few Italians eat like this every day. Even in restaurants you rarely see anyone plowing through all these courses.

People tend to pick and choose to suit themselves—perhaps ordering a pasta and a *secondo* or an antipasto and a *primo*. Seldom, however, does one find a *primo* of soup, pasta or rice omitted from a meal. While Italian families love to feast, it is this first course that is closest to most of their hearts. This is where culinary genius with their beloved pasta and other fascinating dishes really can surprise and delight.

The southern Italian diet was historically based upon *pastasciutta*, or dried pasta, made without eggs. It was almost always the only course. Dried pasta was inexpensive to make, it contained flour milled from

the hard durum wheat (*semola di grano duro*) that grows in the south, it could be dried in the sun and kept for a long time without spoiling, and it cooked quickly and cheaply in boiling water using little fuel. Immigrants from the south of Italy introduced North Americans to pasta, and today we often think of a plate of pasta as the main course in a meal.

Whereas dried pasta was the staple of the southern Italian diet, fresh egg-based pasta was the norm in the wealthier northern regions. Today, the finest fresh pasta is still found in the regions of Piedmont, Emilia-Romagna and parts of Lombardy. In parts of northern and central Italy, pasta is replaced by soups, rice, dumplings and polenta. Tuscany has traditionally been a soup-eating region, and in the vast Po Valley and alpine regions, where corn and rice are grown, risotto and polenta are common. In the northeast of Italy, an Eastern European influence produces a myriad of bread- and potato-based dumplings.

Everyone knows Italians eat a lot of dried pasta, and most of us are more than familiar with the many ways it can be prepared. In this chapter I have tried to bring to light a few of the thousands of other things consumed as a first course, many of which are not as well known. Along with detailed instructions for making homemade fresh pasta, I've included various gnocchi preparations, grain-based risottos, polenta dishes, interesting soups and several other intriguing first courses, all of them every bit as Italian as a plate of spaghetti.

In Italy today the trend is to keep portions small and to serve a first course as part of a sequence of other dishes. The sauce used to dress pasta is called a *condimento* and is used sparingly, meant to enhance the flavor of the pasta, not overwhelm it. It should be made using few ingredients of the best quality, simplicity and a light touch being the key to a successful *primo*.

La Mariconda ✦ Broth with Dumplings from Lombardy

These dumplings are found in eastern Lombardy. This part of the region borders on the Veneto and Trentino, where the kitchen takes its cue from Eastern Europe. They are reminiscent of the matzo ball, and there could easily be some connection between the two.

If you don't bake, make sure you use an artisanal hearth-style loaf to make the dumplings.

SERVES 4

½ lb bread, 1 or 2 days old

1 cup milk

6 tbsp (¾ stick) butter

2 eggs

1 tbsp all-purpose flour

A pinch of freshly grated nutmeg

1 cup grated Parmesan cheese

2 tbsp finely chopped fresh parsley

Salt and pepper to taste

8 cups beef broth

Dice the bread or tear it into small pieces, and soak in the milk for 1 hour. Heat the butter in a large sauté pan and add the bread mixture. Cook over moderate heat, stirring constantly, until the mixture is fairly dry—all the milk should have evaporated. Transfer to the work bowl of your food processor and let sit until it is cool.

Add the eggs, flour, nutmeg, half the cheese, the parsley and salt and pepper and process briefly until it comes together. Shape into walnut-sized dumplings.

Bring the broth to a boil and add the dumplings. Cook for about 5 minutes, until they rise to the surface. Serve broth and dumplings in heated soup plates and pass the rest of the cheese at the table.

"Mai buttare via il pane"

"Never throw out the bread" is a saying I have heard uttered by almost every Italian I have ever worked with in the kitchen. The days when bread formed the mainstay of the diet are still fresh enough in the collective Italian psyche that most people consider it sacrilegious to throw bread away. As an owner of courtyard animals, I'm often given ends of loaves for which there is no other use. Stale bread can be purchased at most feed stores in the country for a small sum. The animals are where the bread buck stops.

I bake my own bread, using natural leavens and the finest-quality stone-ground organic wheat, and it is criminal to throw out the remains of hand-crafted loaves like these. But I've never been a fan of the standard uses for leftover bread I knew in North America—bread puddings and French toast. I find them cloyingly sweet, leaden and all too often indigestible. What's more, they mask both the taste and the texture of really good bread.

Fortunately, there are countless recipes based on stale bread in the Italian repertoire, each region with its own favorites. Most of them are so delicate and delicious I wonder if having the leftovers isn't the whole point of baking the bread in the first place. Over the years I have amassed a collection of savory preparations that make the most out of our day-old homemade bread. Some of my favorites are scattered throughout this chapter. Besides *La Mariconda* (page 117), there is the *canederli* (page 163), *pappa al pomodoro* (page 137), *acquacotta* (page 135) and *seuppa à la Valpelleunentze* (page 130). There is great satisfaction to be had when you can put together an easy meal out of yesterday's loaf. Not only is it economical, it is usually very healthy, not to mention delicious.

La Petraia Minestra di Castagne e Finocchio Selvatico ✦ Chestnut and Wild Fennel Soup

One of La Petraia's prized possessions is fifteen acres of ancient chestnut forest, many of the trees with trunks wide enough to house a small family. And this place does provide both shelter and food for the boar, fox and other animals who call this enchanted forest home. The soil provides perfect conditions for the elusive porcini mushrooms, and in the fall local Raddesi flock here to pick their winter's supply of chestnuts and mushrooms. It is from them we have learned how to harvest and store our own.

Chestnuts were once upon a time the food of the poor in Italy, but in recent years they've gained tremendous status and are found on the menus of the smartest restaurants. This extremely nutritious nut is used in a myriad of ways in the Italian kitchen. It can be roasted or braised in wine, used to make bread, soup, gnocchi, pasta and polenta, added to meat stews and used in many classic desserts.

This soup is a nice combination of the chestnut and the wild fennel that grows in our fields. If you can't find wild fennel, you can use the widely available domestic variety. Celery combined with a dash of fennel seed will also do. Because I usually prefer to serve a pasta dish as a first course, I often offer a small taste of this soup as a starter or an *amuse bouche*, served up in an espresso cup. If you can afford the luxury, a dab of truffle butter on top of each serving adds an elegant touch to finish the dish.

SERVES 6 TO 8

1 onion, minced

A few flakes of hot chili pepper

Olive oil to cover the bottom of your sauté pan

3 or 4 large wild fennel branches (or 1 fennel bulb and some of the stalk and green fronds), chopped

½ tsp fennel seed

1 lb shelled fresh chestnuts (see page 122)

6 cups hot chicken or vegetable broth

2 tbsp butter

Salt and pepper to taste

Croutons, preferably made from homemade bread

Truffle butter or whipped cream to finish

A few small fennel fronds to garnish

Sauté the onion and the chili flakes in the oil until they become translucent. Add the fennel, fennel seed and chestnuts. Cook for a few minutes, until the fennel starts to wilt, then add the hot broth. Simmer for 20 minutes or until the chestnuts and fennel are tender. Purée the mixture using a food mill, passing it once through the large-holed disk and once through the smaller-holed disk. If you don't own a food mill, use a blender or a food processor and then pass the mixture through a fine sieve, pressing on the solids. Add the butter and season with salt and pepper.

Place a few croutons in the bottom of a warm soup plate; add a ladle of the soup and a dollop of truffle butter or whipped cream. To be very stylish, use a piping bag and pipe a rosette of the cream on top of the soup. Garnish with a small fennel frond. Serve immediately.

Chestnuts

EDIBLE CHESTNUTS

The Native American edible chestnut, *Castanea dentate,* was all but wiped out in the early part of the last century by a blight. Imported chestnuts (Italy is one of the world's largest chestnut exporters to North America) are available for a limited time in the late fall and early winter. Do not use domestic horse or buckeye chestnuts.

DRIED CHESTNUTS

Chestnuts have a fairly short growing season and do not keep for very long, so if the fresh nut isn't available you can probably hunt down some dried ones. If you have an Italian grocer in your neighborhood, they may stock them or know where to find them. Chestnuts are usually dried over a wood fire, and the soup will have an interesting smoky taste if you use dried nuts. It will also make things easier, as you won't have to shell fresh chestnuts. The dried nuts need to be soaked overnight before you use them. Use half the amount called for in a recipe. Ideally, the dried nuts should be from the most recent harvest, not more than one year old.

SHELLING FRESH CHESTNUTS

Fresh chestnuts must be either baked or boiled so their tough outer shell and the thin and bitter inner skin can be removed. If your recipe calls for shelled chestnuts, you should start with twice the amount of fresh ones in the shell.

To bake the nuts: Heat the oven to 400°F/200°C. Cut a deep cross on the top of each nut with a sharp knife. Place the nuts on a baking sheet and bake for 25 minutes or until the outer shell and inner skin pop open to reveal the clean nut inside. Remove from the oven. When the nuts are cool enough to handle, remove the shells and skin.

To boil the nuts: Cut a deep cross on the top of each nut with a sharp knife. Place the nuts in a pot along with a bay leaf and cover with water. Bring just to a boil, then reduce the heat and simmer for 25 minutes or until the outer shell and inner skin have opened up enough to reveal the clean nut inside. Transfer the pot to the sink and shell the nuts one at a time while they are still hot, removing both the tough outer shell and the thin inner skin. Rubber gloves make this task easier if you don't have the asbestos hands of a professional chef. If the shell and skin do not easily slip off, put the nut back in the hot water and try another one.

Gran Farro ◆ Farro Soup from the Garfagnana

In the summer I often serve a *farro* salad (see page 300) made with tomatoes, cucumbers and red onions from my garden. In fall and winter this *farro* soup, or the pear and gorgonzola risotto on page 217, are more appropriate.

Versions of this soup are found all over the Garfagnana region and indeed all over Tuscany. This soup contains a few humble ingredients and is very easy to make. It is absolutely divine and makes a very healthy meal on its own with a simple green salad. You can leave out the pancetta for a vegetarian version.

Like most Tuscan soups and stews, *gran farro* is a good keeper and usually improves the next day.

SERVES 6

For the beans

1 cup dried white beans, such as cannellini or Great Northern

For the soffritto

2 tbsp extra virgin olive oil

1 onion, finely chopped

1 celery stalk, finely chopped

1 carrot, finely chopped

1 garlic clove, minced

28 g (1 oz) pancetta, cubed (optional)

1 tbsp finely chopped fresh parsley

For the soup

1 cup pearled *farro* (see page 125), rinsed in several changes of water

3 or 4 peeled, seeded and chopped tomatoes

3 or 4 fresh sage leaves

A sprig of fresh rosemary

1 bay leaf

2 whole cloves

SOFFRITO

Soffritto in Italian means "fried under" and is the base on which most soups, sauces and braises are built. Similar to the French *mirepoix*, a *soffritto* contains finely chopped aromatic vegetables such as onions, carrots, celery, parsley and garlic, which are gently fried in olive oil for about 10 minutes. If pancetta is also added, the mixture is sometimes called a *battuto*.

1 cinnamon stick

About 5 cups boiling water

Salt and pepper to taste

To finish

Extra virgin olive oil

Grated Parmesan cheese to pass at the table

For the beans

Soak the beans overnight in enough water to cover by 2 inches.

For the soffritto

In a pot over moderate heat, gently cook the *soffritto* ingredients in the olive oil for about 10 minutes, until the vegetables start to wilt.

For the soup

Add the *farro* to the *soffritto* and cook, stirring, for a minute or two, then add the tomatoes. Drain the beans and add them to the pot.

Wrap the sage, rosemary, bay leaf, cloves and cinnamon in a piece of cheesecloth or put them into a tea ball and add them to the soup. Add about 5 cups boiling water and simmer, partially covered, for about 1 hour, until the *farro* is tender and the beans are cooked. Check the pot occasionally, adding more hot water if the liquid seems too low. Remove the herb bundle and season the soup with salt and pepper.

The soup should have a dense consistency. If you like a smoother texture, you can remove a cup or two and pass it through a food mill or blender. You can also add more water if the soup seems too thick.

Serve topped with a thin drizzle of the best extra virgin olive oil you can afford. Pass the Parmesan cheese at the table.

Farro

Farro is an ancient grain said to be one of the first ever cultivated in the Fertile Crescent, the birthplace of modern agriculture. It was used by the Greeks, Etruscans and Romans, but in the last century it fell from fashion in favor of modern, higher-yielding wheat varieties. By the 1960s this grain was all but extinct in Tuscany, cultivated only by a few stubborn growers in the remote, mountainous corner of the region called the Garfagnana, and used mainly for feed. It was apparently a few *osteria* owners from the town of Lucca who ventured up into the mountains and tasted this grain. They brought some home with them, and *farro* was given a new life.

Since the rebirth of *farro*, the Garfagnana itself has experienced somewhat of a renaissance. Tucked between the beautiful, marble-rich Apuane Alps and the Tosco-Emilian Apennine range, the region follows the course of the Serchio River. The Garfagnana does not disappoint the traveler looking for an alternative to Tuscany's more popular tourist attractions. The specialties of this area include more than just *farro*. There is an abundance of wild game, chestnuts, several kinds of rare beans, honey, wild berries, pecorino cheese, wonderful pork products like *biroldo*, an excellent blood sausage, polenta made from a rare type of corn called *ottofile*, wild mushrooms and, finally, a wonderful sourdough bread, *pane di patate*, that is baked in wood-burning ovens from a dough enriched with mashed potatoes. The area is littered with rustic *osterie* where these products and more can be sampled.

Today *farro* from the Garfagnana has been awarded an IGP, or protected geographical designation, by the European Union. Its tender pearled grain can be cooked like rice with no need to presoak. With its satisfying nutty flavor, it is used in soups, salads, savory tarts, risottos and even desserts.

If you can't locate Italian *farro*, pearl barley makes a nice substitute. Pearling is the process of polishing a grain to remove its tough outer hull. North American–grown spelt is similar to *farro* but is usually not pearled. It is not suitable for the *farro* recipes in this book, as it requires soaking.

Pasta e Ceci ✦ Pasta and Chick Pea Soup from Napoli

This is Italian "home to mama" food—delicious and addictive. Although technically a pasta dish, its consistency is more like soup. It uses one pot, so cleanup is easy. Don't be tempted to add anything to this recipe. What makes it special is what is not in it.

Versions of this dish are found in many Italian regions. I think the best one I ever had was in the Vomero district of Naples, at the Osteria Da Sica. Its excellence was due to its simplicity and the quality of its two main ingredients: pasta and chick peas. In Naples, this dish is made with a mixture of several different pasta shapes. A mixture I bought there included broken pieces of spaghetti, linguine, bucatini and lasagne as well as fusilli, gemelli, penne, elbow macaroni and ditalini. It came from one of the excellent artisanal pasta producers in the towns of Gragnano and Torre Annunziata just outside Naples. You can make your own mix by saving the bits of pasta left in a package that are not quite enough for a meal. In other regions of Italy the small tube-shaped ditalini are used, or the scraps left over from making homemade pasta called *malfatti* or *maltagliati* (see page 173).

¾ cup dried chick peas, soaked overnight in water

1 small onion

1 garlic clove

1 bay leaf

A few fresh sage leaves

A sprig of fresh rosemary

170 g (6 oz) mixed pasta shapes

Salt and pepper to taste

To finish

Extra virgin olive oil

Grated Parmesan or pecorino cheese to pass at the table

Drain the chick peas and put them in a saucepan with the onion, garlic and a *bouquet garni* made with the herbs. Add enough water to cover by about 3 inches and simmer until the chick peas are tender. The time will vary depending upon the age of the chick peas. Check from time to time and add more water if needed.

When the beans are soft, remove the *bouquet garni*. Use a hand blender, blender or potato masher to roughly purée the chick peas and the onion. You are not looking for a smooth purée—the soup should retain some semblance of the original chick peas.

Bring the soup to a boil, add the pasta and reduce to a simmer. Cover and simmer for about 15 minutes, until the pasta is *al dente*. Season with salt and pepper.

Serve immediately with a drizzle of the olive oil and the grated cheese.

ABOUT CHICK PEAS

The chick peas I buy in Italy often take longer to soak than dried beans, so I usually start soaking them the morning of the day before I plan to serve this dish. Chick peas can also take a long time to cook. If you own a pressure cooker, you can cook them without presoaking. Use a 1:3 ratio of chick peas to water (for ¾ cup chick peas you will need 2¼ cups water) and cook for about 20 minutes along with the *bouquet garni*, onion and garlic. Remove the pressure cooker from the heat and let the pot sit for about 15 minutes before you open it.

Farinata

◆ Bean, Polenta and Kale Soup from the Garfagnana

Farinata (sometimes called *infarinata* in the Garfagnana) is another example of a dish that turns up in different guises all over the peninsula. In the Tuscan Garfagnana it is a cornmeal, kale and bean soup. A few miles away in the Lunigiana and into Liguria, *farinata* is a pancake made with chick pea flour.

I prefer the Tuscan version. It is the kind of satisfying, wholesome food that sticks to the ribs. If you have beans left over from making *fagioli al fiasco* on page 298, you can use them in this recipe.

I make *farinata* in the winter months, using the beans I have dried from my fall harvest, coarsely ground cornmeal from last summer's corn, ground fresh in my grain mill, and newly dug carrots and some celery and kale from the garden. It is always a hit with guests, and when I serve it I am careful to explain that every ingredient comes from the property, hard won after a summer's labor in the garden.

SERVES 4 TO 6

For the soffritto

    1 tbsp olive oil

    28 g (1 oz) finely chopped pancetta

    1 onion, chopped

    1 large carrot, chopped

    1 celery stalk, chopped

    1 garlic clove, crushed

    1 tbsp finely chopped fresh parsley

For the soup

   ½ cup dried white beans, soaked overnight

   A few sage leaves

   1 garlic clove, unpeeled

   1 large potato, unpeeled, scrubbed clean and cut into small cubes

   Several leaves of kale or *cavolo nero*, tough stems and center ribs
      removed, and leaves washed and finely chopped

   A sprig of fresh rosemary, a sprig of fresh thyme and 1 fresh or
      dried bay leaf tied together with a string

   Salt and pepper to taste

   ½ cup coarsely ground cornmeal

To serve

   Thick slices of Tuscan bread, grilled and rubbed with a clove of
      garlic

   Extra virgin olive oil and grated Parmesan cheese

Drain the beans and put them in a large pot with the sage and garlic clove. Add enough water to cover by about an inch and simmer until the beans are tender. (Cooking time will depend on the age of the beans, but usually about 45 minutes to an hour should be enough.) Do not drain the beans.

For the soffritto

In a large, heavy-bottomed saucepan or Dutch oven (I use an enameled cast-iron or a glazed terra-cotta Dutch oven), gently cook the *soffritto* ingredients in the oil over moderate heat until the vegetables start to wilt—about 15 minutes. Meanwhile, place a kettle of water on the stove to heat.

Add the beans and their cooking liquid, the potato, the kale and the herb packet to the *soffritto*. Add enough hot water to cover. Simmer very gently for about 30 minutes or until the potato and kale are tender. Remove the herb bundle and add 1 more cup of hot water.

Add the cornmeal to the mixture in a steady stream, stirring constantly. Once incorporated, cook over low heat, stirring frequently, for another 30 minutes. The *farinata* will thicken as the cornmeal cooks. Season with salt and pepper.

Spoon a ladleful of *farinata* over a slice of grilled Tuscan bread. Drizzle with a generous amount of extra virgin olive oil and pass freshly grated Parmesan cheese at the table.

Variation

This recipe produces a moderately thick soup. You can adjust the thickness to suit your taste by varying the amount of cornmeal you use. A little more produces a thicker porridge. I sometimes thicken leftovers for the next day. On day 3 any remains can be cut into slices and fried lightly in extra virgin olive oil.

Seuppa à la Valpelleunentze
+ Cheese Soup from the Val d'Aosta

The exploration of Italy's border regions is a passion of mine. Whether these are *comunali*, provincial, regional or national, there is inevitably a no-man's-land where a bit of confused identity governs the local kitchen.

The cuisine of the alpine regions of Aosta, Alto Adige, Lombardy, Piedmont and Friuli, whose borders include France, Austria, Switzerland, Slovenia and the Istrian Peninsula of Croatia, are especially interesting.

The presence of lush mountain pastures for grazing provides for excellent dairy products, and from the highest vineyards in Europe come some top-quality and virtually unknown wines. The gastronomic traveler who ventures into these parts is unlikely to be disappointed.

Important mountain passes historically brought to these regions sophisticated travelers who influenced the local culinary tradition. At the same time, the isolation of more remote mountain valleys meant that in these parts time more or less stood still. As a result, these areas today are advanced and wealthy, but their cultural heritage is proudly preserved.

These parts of Italy were often the subject of disputes, and borders were constantly changing. Such struggles have resulted in a fiercely independent people, who do not always consider themselves Italians first. In Aosta, which once belonged to the House of Savoy, the dialect and the cuisine both reference those of its French neighbor.

Aosta is the smallest Italian region and has a bilingual French-Italian population. It is surrounded by Monte Bianco, Monte Rosa and the Matterhorn, the highest peaks in the Alps. Aosta is famous for its fontina cheese, which has been awarded a DOP denomination by the European Union. This wonderful melting cheese is used to make *fonduta* (see page 273), perhaps the region's most famous export.

Seuppa à la Valpelleunentze is a rich, rustic soup that goes down nicely on a cold winter evening. It is from the Valpelline in the Val d'Aosta. This valley winds its way up into the high Alps from the San Bernardo pass. The road ascends through several scenic alpine villages before it dead-ends at an alpine lake nestled just below the glaciers of the Matterhorn on the Swiss border. The soup combines traditional mountain ingredients— cheese, rye bread and cabbage—to marvelous effect. It pairs beautifully with a glass of Blanc de Morgex if you can find it—a pale, straw-colored white wine that is grown on rock-terraced vineyards at up to 3,000 feet.

The rocks absorb the heat from the sun and warm the earth, allowing the vine to be cultivated even at the foot of Europe's highest peaks.

The soup is made with a rich bouillon that is one of the hallmarks of Aosta cuisine and was traditionally kept bubbling away on the back of the stove for weeks, constantly being added to and then used as a base for whatever soup was being prepared. Soup, not pasta, forms the basis of the Val d'Aosta kitchen. How many soups are there from this region? "*Nessuno è mai riuscito a contarle*"—no one has ever been able to count them—says one of the region's classic cookbooks, *Val d'Aosta in Cucina*.

SERVES 4 TO 6

For the broth
    1 kg (2¼ lb) meaty beef bones
    1 carrot
    1 leek
    1 onion
    1 celery stalk
    1 garlic clove
    A cinnamon stick and a grating of nutmeg

For the soup
    Butter for the bread and to grease your casserole
    About 8 thin slices stale rye or whole wheat bread (the rye
        sourdough on page 49 is perfect)
    225 g (8 oz) fontina cheese, grated
    The leaves from half a large Savoy cabbage, center ribs removed,
        the leaves cut into shreds and blanched
    6 cups beef broth

For the broth

Place all of the broth ingredients in a stock pot and add cold water to cover by about 2 inches. Simmer for 4 to 5 hours on very low heat. Use a skimmer or a spoon to skim the surface from time to time. Strain.

For the soup

Preheat the oven to 350°F/175°C.

Butter the bread and place half of it in a layer in a well-buttered casserole. Top with a layer of the cheese and one of the cabbage. End with a layer of bread and a final layer of the cheese.

Pour the broth over it all and bake, uncovered, for about 30 minutes or until the cheese on top starts to bubble and turn golden. Serve immediately.

Carabaccia ◆ Florentine Onion Soup

Tuscany is one of the few regions in Italy where pasta was never embraced. I suspect this has something to do with the fact that once Caterina de' Medici married and moved to France, all things French gained a certain status here. By the influential cookbook author Pellegrino Artusi's time, in the late 1800s, the Italian aristocracy had French-trained chefs. Fabio Picchi, owner of the legendary Cibreo restaurant in Florence, is known for his refusal to include pasta on his menu because it is not traditionally Florentine. It is true that the Tuscan first course is often soup. There is the famous *ribollita* or *zuppa di pane*, as well as *pappa al pomodoro, gran farro, acquacotta* and countless others.

Carabaccia is a dish that dates from the Renaissance, sugar and cinnamon being the telltale ingredients. A common version today uses, strangely, green peas instead of almonds, omits the sugar and cinnamon and is thickened with eggs. The recipe below is an attempt at something closer to the original.

Carabaccia is an example of the Italian genius for combining simple ingredients to produce supremely elegant results. Here at Petraia I make it towards the end of the cold winter months, as my year's supply of red onions are in danger of spoiling in the *cantina* and need to be used up. Onions lose moisture over time, and their flavor becomes much more concentrated, making them more suitable for cooking and perfect for this soup.

SERVES 6

2 lb red onions, very thinly sliced
A few flakes of hot chili pepper
½ cup olive oil
½ cup Marsala or port
8½ cups hot chicken broth
2 cups ground almonds
2 tsp mild liquid honey
½ tsp cinnamon, plus extra for garnish
A few pinches of grated nutmeg
Juice of 1 lemon
Salt and pepper to taste
Croutons for garnish

Sauté the onions and chili flakes in the oil until the onions start to wilt, then add the Marsala. Cook, partially covered, stirring occasionally, until the liquid has evaporated, then add the hot broth and the almonds. Reduce the heat to moderately low and cook, stirring occasionally, for 1 hour.

Pass the mixture through the fine disk of a food mill. Return to the pan and add the honey, cinnamon, nutmeg and lemon juice. Season with salt and pepper. Cook for another 10 minutes over low heat.

Serve the soup in heated soup plates, garnished with croutons and a light sprinkling of cinnamon.

Acquacotta ✦ Tuscan Cooked Water

Acquacotta is one of many Tuscan bread-based soups. It is found in southern Tuscany, especially in the Maremma region. This effortless soup, made with a few slices of day-old bread cooked in some aromatic vegetables and lots of water, illustrates the economy of the Tuscan kitchen, and recalls a time not so long ago when a little bit had to go a long way. These days this humble soup appears on the menu of many of the area's finest restaurants, and for good reason. It is delicious.

This is one of my favorite soups at Petraia because our soil is wonderful for growing peppers. Peppers don't mind cool weather, and my plants often continue to produce fruit well into November, even standing up to a light frost. I roast and freeze the overflow to use them in this lovely soup all through the winter. Yet this is also a wonderful summer soup when made using fresh tomatoes and peppers from the garden. It is lovely before a second course of grilled meat.

Whatever season you serve it in, it is best prepared using a saltless Tuscan-style bread (see page 31). If you don't bake, make sure you use an artisanal hearth-style loaf.

SERVES 4

2 red peppers
2 tbsp extra virgin olive oil, plus extra for brushing the peppers
1 red onion, minced
2 celery stalks, finely chopped

Roasted peppers can be frozen after they are cooled and skinned. They will keep for 2 months in the freezer.

2 garlic cloves, minced

Several sprigs of fresh parsley, chopped

3 ripe tomatoes, peeled, seeded and chopped (or 3 canned tomatoes, seeded and chopped)

Salt and pepper to taste

To serve

4 slices Tuscan bread, toasted and rubbed with a clove of garlic

4 free-range organic eggs

Extra virgin olive oil

Freshly grated Parmesan cheese

Preheat the oven to 350°F/175°C.

Cut the peppers in half, remove the stems, white pith and seeds and rub the peppers all over with some olive oil. Place them cut side down in an ovenproof dish and roast for half an hour. Remove from the oven and, when cool enough to handle, peel off the skins. Finely chop the peppers.

Put 4 cups of water on to boil. Heat the olive oil in a large casserole over low heat and add the onion. Cook for a few minutes, stirring occasionally, until the onion becomes transparent but does not brown. Add the celery, garlic and parsley and cook for another few minutes. Add the roasted peppers and the tomatoes and cover with the hot water. Bring to a boil, then reduce the heat. Let simmer over low heat for 30 minutes. The soup can be puréed if you prefer a smoother texture. Season with salt and pepper.

To serve

Warm 4 soup plates. Place one piece of toast in each soup plate, and crack an egg on top of it. Bring the soup to a boil and ladle into the bowls. Drizzle with olive oil and serve immediately.

Pass the cheese at the table. Each person should stir the soup before eating—the egg will cook and thicken the soup.

Pappa al Pomodoro ✦ Tuscan Bread and Tomato Soup

Pappa al pomodoro is found in central Tuscany, especially in Florence and in the Chianti area, where I live. It is referred to as a "pap" because it is so thick it is often served on a plate and eaten with a fork.

Here is another example of the thrift that governs the Tuscan kitchen. Once again it is stale, saltless Tuscan bread that forms the basis for this thick porridge-like soup that boasts the divine essence of fresh tomatoes. This is food that sticks to the ribs on a cold winter day when there is finger-numbing work outdoors trimming grape vines and olive trees. It can be made in almost an instant, so it is perfect for those times when busyness threatens to get in the way of cooking a nutritious hot meal.

I make *pappa* with the bottled tomato purée of our summer crop. Our tomatoes are picked at their absolute ripest and then put through an electric food mill. This is a gadget owned by almost every Italian family. It looks a bit like a meat grinder, and in a matter of minutes it can process hundreds of tomatoes, spitting out the indigestible seeds and skins and leaving the succulent juice and pulp. But you can also make tomato purée if you own an inexpensive manual food mill. Otherwise, it is available in most supermarkets. Italian tomato purée is called *passata*.

This is the rare Italian preparation that does not involve a *soffritto*, and is made with only a few ingredients. Its texture and taste depend on the use of stale saltless Tuscan-style bread (page 31) and the very best-quality ripe tomatoes and extra virgin olive oil. If you don't bake, make sure you use an artisanal hearth-style loaf. This is the perfect first course to serve with a *bistecca* (see page 263).

SERVES 4 TO 6

1.5 kg (3⅓ lb) ripest tomatoes (or 5 cups of ready-made tomato purée)
6 oz day-old saltless Tuscan bread, sliced
1 garlic clove, minced
¼ cup extra virgin olive oil
Leaves from 1 small bunch fresh basil, roughly torn
2 cups water
Salt and pepper to taste

To finish
Extra virgin olive oil
Fresh basil leaves

If you are using fresh tomatoes, wash them and cut them in half. Place in a saucepan large enough to hold them all and add 1 cup of water. Cook for about 15 minutes over moderate heat—just long enough to loosen the skins and slightly cook the tomatoes so they will pass through a food mill easily. Pass the mixture through a food mill. You will need 5 cups of the resulting purée.

I sometimes prefer a creamier consistency and use a hand blender to purée the finished soup.

Place all of the soup ingredients in a saucepan and bring to a boil. Reduce the heat to low and simmer slowly for about 30 minutes. Stir from time to time with a wooden spoon, mashing up the bread so that it dissolves into the soup and thickens it. Season with salt and pepper, and serve drizzled with extra virgin olive oil. Garnish with a basil leaf.

Crema di Zucca ✦ Pumpkin Purée

A *crema* (sometimes called a *passato*) is not a cream soup, as one might expect, but a vegetable purée—vegetables cooked in broth or water and then passed through a food mill. A *crema* is meant to highlight the distinctive flavor of one vegetable.

This basic formula can be used with other vegetables such as carrots, parsnips, roasted yellow or red peppers or green peas. Look for a late-harvest sweet winter squash with deep orange flesh, such as a Hubbard. Simple, elegant and delicious, this soup is perfect for a winter evening.

SERVES 4

1 winter squash (approx. 1 kg/2¼ lb)
2 medium potatoes (any kind will do)
Freshly grated nutmeg
Salt and pepper to taste

To finish

Croutons
Heavy cream or butter (optional)

Peel and seed the squash and cut it into chunks. Peel the potatoes and cut them into chunks. Place the vegetables in a saucepan and barely cover with water. Bring to a boil, then reduce the heat and simmer until the vegetables are tender. Purée the mixture in a blender or pass through the fine disk of a food mill. Add a little freshly grated nutmeg and season with salt and pepper.

Serve in heated soup plates and top with a couple of croutons. A drizzle of cream or a dab of butter can be added at the end.

Zuppa di Sedano ✦ Celery Soup

This soup highlights the subtle taste of celery, a vegetable we seldom place center stage despite its star potential. It can be hard to find really flavorful celery unless you grow it yourself or frequent a farmers' market or quality purveyor of fruits and vegetables. Look for small dark green stems and abundant healthy foliage.

SERVES 4

1 bunch celery (about 10 stalks), including some of the leaves,
  finely chopped
1 onion, minced
1 garlic clove, minced
1 tbsp finely chopped fresh Italian parsley
5 tbsp butter
1 medium potato, scrubbed and cut into small dice
4 cups hot vegetable or chicken broth
Salt and pepper to taste

To finish
Croutons (preferably made with homemade sourdough)
Whipped cream or truffle butter (optional)

Cook the celery, onion, garlic and parsley in the butter over moderate heat, stirring occasionally, for about 10 minutes, until the onions wilt and become transparent. Add the potato and the hot broth and simmer for 45 minutes or until the potato and celery are very soft. Season with salt and pepper.

Pass the mixture through the large disk, then the small disk, of a food mill. If you don't own a food mill, purée the mixture in a blender and then press it through a sieve.

Serve in heated soup plates, topped with a couple of croutons and a spoonful of whipped cream or dab of truffle butter, if desired.

Zuppa al Vino ◆ Wine Soup from the Alto Adige

The Alto Adige, or South Tyrol, as it is also known, belonged to the Austro-Hungarian Empire until the First World War, when it was occupied by Italy and subsequently annexed. Thus began a long and turbulent history for the region. Under Mussolini, a program of Italianization was implemented. Thousands of Italians from other parts of the country were relocated here, place names were changed and even some family names were translated into Italian. The region became rife with unrest. In 1946, with the Gruber–De Gasperi Agreement, the German-speaking population was given limited recognition, but the problems were far from over. Unrest came under increased international scrutiny when a series of bomb attacks were carried out by South Tyrolean activists targeting electricity plants supplying the region and other parts of Italy with hydro. In 1972 an Autonomy Statute was passed, giving the region a degree of independence from the rest of Italy. Today the Alto Adige is often considered a model example of conflict resolution.

The population here is about 70 percent German-speaking, followed by Italian and a small (around 4 percent) Ladino population. Ladino is a Romansch language spoken in a few mountain communities in the Dolomites. It is no wonder the area was so prized, for here we are in one of the most pristine and beautiful parts of the Alps. There are the fashionable ski resorts and the picturesque mountain valleys famous for their fruit and wine. Beautiful cities such as Bolzano and Merano along with countless picture-perfect Alpine villages dot the landscape.

This region is deeply religious. Alpine roads are often marked at each kilometer by beautiful hand-carved crucifixes. Onion-domed churches dominate the landscape, and, unlike in other parts of Italy, they are not museums where tourists flock to adore famous artworks but still an active part of daily life.

There is also the sense in this part of Italy that things run a little smoother, with less of the bureaucracy that seems to bog down other parts of the country. Houses are freshly painted and lawns meticulously kept. Window boxes are full of pretty geraniums, and now and again in the mountains one still catches a glimpse of people wearing traditional costume. The cuisine is rich and varied, as is usually the case in the mountains, each small valley having its own specialties. The area is famous for its wine and produces excellent white and red varieties.

This soup is traditionally made with the white Terlano from the town of the same name in the Alto Adige. It is a little on the rich side, but all that means to me is that you consume it in small amounts.

Zuppa al vino is wonderful served in the winter as a first course, followed by the *stockfischgrostl* on page 228. It has a rich, smooth texture and makes a refined and elegant preface to a special meal. Serve with a chilled bottle of white wine, preferably from the Alto Adige, such as a Terlano or a Müller-Thurgau.

SERVES 4 TO 6

2 cups beef broth
2 thick slices day-old, preferably homemade, whole wheat bread
1 tbsp butter

4 egg yolks

1 cup light cream

1 cup white wine

Salt to taste

A pinch of cinnamon

Bring the broth just to a boil and then reduce the heat to low.

Cut the bread into croutons. Melt the butter in a nonstick pan and sauté the croutons until they are browned on all sides. Drain on paper towels.

Whisk together the egg yolks, cream and wine. Pour this mixture into the hot broth, whisking the whole time. Continue to whisk the soup until it is warm enough to serve. Be careful not to boil it. Season with salt and ladle into warm soup plates. Top with the croutons. Sprinkle with the cinnamon and serve.

Crema di Ceci e Gamberi
✦ Chick Pea Purée with Shrimp

This is an easy, elegant chick pea purée with a few shrimp added for color and flavor. Seafood and chick peas often turn up together along the Tuscan coast. If you happen to own a pressure cooker, you can cook the chick peas without presoaking them, which makes this already simple preparation even easier.

I sometimes serve this soup topped with a thin sliver of my home-made *lardo*, which melts on top of the hot soup. I make *lardo* with the fat of a special breed of local pig I raise called the Cinta Senese (see page 145).

Fortunately, this mouth-watering *zuppa* does not fail to enchant, *lardo* or not. If you want to be authentic, seek out a peppery Tuscan extra virgin olive oil from the latest harvest to drizzle over the soup just before you serve it.

SERVES 4

1 cup dried chick peas
1 garlic clove, unpeeled
1 small onion, peeled
A sprig of fresh rosemary or thyme
8 large shrimp, peeled and deveined
Salt and pepper to taste

To finish

Extra virgin olive oil
Small sprigs of fresh thyme or rosemary to garnish

Soak the chick peas overnight. The next day, cook them with the garlic, onion and rosemary or thyme, in enough salted water to cover by about an inch. The cooking time will vary depending on the age of your chick peas, but you will need at least an hour, and possibly two or three. You may need to add more water from time to time.

When the chick peas are tender, remove the herbs. Purée the peas and then pass the puréed mixture through the fine disk of a food mill or press it through a fine sieve. Bring the soup to a boil and add the shrimp, cooking them briefly—about 4 minutes—just until they turn pink. Season with salt and pepper.

To serve, place a ladleful of soup in each heated soup plate, making sure each serving has 2 shrimp. Drizzle with a generous ribbon of olive oil and garnish with a small sprig of fresh thyme or rosemary.

Cinta Senese

These pigs used to roam the chestnut and oak forests that cloak our part of Tuscany, but in the last century the breed fell out of favor with modern tastes, almost to the point of extinction.

Cinta are not able to live in stalls and must be reared in a semi-wild state, preferably on chestnuts and acorns. They take over a year to mature, produce a very fatty meat and require a lot of land. Although they were once a common sight on Chianti farms, by the 1980s only a handful of breeders were still rearing them. They were considered uneconomical in the face of the modern large white breed of pig that could be raised in stalls, ate commercially available feed, produced lean flesh and was ready to slaughter sooner.

All of the Cinta alive today are descendants of just a few pigs that were kept by these stubborn breeders. Fortunately, in recent years these farmers have provided the inspiration for a new generation of breeders, and today, happily, several hundred Cinta are once again roaming the forests of their ancient homeland. But the story is not finished; Cinta breeders still struggle with the problems created by inbreeding, when the gene pool of a breed shrinks to almost nothing. As this pig's numbers and popularity increase, however, so too does the likelihood that it will survive.

The Cinta is a handsome black pig with a belt of white skin (*cinta* means "belt") around its neck. The fat—and these pigs have a lot of it—is delicious and melts in your hands at body temperature. Similar to its famous Iberian cousins from Spain, the Cinta's diet of acorns, rich in oleic acid, lowers the melting point of its fat, making it more healthful than most lard. The meat of the Cinta is a rare delicacy, selling for much more than regular pork.

Eaten fresh or cured, Cinta is made into prosciutto, salami, *lardo* and other specialties. Its meat is easily identified by the large amount of fat it contains. I cure *lardo* in the winter months at Petraia and hang it in my *cantina,* along with wild boar prosciutto and pancetta. The *lardo* is wonderful sliced sliver thin and laid to melt over a thick slice of hot Tuscan bread or on top of a bowl of *crema di ceci* soup (page 143).

POLENTA

I avoided polenta for a long time. It seemed like nothing more than glorified cornmeal porridge, and I couldn't understand the fuss made over it. Then I tasted polenta made from an ancient variety of corn called *ottofile* and had an epiphany. This type of corn, whose name means "eight rows," is said to be the same type of corn Columbus introduced here centuries ago. An ancient variety, it has managed to survive, escaping the hybridization that today produces corn varieties containing many more rows per cob. This polenta flour had been ground fresh in a stone mill. It had a nutty taste and still possessed a hint of the fresh corn it once was. It was so good, so different from anything I had eaten before, I became an instant convert, understanding immediately after my first bite that there is polenta and then there is POLENTA.

Quality and freshness are the two most important ingredients in polenta. Always use the best-quality cornmeal you can find, and check the "best before" date to make sure that it is fresh. Like whole wheat flour, the corn oil contained in the germ of the kernel will go rancid if it sits too long after having been ground. Ideally, you are looking for a fresh, coarse meal that has been ground using a stone. At Petraia, I grow my own corn and make my own polenta flour in a home grain mill.

When it runs out, I buy flour from the northern Italian regions of Aosta, Piedmont, Lombardy, the Alto Adige or Friuli. In these parts polenta forms a staple part of the local diet. Corn, a crop that can withstand cold weather and a short growing season, is cultivated along with buckwheat and rye on mountain terraces. The area is littered with small family-run mills where growers can take their harvest to be ground for their own use. Houses are often decorated throughout the fall and winter with corn cobs hung to dry on wooden balconies or left to hang from beams, replacing the characteristic red geraniums of the summer months.

Polenta is one of those versatile foods that can appear in almost any course of an Italian menu, from antipasto to dessert. After the following basic recipe, I have included two of my favorite polenta dishes. They can be served as an antipasto, *primo, secondo, contorno* or *piatto unico.* Technically *primi,* they are fairly robust and best served either in very small servings or on their own as a one-course meal with a green salad.

Polenta can be used as a base for some of the hearty game stews in the *Secondi* chapter: *Peposo dell'Impruneta* (page 249), *Cinghiale in Dolce e Forte* (page 251) and *Scottiglia* (page 260). It can also be sliced and used in the place of noodles to make lasagna, or grilled with a thin slice of pancetta on top to serve as an antipasto. Or you can slice it thinly, deep-fry it, sprinkle it with salt and eat it hot.

I use a 1:4 volume ratio of cornmeal to water. One cup of cornmeal makes enough for two people as a main course or four as a side dish or *primo.* The taste of polenta made with quality stone-ground cornmeal should be reminiscent of creamed fresh corn. Polenta this good hardly needs any garnish but a drizzle of extra virgin olive oil and a pinch of sea salt.

This recipe yields a fairly stiff polenta that can be cooled and sliced for grilling or baking.

SERVES 4

MAKE-AHEAD NOTE

If you want to make the polenta ahead, you can reheat it in the top of a double boiler half an hour before you plan to serve it. Cover loosely with a piece of foil and stir the polenta from time to time while it is reheating.

4 cups boiling water

1 tsp salt, plus more to taste

1 cup coarsely ground yellow cornmeal

Place the boiling water in a large, heavy-bottomed saucepan over high heat and add the salt. Take a fistful of cornmeal and add it in a fine stream to the water, whisking constantly so it doesn't form lumps. Continue in this way until you have used up all the cornmeal, then replace the whisk with a wooden spoon and reduce the heat to low. Continue to stir, fairly constantly, although now you do not need to be quite the slave to the pot. Coarsely ground cornmeal will take about 45 minutes to thicken and cook completely. When it is done it should start to come away from the sides of the pot as you stir. Taste for salt.

If you plan to grill, fry or slice the polenta, turn it out onto a lightly oiled work surface or into an oiled loaf pan to cool. Polenta can be kept for a day or two in the fridge.

Variations

Once you start to make polenta, you will discover the exact texture you prefer. You can achieve a creamier texture in a couple of ways. The easiest is to cook the polenta for a slightly shorter time—remove it from the heat before it cleans the sides of the pot (about 35 minutes). Alternatively, you can use a little more liquid. For a richer-tasting polenta, add a dab of butter, a little hot milk and/or some grated cheese near the end of the cooking time.

pages 240, 241

Polenta with Greens

I love the combination of polenta, greens and cheese. Uncomplicated yet full of flavor, this is healthy, comfort-giving food.

SERVES 4 TO 6

1 onion, finely chopped

2 tbsp butter

4 cups boiling water

1 cup cornmeal

140 g (5 oz) finely chopped steamed greens (spinach, chard or
    beet greens)*

1 cup grated cheese (Gruyère, fontina or Parmesan all work well)

Salt and pepper to taste

See note on page 165 for cooking greens.

Preheat the oven to 350°F/175°C.

In a large, heavy-bottomed saucepan, over moderate heat, cook the onion in the butter until it wilts. Add the boiling water, and then slowly add the cornmeal, whisking constantly until it is all absorbed and there are no lumps. Add the greens and stir well.

Proceed with making a creamy polenta as described on page 148. When it is cooked, stir in half the grated cheese and the salt and pepper. Stir the mixture until the cheese has melted and transfer to an oiled baking dish. Top with the remaining cheese.

Bake until the cheese melts, about 15 minutes, then broil for about 5 minutes or until the cheese is golden brown. Serve hot.

MAKE-AHEAD NOTE

This recipe, up to the point where it is transferred to the baking dish, can be made ahead and kept in the fridge for several days. When you are ready to put together the finished dish, simply top with the remaining cheese and proceed to bake it. Leftovers can be reheated to make a nice lunch with a green salad and a glass of wine.

Polenta Concia ◆ Baked Polenta with Cheese

This is a hearty first course from the Val d'Aosta. The best rendition of this dish I've tasted was in the Val Veny, at the charming hotel and restaurant La Grolla, just outside the fashionable ski resort of Courmayeur. Wonderful mountain food, *polenta concia* features the local fontina cheese and goes best with a good appetite. *Concia* refers to "dressing," "tanning" or "curing" something. For centuries polenta was a staple in the diet of the poor. Dressing it up with a bit of butter and cheese every once in a while turned the ordinary porridge into a special treat, a good cure for those in danger of getting sick of it.

SERVES 4 TO 6

2 cups warm milk
2 cups boiling water
1 cup cornmeal
2 tbsp butter
Salt and pepper to taste
100 g (3.5 oz) thinly sliced fontina cheese
⅓ cup grated Parmesan cheese

Preheat the oven to 350°F/175°C.

Prepare the polenta as described in the variations on page 148, using the milk and the water. When done, stir in the butter, salt and pepper and transfer to an oiled large, shallow baking dish or individual baking dishes. Layer the fontina on top and sprinkle with the grated Parmesan.

Bake for about 20 minutes or until the cheese has melted. Broil for 5 minutes to achieve a golden brown crust and serve.

CRESPELLE, GNOCCHI, TESTAROLI ...

Gnocchi, crêpes, dumplings, pancakes . . . just a few more of the many things that might turn up as a first course.

Gnocchi di Ricotta con Piselli e Menta
✦ Ricotta Gnocchi with Spring Peas and Mint

Italians make gnocchi out of a thousand different things. Sometimes the mixture is simply flour bound with an egg, other times it is made with potatoes, polenta, chestnut flour or ricotta cheese. Squash, beets or other vegetables are incorporated to add color and flavor. While few of my Italian friends can make fresh pasta, almost all of them can whip up a batch of gnocchi in no time flat. And for every gnocchi maker there is a different secret technique. I've also yet to meet an Italian child who does not adore gnocchi. Even the fussiest of eaters gobble them up. This is Italian soul food. It's made in a minute and it disappears that fast too.

My favorite gnocchi are the delicate ones made with ricotta cheese. Use the best quality and freshest ricotta, preferably made from sheep's or buffalo's milk. These feather-light dumplings melt in your mouth and are best adorned with judicious restraint. A simple condiment of lightly sautéed seasonal vegetables is enough.

SERVES 4 TO 6

For the gnocchi

    225 g (8 oz) fresh ricotta cheese
    70 g (2.5 oz) (¾ cup) grated Parmesan cheese

Ricotta cheese sometimes
contains excess whey that
needs to be drained off
before you can use it. If
your ricotta appears runny,
it will need draining.
Place it in a fine sieve and
let it sit for 30 minutes to
remove any excess whey.
More often than not today,
ricotta is sold already
drained. Drained ricotta
cheese is thick rather than
runny, and if you place
it in a strainer almost no
liquid will come off it.

½ cup bread flour, plus more for rolling out the dough

1 egg, lightly beaten

¼ tsp salt

For the sauce

1 small onion, minced

½ garlic clove, minced

28 g (1 oz) pancetta, thinly sliced or finely diced

1 tbsp extra virgin olive oil

½ cup fresh or frozen green peas

To finish

Several leaves of fresh mint, rolled tightly one on top of the other
into a cigarette shape and finely sliced into a *chiffonade*

For the gnocchi

Mix all of the gnocchi ingredients together. This can be done by hand or
in a mixer using the paddle attachment. The dough will be a bit sticky.
Refrigerate the dough for at least 1 hour.

When you are ready to shape the gnocchi, you will need a bowl of
cold water and two wet hands. Sprinkle your work surface with flour and
divide the dough into 3 or 4 parts. Take one piece of the dough and, with
wet hands, roll it into a slender log about ½ inch wide. Using a sharp
knife dipped in the water, cut this log at bite-sized intervals—about ½
inch. Place on a piece of wax or parchment paper while you proceed to
shape the rest of the dough. If you like, you can experiment with shaping
the gnocchi by rolling them over the tines of a fork or, alternatively, rolling them into a ball using wet hands. The gnocchi can be kept for several
hours in the fridge until you plan to cook. Better yet, freeze them on a

tray lined with parchment or wax paper. The frozen gnocchi are not the least bit sticky and are much easier to transfer into the boiling water.

Cook the gnocchi in a large pot of rapidly boiling salted water until they rise to the surface—just a couple of minutes. Drain, reserving 1 cup of the hot water for the sauce.

For the sauce

Make this quick and easy sauce by sautéing the onion, garlic and pancetta in the olive oil until the onion wilts and the pancetta begins to crisp slightly. Add the peas along with some of the reserved water from the gnocchi, if needed to form a sauce consistency. The peas will take just a couple of minutes to cook. Serve garnished with the fresh mint.

Variations

You can experiment with the sauce. I sometimes add a dash of cream at the end, and certainly many other vegetables will work in place of peas—zucchini, asparagus, fava beans, winter squash, or red or yellow peppers, just to name a few. This is an easy and whimsical sauce, so follow your instincts and the season and you will not be disappointed. The mint marries well with spring and early-summer vegetables such as peas and fava beans. Zucchini and peppers love basil, and sage is wonderful with winter squash.

Gnocchetti di Grano Saraceno ◆ Buckwheat Gnocchi

Tiny dumplings made of buckwheat flour are found in the alpine regions of northeastern Lombardy and in the autonomous regions of the Alto Adige and Trentino, where they are often called *spatzli*, the local version of their German name.

Buckwheat is a hearty grain that is a staple in the diet in these regions. Similar to the Swiss/German *spätzle* or *knöpfle*, these *gnocchetti* are made with a thick batter passed through the small holes of a grater, colander or *spätzle* maker and into a pot of boiling water. Alternatively, the batter can be sliced into the water from a bread board held over the pot. They are often served in place of potatoes as an accompaniment to hearty stews and braises rather than as a stand-alone first course.

SERVES 4 TO 6

For the gnocchetti

    140 g (5 oz) (1 cup) unbleached all-purpose flour

    100 g (3.5 oz) (¾ cup) buckwheat flour

    A generous pinch of freshly grated nutmeg

    A pinch of salt

    2 eggs, lightly beaten

    ½ cup milk

    2 tsp extra virgin olive oil

For the sauce

    1 tbsp extra virgin olive oil

    1 tbsp butter

    56 g (2 oz) pancetta, cut into small dice

    ½ cup heavy cream

To finish

    2 or 3 leaves of fresh sage, stacked, rolled like a cigarette and
        cut into a fine *chiffonade*

    Freshly grated Parmesan cheese to pass at the table

For the gnocchetti

Sift the flours, nutmeg and salt into a large bowl. Whisk in the eggs, milk and oil to form a thick batter.

For the sauce

Heat the oil and butter over moderate heat and add the pancetta. Cook the pancetta until it begins to give off its fat and get a bit crispy, about 5 minutes. Stir in the cream. Bring slowly just to a boil. Keep warm while you cook the *gnocchetti*.

To cook

Bring a large pot of salted water to a boil. If you own a *spätzle* maker, use it to make the *gnocchetti*. Otherwise, push the batter through the holes of a colander or grater into the boiling water. A rubber spatula is a perfect tool for this. Alternatively, place the batter on a bread board over the pot and use a knife to cut thin strips of it into the boiling water. The *gnocchetti* will take just a few minutes to cook—they are done when the water has returned to a rolling boil and they rise to the surface. Drain the *gnocchetti* and transfer to heated individual serving plates.

To finish, drizzle the sauce over the dumplings and garnish with the sage. Pass the Parmesan cheese at the table.

Crespelle alla Fiorentina ◆ Spinach Crêpes

The Tuscans, especially the Florentines, are spinach eaters. You can get a first-class plate of cooked spinach (or Swiss chard) to accompany a meal almost anywhere (see page 304). The French even adopted the term *à la Florentine* to identify dishes containing spinach, such as eggs Florentine and chicken Florentine.

In and around Florence today, one often finds these excellent *crespelle*. The béchamel sauce can be made the day before and kept in the fridge with a sheet of plastic wrap tight over its surface so that it does not form a crust. The crêpe batter and the filling can also be made ahead and kept overnight in the fridge. Once assembled, the unbaked dish freezes beautifully for up to a month. No defrosting is necessary. The crêpes can go directly from the freezer to the oven.

MAKES 8 TO 10 CRÊPES

For the filling

    112 g (4 oz) cooked spinach,* squeezed dry

    225 g (8 oz) fresh ricotta cheese (see page 152)

    ⅓ cup grated Parmesan cheese

    1 egg

    A pinch of freshly grated nutmeg

    Salt and pepper to taste

*See note on page 165 for cooking greens.

For the crêpes

    1 cup all-purpose flour

    1⅓ cups milk

    2 eggs, beaten

    A pinch of salt

To finish

    1 tbsp tomato paste

    1 recipe béchamel sauce (page 312)

    ½ cup grated Parmesan cheese

For the filling

Place all of the filling ingredients in a food processor and process briefly until you have a smooth paste. Refrigerate the mixture for at least 1 hour.

For the crêpes

Make a thin batter by whisking together the crêpe ingredients. Let sit for 1 hour at room temperature.

Lightly grease a large nonstick frying pan with a little olive oil and heat the pan over moderate heat. Pour about ¼ cup of the crêpe batter into the pan and swirl to evenly distribute the batter over the bottom. Cook the crêpe until it is lightly colored on the bottom and set on the top—just a few minutes. Flip over and briefly cook the other side.

Remove to a plate and continue to make crêpes with the remaining batter.

To cook

Preheat the oven to 400°F/200°C. Grease an 8-inch square baking dish with olive oil.

Whisk the tomato paste into the béchamel sauce.

Spread a thin, even layer of the filling over the entire surface of each crêpe, then fold the edges of the round shape inward to form a square. Then fold the square in thirds (see photos).

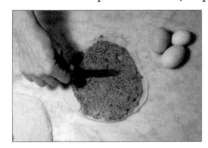  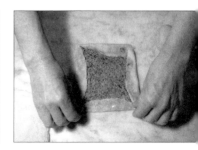

Place the crêpes in the baking dish. Spread the tomato-béchamel mixture evenly over the crêpes and top with the Parmesan cheese.

Bake for 15 minutes or until the top is bubbly and lightly browned.

Variation

These *crespelle* are marvelous finished with *fonduta* (page 273) in place of the béchamel mixture. Ladle it over the stuffed crêpes and bake until golden. (You do not need the Parmesan cheese sprinkled on top).

Testaroli col Pesto Genovese
✦ Ligurian Pancakes with Basil Pesto

Testaroli with pesto is a fascinating dish from the eastern Ligurian *entroterra* (inland) and the Lunigiani region of nearby Tuscany. These crêpe-like pancakes are traditionally cooked in terra-cotta plates that are first heated to a very high temperature over the embers of a wood-burning fire. The plates are removed from the heat, the *testaroli* batter is ladled on, and the plates are stacked up one on top of the other to bake. The plates are so hot by now that the *testaroli* cook very quickly. The round pancakes are divided into triangles and served warm as an antipasto with a drizzle of olive oil and a sprinkling of grated cheese or a dollop of pesto. As a first course, they are cut into strips and boiled like pasta and then topped with either the basil pesto or with olive oil and Parmesan.

The recipe for the pesto below does not include cheese or pine nuts, two ingredients normally found in basil pesto. I like the simplicity of it—the pure taste of basil and extra virgin olive oil together. If I have any in my pantry, I sprinkle a few toasted pine nuts on the finished dish at the end. The cheese I add at the table. As it is unlikely you will find authentic *testaroli* saucers, they can be made in a cast-iron or nonstick frying pan.

SERVES 4

For the testaroli
 1 cup all-purpose flour
 1 cup water

For the pesto
 A handful of fresh basil leaves
 1 garlic clove
 A pinch of salt
 Extra virgin olive oil (preferably from Liguria)

To finish
 1 tbsp toasted pine nuts
 Grated Parmesan cheese to pass at the table

For the testaroli
Whisk together the flour and water and let sit for half an hour at room temperature.

Heat a lightly oiled 8- to 10-inch nonstick or cast-iron frying pan over moderately high heat. When the pan is hot, pour in about ⅓ cup of your batter and twirl the pan so the batter spreads evenly over the bottom.

You are looking for a pancake about 6 inches in diameter with a thickness somewhere between a thick crêpe and a thin griddlecake. When the pancake is set on the bottom and has developed a white skin that is slightly flecked with gold, flip it over and briefly cook the other side until it is the same color. Continue to cook the *testaroli* with the remaining batter, adding a little more oil to the pan if necessary. Stack the finished *testaroli* on a plate until you're ready to cook them. They keep well in the fridge for several hours.

For the pesto
If you own a mortar and pestle, place the basil, garlic and salt in the mortar and pound to a paste, gradually drizzling in enough olive oil as you work to get a fairly homogenous sauce. Alternatively, add the ingredients to a blender or the measuring cup of a hand blender and process to a smooth sauce. You can adjust the pesto ingredients to suit your taste.

To cook
Bring a large pot of water to a boil. When it reaches a boil, add 1 tbsp salt.

Cut the *testaroli* into strips 1 inch wide, to resemble noodles. Boil until the noodles float to the surface—usually about a minute or two. Drain and transfer to a warm serving bowl.

Dilute the pesto with a bit of the cooking water and drizzle over the *testaroli*. Serve garnished with the toasted pine nuts and pass the cheese at the table. Although it is not traditionally done, I often garnish this dish with quartered cherry tomatoes from my garden for added color and flavor.

To serve testaroli as an antipasto
Make smaller *testaroli*, about 3 inches in diameter. For each serving, place one warm *testarolo* on a warm plate, drizzle with some olive oil and

sprinkle some Parmesan cheese over the top, or spread with a thin layer of the pesto. Place another *testarolo* on top and repeat the topping.

My Search for Testaroli

I found a recipe for *testaroli* in a Ligurian cookbook and had been making them for years before I tasted the real deal, that is, *testaroli* made for me by a Ligurian. They actually do exist, these elusive pancakes, but they are increasingly hard to find, perhaps even an endangered Ligurian-Luni specialty.

I got to taste authentic *testaroli* at Osteria La Brinca in the small village of Ne. Ne is perched above the elegant old resort town of Chiavari, just a few winding miles into the hills but worlds away from the glam and glitter of the Riviera. On my last visit, 25 euros bought a seemingly endless meal. There was no printed menu, and no choice. This is usually a good sign—no guessing, no tough decisions. All you need to do is sit back and be prepared to enjoy whatever the cook has in store.

Platters laden with food, and bottles of the local red and white wine, soon appeared, and kept appearing until finally, mindful of the tiny, winding mountain roads we had to negotiate home, we signaled our waiter that we were finished. We left the place astonished and delighted. So much food—all of it exquisite and perfectly prepared, most of it demonstrating the Ligurian love affair with the vegetable: intricately prepared stuffed vegetables; *testaroli* served with a dollop of the region's signature basil pesto; thin wedges of several different kinds of savory vegetable tarts (see page 94); tasty Ligurian rabbit braised in olives and white wine; delicate homemade stuffed pastas; vegetable flans. Someone in the kitchen, or more than likely several generations of women from this village, had gone to a whole lot of trouble to produce that meal. And this was a meal that, if you could find it, which is highly unlikely, would cost a small fortune anywhere else.

When we left, we noticed the steep terraces the restaurant was perched above and understood then that the labor in the kitchen was only the beginning. Here was a perfectly tended vegetable garden and a *pollaio* full of healthy-looking free-ranging poultry. A fruit and olive orchard completed the picture. No wonder everything tasted so good—look how fresh it all was! But for me the *testaroli* were the highlight of the meal. Finally, I had tasted an authentic version of the delicious pancake that had been eluding me all these years.

Recently my quest for *testaroli* came full circle when I found some of the terra-cotta saucers they are traditionally made in. I had heard these were a thing of the past and could no longer be found. I was visiting the town of Varese Ligure, in the Val di Vara in the eastern Ligurian *entroterra* near the Tuscan border, not far as the crow flies from the town of Ne, where I had eaten my first *testarolo*. The valley promotes itself as an organic valley (*valle del biologico*). One of Liguria's largest and least populated valleys, its capital is the town of Varesa Ligure, sometimes called Europe's most organic *comune*.

I was curious to visit such a paradise. I was especially keen to seek out the fairly new organic cheese cooperative, the Cooperativo Caseraria Val di Vara, and the Cooperativo San Pietro Vara, a point of sale for locally raised organic beef. Having found the meat co-op closed, I was wandering around Varese Ligure, admiring its famous medieval *borgo rotondo*. On the circular main square of that beautiful town was a hardware store, and there in the window was a stack of thick terra-cotta saucers. I went in to inquire. Yes, the owner told me, these are what we use to make *testaroli*, and he went on to describe to me exactly how they're made. I bought a dozen of these pretty saucers and am now stacking them up near the hearth of my own fireplace.

Canederli agli Spinaci
◆ Spinach Dumplings from the Alto Adige

The farther north and east one travels in Italy, the more dumpling-type preparations replace pasta and rice as a first course. *Canederli* (ca–nay–der–lee) are dumplings made from day-old bread that are found in Trentino and the Alto Adige (or South Tyrol). They are usually available in different varieties, including spinach, liver, mushroom and cheese. There are even sweet versions made with apricots and served for dessert.

Even those who claim to dislike spinach often love these pretty green dumplings. Spinach *canederli* are easy to make, healthy and a good way to use up some of your (preferably homemade) day-old bread. They are surprisingly light, but two or three per person will make a substantial first course.

The mixture can be made one day ahead and stored in the refrigerator overnight, then shaped and cooked the next day. This dish is perfect food for the gourmet bachelor or family of two. Often I mix up a batch of *canederli* to keep in the fridge, dipping into it to make a few dumplings for lunch or dinner over the course of a few days. Some bread, spinach, milk and an egg thrown together like this never tasted better.

SERVES 4

6 oz day-old hearth-style bread, preferably homemade (the rye bread on page 49 or the crusty loaf on page 31 is perfect)

MAKING PERFECT CANEDERLI

- The spinach must be cooked long enough to evaporate any excess moisture.
- The bread should be neither too fresh nor too stale. Day-old bread is ideal.
- The seemingly small amounts of flour and bread crumbs are important to the final texture.
- Do not over-process the mixture, or too much water will be released from the spinach, resulting in a texture that is too smooth.
- The mixture needs to be refrigerated for 1 hour before shaping.

¾ cup warm milk

2 tbsp butter or extra virgin olive oil

1 garlic clove, minced

1 small onion, minced

250 g (9 oz) finely chopped steamed spinach (see page 165)

1 egg, lightly beaten

1 tbsp bread flour

1 tbsp dry bread crumbs

Salt, pepper and grated nutmeg to taste

To finish

Melted butter or olive oil (optional)

Grated Parmesan cheese

The evening before you plan to make the *canederli*, slice the bread and leave it out all night to dry completely. The next day, a couple of hours before you plan to cook, break up the bread and place it in a large bowl. Cover with the warm milk and let sit.

Melt the butter in a sauté pan over moderate heat and add the garlic and onion. Cook for a few minutes, until the onion becomes soft but does not brown. Add the spinach and cook for about 7 minutes, until the spinach is tender and any excess water it contained has been cooked off. Remove from the heat and let cool.

By now the bread should have absorbed all the milk. To the bread, add the spinach mixture, egg, flour and bread crumbs. Season with the salt, pepper and nutmeg. Using wet hands, mix the ingredients together, or place the whole lot in your food processor and process very briefly—just until things are well combined. Be careful, because if you over-process you will ruin the *canederli*. You are looking for a mixture that has some texture, not a smooth paste. Refrigerate for at least 1 hour or up to 2 days.

Using wet hands, form 8 to 12 balls, about the size of a golf ball, from the mixture. At this point, the *canederli* can be kept in the fridge, on a plastic-lined tray and covered with a clean tea towel, for several hours until you are ready to cook them.

Bring a large pot of water to a rolling boil. Add the *canederli*, reduce the heat to moderate, and cook for 5 minutes. The *canederli* will rise to the surface when they are cooked. It is a good idea to remove one and test it for doneness by tasting it. It should be completely cooked through, hot inside and out. The cooking water turns green while the dumplings cook. Drain.

Serve 2 or 3 per person, with melted butter or olive oil drizzled over the top and sprinkled with the grated cheese.

Cooking Greens

Most of the recipes in this book that call for spinach or other greens call for the amount of greens weighed *after* they have been cleaned, stemmed and steamed and much of the moisture removed. This is because greens can vary tremendously in the weight they cook down to, depending on what kind you use, how much of what you buy is stem and ribs that you discard, and the age and size of the leaf. If you are using fresh greens, a good rule of thumb when a recipe calls for steamed greens is to start with three times the stated weight.

To steam greens, wash them in several changes of water and remove all the tough stems and thick center ribs. Do not dry them. Place them in a large sauté pan and cook over moderate heat, turning them occasionally with a pair of tongs so they steam evenly. The water clinging to their leaves should be enough to cook them. Cooking time will vary depending on the type of green chosen, but count on at least 5 minutes. Tougher greens like kale may need longer. Remove to a colander and run under cold water to stop the cooking. If the greens are to be used to stuff pasta, squeeze as much of the water out of them as you can. If the next step in the recipe calls for the greens to be sautéed, it is best to leave a little of their water clinging to the leaves.

Many Italians rely on precooked greens bought in the local *gastronomia*. These balls of chopped, blanched greens make life very easy for the home cook who does not want to bother cooking and cleaning mounds of fresh greens. In North America, frozen chopped organic spinach or chard offer the same convenience.

Don't throw away the stems! If you are using thick-stemmed greens like chard or beets, you can make a tasty side dish by cutting the stems into pieces about 1½ inches long and boiling them until they are tender in 2 parts water to 1 part wine vinegar. Drain, season with salt and pepper and serve at room temperature with a drizzle of extra virgin olive oil and some finely chopped basil.

PASTA

Pasta is Italian comfort food. Anyone who has been invited to an Italian home for dinner can testify to this. It is only after the pasta course has been delivered and seemingly instantly consumed that tensions seem to ease and a relaxed atmosphere takes hold. The meal has begun properly. For most Italians, to not eat pasta at least once a day is to not live. There are as many ways to prepare it as there are people who eat it. Everyone has his or her own special recipe. Everyone is an expert when it comes to pasta.

Sometimes I find myself in Florence or Siena over the lunch hour, not able to get home for the midday meal. Not much of a breakfast fan, I'm always hungry for lunch, so I often eat in one of the bars I know has a good *tavolo caldo* (hot table). The best ones are generally packed with young, stylish businesspeople, the men squeezed into pencil-thin trousers and pointy-toed shoes and the women with spiked heels, coiffed hair and stylish handbags. But these fashionistas, unlike so many of their North American counterparts, seem to enjoy a healthy relationship to the plate. Famished, they eat, and what they eat is more often than not *la pasta*. They eat standing, not sitting, talking loudly and gesticulating wildly, in one hand a plate of pasta, in the other a fork. Italian fast food. Here a quick lunch is a steaming plate of delicious pasta. If you can't get home to *la mamma*, that is.

Pasta Fatta a Mano ✦ Fresh Pasta

I've found that if you want to learn how to make fresh pasta, you'll do well to find yourself a *nonna*. Very few people know how or can be bothered to make it at home anymore. Like most of the white arts, homemade pasta is something refined and perfected only after years spent with a *mattarello*—a rolling pin—and a wooden board. People in Italy today who want to eat fresh pasta are more apt to buy it at their local pasta shop or supermarket. Even in fine restaurants one has to read the menu carefully. There is a difference between *pasta fresca* (fresh pasta) and *pasta fatta in casa* (house-made pasta). The former is often purchased from a wholesale supplier. To find handmade pasta anymore, it seems you

My rule of thumb for pasta is to cook 100 g (3.5 oz) per person if served as a main course. If as a *primo* and part of a larger meal, I cook 60 to 70 g (about 2.5 oz) per serving. If you are making stuffed pasta, you will need roughly half these amounts per person.

need to search for an authentic *osteria* where *la nonna* is still gainfully employed as the *sfoglina*, or pasta chef. I wonder what will happen to this art once all of these women are gone.

I've learned a few tricks from watching some of these grandmothers. First and foremost is to do away with a pasta-rolling machine and take up the rolling pin. Like most things made by hand, the results are superior, and once the technique is mastered, just as fast—not to mention easier, since there is no machine to buy, store or clean. Dough rolled out by hand with a wooden pin develops a texture that is difficult to achieve using a machine with metal rollers. This is important, because texture is what is required if the sauce is to penetrate the pasta and impart flavor to it. It is also easier for the cook to control the thickness and the width of hand-rolled pasta, resulting in delicate, less uniform-looking noodles with immense visual appeal.

Since fresh pasta usually contains only two ingredients (flour and eggs or water), its goodness largely relates to the quality of those things. Look for the freshest free-range eggs, with deep yellow yolks. The yolks of the eggs I get from my corn-fed chickens are bright orange, making my pasta almost fluorescent. In Italian supermarkets you can buy eggs especially for making pasta, and their yolks are almost red.

Fresh Pasta: The basic formula

This formula produces enough pasta to feed two people as a first course and can easily be multiplied. If you plan to stuff the pasta to make *ravioli* or *agnolotti*, the basic formula is sufficient for four servings. The standard formula for making homemade pasta is to use 1 large egg (weighing approx. 65 g or 2.3 oz out of its shell) for every 100 g (3.5 oz) (¾ cup) of flour.

100 g (3.5 oz) (scant ¾ cup) all-purpose flour

65 g (2.3 oz) (approx. 1 large) egg, weighed out of its shell

If you own kitchen scales, be sure to use them when you make pasta. Getting the right hydration in the dough makes all the difference in the world, so the more accurate you can be, the better. If your eggs weigh less than the required amount, then you need to add enough liquid to make up the difference. You can use water, olive oil, more egg or a combination of them all. Olive oil tends to lend a silkiness to fresh pasta, but don't overdo it. I never add more than a teaspoon per egg.

If you do not own scales, you can still make excellent pasta. I once ate perfect homemade pasta at the home of a friend. When I asked her how much flour per egg she used, she couldn't say. "*Facciamo ad occhio,*" she said—we do it by eye. Roberta learned to make pasta as a youngster from her mother, and the two of them still make it together often, especially in early summer when the hens are busy laying eggs. Learning the right texture of the dough is what really matters. Perfect pasta dough is silky smooth without being sticky. It comes together into a firm ball yet is very malleable and easy to roll out. It is strong and elastic so that it can be rolled out very thinly without tearing.

Mixing the dough

BY HAND:

To be really authentic, make the dough by hand, at least the first few times. Once you get comfortable with the process, you'll be surprised how quickly it comes together. Dump the flour into a mound on your work surface and make a well in the middle. Dump the eggs in the well and, using a fork, start to beat them lightly. As you beat, start to incorporate the flour from the sides of the well.

FLOUR FOR PASTA

Use unbleached all-purpose flour, with a protein content around 11.5 percent (see page 15).

Once the eggs and flour are incorporated, you can start to knead the dough. A bench scraper is handy to have on hand at this point to scrape up any dough that sticks to your board. Knead the dough for 10 minutes or until it is smooth and fairly stiff yet still pliable—think playdough consistency. You should be able to see small bubbles on its surface. Wrap the ball of dough in plastic and let it rest for about half an hour at room temperature. During this time it will become more extensible, and easier to roll out.

USING A MIXER:
Place the flour and eggs in the mixer and knead with the dough hook on medium speed for 6 to 8 minutes. The dough will form a ball. Wrap the dough in plastic and let it rest for half an hour.

Rolling out the dough

Professional *sfogline* make large quantities of fresh pasta using a series of rolls and turns that take them years to master. They use long rolling pins and have large wooden tables dedicated to the task. For the home cook working with fairly small quantities of dough, I have adapted a simpler method of hand rolling that achieves comparable results.

When you begin making homemade pasta, it is best to work with small pieces of dough. Once you become more practiced, you can increase the amount you roll out at one time, and the whole business will become much faster, although you may need a longer rolling pin. If you don't own one, you can make an inexpensive one using a piece of wood cut from a 1½- to 2-inch-wide dowel. It is best to work on a wooden surface to give the noodles texture.

Lightly flour your work surface, and put one ball of dough on it. Press down on it to form a flat circle, and lightly flour the top. Place your rolling pin in the center of the round, press down and roll the pin up (away from you). Use as much of your weight and strength as you can as you roll. Place the pin back in the middle and roll down (towards you). Again, it is important to use all your strength.

Now, always beginning from the middle of your circle, begin rolling in a clockwise direction, working around the dough circle at 45-degree intervals, covering half of the circle with each roll. If the dough starts to feel like it may stick to the board, lift it using your rolling pin and lightly sift a thin veil of flour on the work surface underneath. Flip the dough over and continue rolling on the other side. Be miserly with the flour at every stage, or the pasta will get dry and tough.

The dough will tell you when it's done. It will stop increasing in size as you roll. Now must you stop too, or you risk tearing it. You should have an almost paper-thin sheet of dough. Let it dry briefly on a clean kitchen towel or on a cooling rack before you begin cutting it—15 minutes or so is usually long enough for the sheet of pasta to develop a light skin so it won't stick together when you fold it. If you leave it too long, it will become dry and brittle, impossible to fold and to cut without breaking.

For Pappardelle and Tajarin

Fold up your sheet of dough like a jelly roll into a flat roll. Cut pappardelle a little less than 1 inch wide and *tajarin* about ⅛ inch wide, or as thin as you can cut.

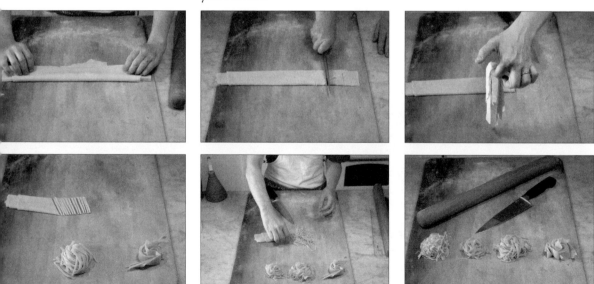

Dry the noodles on a pasta-drying rack or a tea towel that has been lightly sprinkled with flour (semolina flour is best for this) until they are dried out just enough so they will not stick together—about 15 minutes. If you're not ready to cook them yet, you can twirl them into one nest per serving, transfer them to a parchment-lined baking sheet and cover with a clean kitchen towel. Fresh pasta will keep for a few hours like this in the fridge. The longer it sits, the drier it gets and the more time it will take to cook, so it is ideally made as close to cooking time as is practical.

For stuffed pasta

Roll out the dough as described above. Use a cookie cutter or pastry wheel to cut the dough into the appropriate shape and follow the recipe instructions.

Sugo

After you've mastered the art of making your own pasta, the next thing to do is make a long, slow pot of *sugo*. *Sugo* simply means "sauce" in Italian, but the specific sauce it usually refers to is the rich meat *ragù* that is the favored condiment for a plate of freshly made pasta up and down the *stivale* (boot). There are as many recipes for it as there are cooks who make it.

Sugo is an honored, festive sauce served at all the important family get-togethers. In Emilia-Romagna, which is home to most of Italy's dairy cows, the liquid ingredient is often milk. In Tuscany, of course, it is red wine. In southern Italy, where tomatoes develop an uncommon sweetness, they are added to the *sugo*. Other *sugo*-type sauces for fresh pasta are derived from the braising liquid of a main-course meat dish like the *scottiglia* on page 260. Couples argue to their graves about the best way

**WHAT TO DO WITH
THE UGLY BITS**
Don't reroll your badly cut scraps; they become tough. I keep mine in a bag in the freezer to add to broth for a delicious light soup. They can be used to make *pasta e ceci* on page 126. Or deep-fry them in extra virgin olive oil; drain on paper towels, toss with sea salt and serve hot with a glass of sparkling wine as a before-dinner tease. The Italians fondly call these scraps *maltagliati*, or "badly cut." Because they indicate a handmade pasta, they are given pride of place at the Italian table. So don't throw them away—show them off!

to make *sugo*—he likes it with pancetta added to the *soffritto*, she doesn't. And so go endless debates and discussions about what constitutes a perfect *sugo*.

What follows is a Tuscan-style *sugo* I make at Petraia using red wine as the liquid. I like to add a few dried porcini mushrooms because here we are surrounded by woods full of them.

When you make this *sugo*, buy your meat from a reputable butcher and explain that you do not want finely ground hamburger but minced meat. This means it is passed once through the larger holes of the mincer. The meat wants some texture and bite. If minced meat is not available, the next best thing is to buy the meat whole and chop it up yourself into a very fine dice, the method often preferred by home cooks in Italy.

Finally, *sugo* is not a dish to rush. Time is the most important ingredient, so it makes a perfect project for the weekend cook.

SERVES 8 TO 10

15 g (½ oz) dried porcini mushrooms

¼ cup extra virgin olive oil

1 onion, minced

1 celery stalk, finely chopped

1 carrot, finely chopped

1 garlic clove, minced

2 tbsp finely chopped Italian parsley

450 g (1 lb) minced beef (from a shoulder cut such as chuck, brisket or top blade)

112 g (¼ lb) minced pork shoulder (or the equivalent weight of Italian sausage if you have a good source)

2 chicken livers

1 cup red wine

2 to 3 cups beef broth

2 ripe tomatoes, peeled, seeded and chopped (or 2 canned
   tomatoes, seeded and chopped)

Salt and pepper to taste

To finish

Fresh basil or parsley leaves to garnish

Grated Parmesan cheese to pass at the table

Rehydrate the mushrooms in warm water to cover for 20 minutes. Drain the mushrooms, reserving their soaking liquid. Rinse the mushrooms to remove any dirt and finely chop. Strain the soaking liquid through a coffee filter or a sieve lined with a paper towel.

Heat the oil in a large sauté pan or Dutch oven over moderate heat. Add the onion, celery, carrot, garlic and parsley and cook this *soffritto*, stirring occasionally, until the vegetables start to soften and the onion is transparent—10 to 15 minutes. Add the beef, pork and chicken livers and reduce the heat. Cook until the meat has released all of its fat and has browned nicely, about 20 minutes. As the meat browns, use a wooden spoon to mash up the chicken livers.

Add the wine and continue to cook. Place the broth in a saucepan and heat it up. Once the wine has evaporated, add the tomatoes, the mushrooms and their soaking liquid. Turn the heat to the lowest possible setting and add 1 cup of the hot broth. Leave the pan partially covered and cook on a very low simmer for about 2 hours. Check the level of the liquid occasionally and add more of the broth as needed. The finished sauce should be very thick. Season with salt and pepper.

To serve

Italians don't drown their pasta in *sugo,* nor do they pre-toss it. It is best served ladled on top of individual plates of fresh pasta, about ⅓ cup per serving. Add a leaf of fresh basil or parsley to garnish. Pass Parmesan cheese at the table.

Variations

I like to place a teaspoon of butter on top of the *sugo* when I serve it. If I have truffle butter, I use a tiny dab of that instead to add a subtle truffle flavor. This *sugo* is also nice on top of a plate of polenta.

In the winter I sometimes toss a few thawed frozen peas on top of the dish before I serve it to add a bit of color.

White Truffle Butter

In Italy white truffles are available for a short period in October and November. They are found in various regions, but the most famous ones come from the area around the town of Alba, in Piedmont. Tuscany also boasts several areas famous for white truffles. Unfortunately, La Petraia is not one of them. Or, if it is, I'll be the last to know.

Fresh truffles are ridiculously expensive, but there are ways to get their essence into your cooking without breaking the bank. I'm not fond of the truffle oil that a lot of cooks use, as I find it sometimes has a rancid taste. But I like white truffle butter. This condiment is sold from a refrigerated shelf in tiny jars that contain just an ounce or two. Make sure you're buying the white truffle butter (not black, which is not as flavorful or as prized in Italy). Check the "best before" date to make sure you're buying a fresh product. A small jar in Italy can set me back 12 euros, but a little bit goes a long way. It is wonderful with potatoes, eggs and many pasta dishes, and should be added only to the finished dish or the truffle flavor will be lost in the cooking. I usually put an amount that fits on the end of a teaspoon on top of a pasta or soup before I serve it so that diners can stir it in themselves.

Pappardelle Mare e Monte
✦ Mountain and Sea Sauce for Pappardelle

A *mare e monte*, or sea and mountain, sauce simply means a sauce made from an ingredient you find at the sea and one you find in the mountains. Other than that, it's up to the cook to come up with the rest. Here's my version, which highlights the fresh peas of my spring garden, the porcini mushrooms that are available in spring and fall on our mountain, and the beautiful fresh shrimp I get from the mobile fishmonger who visits us every Friday morning.

This is a good pantry dish for those times when you have nothing fresh in the house, because it uses dried mushrooms and the peas and shrimp can come from a well-stocked freezer. Naturally, if you don't have time to make the pasta, you can purchase it fresh or dried.

SERVES 4

For the pappardelle
   200 g (7 oz) (scant 1½ cups) all-purpose flour
   2 large eggs
   1 tsp olive oil

For the sauce

  28 g (1 oz) dried porcini mushrooms

  Leaves from 1 bunch fresh basil

  2 tbsp extra virgin olive oil

  1 onion, minced

  1 garlic clove, minced

  A few flakes of hot chili pepper

  1 Italian sausage, casing removed

  ½ cup fresh or frozen peas or other vegetables (see Variations)

  4 large shrimp, peeled, deveined and cut into small pieces

  ¼ cup heavy cream

  Salt and pepper to taste

  White truffle butter to finish (optional; see pages 176 to 177)

For the pappardelle

Make the pasta and cut pappardelle as described on pages 168 to 173. (Or you can use about ¾ lb purchased fresh noodles.)

For the sauce

Soak the porcini mushrooms in warm water to cover for 20 minutes (see page 179). Place the basil leaves one on top of the other. Roll them up into a thin cigar shape and cut into a fine *chiffonade*. Set aside.

Heat the oil in a sauté pan over moderately high heat. Add the onion and sauté for about 5 minutes. Add the garlic, the chili flakes and the sausage. Cook for a few more minutes, using a wooden spoon to break up the sausage, until it begins to brown. Add the mushrooms along with their strained soaking liquid. Reduce the heat to low and cook until the mushrooms are tender and about half the liquid has evaporated.

In the meantime, bring a large pot of salted water to a rolling boil for the pasta.

If using fresh peas, add them to the pan now and cook for a few minutes, until they are just tender. Add the shrimp and frozen peas if using. Cook briefly—about 30 seconds, just until the shrimp turn pink. Add the cream and half of the basil and let the mixture simmer slowly while you cook the pasta in the boiling water. You can add a bit of the pasta water to the pan if things look like they are getting too dry.

Drain the pasta when it is cooked (2 to 3 minutes) and add it to the pan. Toss the ingredients together and cook briefly. Season with salt and pepper.

To serve

This pasta is best served in warm soup plates. Place the pasta in the plate, top with a tiny drop of the truffle butter, if desired, and garnish with the remaining threads of fresh basil.

Variations

You can vary the vegetable according to the season. In winter the peas can be replaced by finely shaved Savoy cabbage, in summer by zucchini. In the fall I like to use diced red and yellow pepper. Don't be tempted to add more than one kind of vegetable, though, or the dish gets too busy.

Dried Porcini Mushrooms

When buying dried porcini mushrooms, look for the freshest possible mushrooms. Check the date on the package. Ideally they should be no more than a year old. The slices should look like mushroom slices—not shriveled up and unrecognizable. The fleshy parts should still be a bit plump and a pretty ivory color—not dark brown and descending into dust. In Italy quality dried porcini are always available, and they are cleaned so well before being dried that I never find it necessary to strain their soaking liquid. However, it is prudent to do so if you suspect that the mushrooms contain a lot of grit.

When I see the dried porcini for sale in North America, I sometimes wonder if they aren't the seconds, the ones too small and fussy to be cleaned and so get packaged for export. Often they are full of sand, dark in color, shriveled almost beyond recognition and older than they should be. At Petraia, when our guests ask me what local specialties they should take home with them, I always suggest a bag of dried porcini. They weigh next to nothing and cost a small fortune to acquire back home. A 100-gram bag can be stretched a long way, and so can the memories of a visit to Italy.

Having said all of this, if you are using less than desirable mushrooms, they may need to be soaked longer than the time recommended in a recipe to reconstitute. Strain their soaking liquid several times through a coffee filter or a sieve lined with paper towels.

Pappardelle con Ragù di Cinghiale
◆ Pappardelle with Wild Boar Ragù

The boar-hunting season in our township begins in December and runs until the end of January. In Radda there are several hunting squads, and the one that uses our property usually gets, in a good year, hundreds of boar. Boar meat is dark, and tastes more like beef than pork. Because the animal lives in the wild, the meat is tough, and the best way to cook it is in a *ragù* or a slow braise.

Locals complain that Tuscan *cinghiale* don't taste so wild anymore, and they're right. Wild boar eat less of their natural diet these days, and their taste reflects that. Hunters often leave feed in the woods during the summer months when food is scarce, and boar are notorious for eating the crops of local farmers. They cause thousands of dollars of damage for many of us each year. I planted a field of grain a few years ago with the hopes of harvesting enough wheat for flour for my Petraia baking. But instead, in less than a month, wild boar had eaten the whole crop. Even though I placed an electric fence around the field, they were not deterred. They were hungry, and since they are such tough creatures, an electric shock was not enough to stop them.

A wild boar *ragù* is a classic dish in Tuscany. Most people I know have a freezer full of boar that they either hunted themselves or were given by a friend or relative. I rely on our farm manager, Alessandro, to provide the boar at Petraia. He always has several freezers full of it, being an avid hunter and a famed shot.

But this animal is increasingly becoming a rodent in Chianti Classico, its population soaring steadily out of control in recent years. As the region becomes more gentrified, the *contadini* and small landholders that once kept the population in check are fewer. Legend also has it that many animals have immigrated here from other parts of Italy and Eastern Europe. Whatever the reason, I don't feel bad about eating them, nor do most people I know. As a winemaker neighbor of ours replied when we invited him for dinner and inquired if he ate *cinghiale*, "They eat my grapes so I eat them." Sounds like a fair trade to me.

If you can't find wild boar, this *ragù* can be made with venison, moose, elk, buffalo, pork or even beef. The meat should not be minced but should be cut into small cubes. The sauce is used as a condiment for the pappardelle, and the meat is served as a second course, ideally to top a dollop of polenta, but mashed potatoes or grilled or toasted bread will also work. The *ragù* tastes better the next day, so this is a great dish to make ahead of time. This recipe makes a large batch of *ragù*, and I usually freeze half.

SERVES 8 TO 10

For the marinade

   1 onion, peeled and halved

   1 carrot, peeled and cut in 2 or 3 pieces

   1 garlic clove, crushed

   A few leaves of fresh sage

   A sprig of fresh rosemary

   2 cups red wine

   2 tbsp red wine vinegar

   2 tbsp olive oil

   1 kg (2¼ lb) boneless boar (a shoulder cut, if possible), trimmed of any excess fat and cut into ½-inch cubes

For the ragù

   ¼ cup extra virgin olive oil

   1 onion, minced

   1 celery stalk, finely chopped

   1 carrot, finely chopped

   3 or 4 juniper berries

   2 or 3 whole cloves

   1 bay leaf

   A sprig of fresh rosemary

   Several leaves of fresh sage

1 garlic clove, minced

Salt and pepper to taste

2 ripe tomatoes, peeled, seeded and finely chopped

2 cups beef broth or water

For the pappardelle

Enough fresh pappardelle—either homemade (see pages 168
to 173) or purchased—for the number of people you will be
feeding (see page 168)

For the marinade

Combine all of the marinade ingredients in a resealable plastic bag or non-reactive bowl and add the meat. Marinate overnight in the refrigerator.

For the ragù

Drain the meat from the marinade. Strain and reserve the liquid. Heat the oil in a large pot over moderate heat and add the onion, celery and carrot. Cook, stirring occasionally, for about 5 minutes. Add the meat and brown it well on all sides—about 15 minutes.

Place the juniper berries under the blade of a chef's knife and apply enough pressure to slightly crush them. Tie the juniper berries, cloves, bay leaf, rosemary sprig and sage leaves in a piece of cheesecloth, or place them in a tea ball, and add to the pot with the garlic and salt and pepper. Cook for 5 more minutes before adding a ladleful of the marinating liquid. Scrape any browned bits from the bottom of the pan with a wooden spoon, and cook until the marinade has almost evaporated. Continue to add the marinade a ladleful at a time, letting it simmer until it is almost evaporated before you add more. Reduce the heat to low and add the tomatoes and the broth. Partially cover the pot and simmer the *ragù* very slowly for about 3 hours. Check the pot every now and again and add more wine or broth if need be. Remove the spice packet before serving.

For the pappardelle
While the *ragù* simmers, make the pasta and cut pappardelle as described on pages 168 to 173.

Cook the pasta in a large pot of boiling salted water. It will be ready in 3 to 4 minutes.

To serve
I prefer to serve this pasta in individual heated soup plates, with about ⅓ cup of the *ragù* sauce drizzled over the top. Alternatively, you can serve it family style in a large heated pasta bowl, tossing the *ragù* into the noodles before serving.

Tajarin con Gorgonzola e Nocciole
✦ Tagliolini with Gorgonzola and Hazelnuts

Tajarin are the fine tagliolini made in the Piedmont region of northern Italy. Traditionally they were made using up to 40 egg yolks per kilogram of flour. The yolks give a deep yellow color to the noodles.

The combination of hazelnuts and gorgonzola cheese is a noble one. The cheese, made in Piedmont and nearby Lombardy, is a common ingredient in the Piedmont kitchen, as are the nuts that grow beside the region's famous vineyards. I don't know if you'll find an easier, more elegant sauce for these rich, fresh noodles. Naturally, if you aren't up to making pasta, you can buy fresh or dried egg noodles.

For the tajarin

200 g (7 oz) (1½ scant cups) all-purpose flour

8 to 10 large egg yolks

1 tsp olive oil

For the sauce

Scant ½ cup hazelnuts

⅓ cup milk

112 g (4 oz) gorgonzola cheese

2 tbsp butter

Salt and pepper to taste

To finish

Chopped fresh parsley to garnish

For the tajarin

Make the pasta dough as described on pages 168 to 170, using egg yolks and oil. The number of yolks you will need will vary depending on the humidity and your flour. This pasta dough is a bit stiffer than that made with whole eggs, so the rest period after the kneading is critical. Roll out and cut the *tajarin* as described on page 170 to 173. Make the sauce while the cut noodles dry.

For the sauce

Toast the hazelnuts on a baking sheet in a 300°F/150°C oven for about 10 minutes. Rub them in a clean kitchen towel to remove the skins. Let them cool, then chop roughly. Set aside.

In a small pan, slowly heat the milk. Add the gorgonzola in 3 or 4 pieces and stir just until the cheese melts. Swirl in the butter, season with salt and pepper and keep warm while you cook the pasta.

To finish

Cook the noodles in a large pot of boiling salted water. Drain the pasta, transfer to a heated serving bowl and toss with the sauce. Sprinkle the toasted hazelnuts on top. Garnish with parsley and serve.

Variation

A variation of this dish is served in Greve in Chianti, a village not far from us, at one of my favorite restaurants, Mangiando Mangiando (Eating Eating). There they use pistachio nuts, rather than hazelnuts, to marvelous effect.

Pasta Fresca Ubriaca al Chianti
◆ Fresh Pasta, Drunk on Chianti, with Peas and Pancetta

This recipe produces lovely wine-colored pasta. Served against a backdrop of cream, bright green peas, pancetta and fresh mint, it produces a pretty dish that is easy to make and very elegant.

I came upon the idea of coloring pasta with red wine while making a batch of *Chianti Caldo* (page 403). The deep burgundy color of the jelly, made by reducing our local Chianti, was my inspiration. The next time I made pasta, I added a bit, and the result was a lovely ruby to violet dough that seemed to be asking for some of the fresh peas and mint I had in the garden and a slice of my home-cured pancetta.

Normally, I am not keen on gilding the lily by coloring fresh pasta. Using the fresh eggs my hens provide produces silky saffron-colored noodles. Coloring perfection such as this seems absurd, but I make an exception in this case only to offset the vibrant green of my spring peas.

Naturally, this dish can be prepared using dried pasta or store-bought fresh pasta if you don't have time to make your own—you'll need ¾ pound. But then you won't get the artist's palette on the plate these burgundy-colored noodles produce.

SERVES 4

For the pasta
>   1 cup red wine
>   180 g (6.5 oz) (1⅓ cups) all-purpose flour
>   2 egg yolks
>   2 tsp olive oil

For the sauce
>   2 tbsp extra virgin olive oil
>   1 small onion, minced
>   28 g (1 oz) pancetta, chopped
>   ½ cup fresh green peas
>   ¼ cup heavy cream
>   Salt and pepper to taste

To finish
>   A few fresh mint leaves to garnish
>   Grated Parmesan cheese to pass at the table

For the pasta

Boil the wine in a small saucepan over high heat and reduce to ⅓ cup. Let cool. Make the pasta as described on pages 168 to 170, using the wine, egg yolks and oil in place of the whole eggs. Roll out and cut the pasta, as described on pages 170 to 172, for any size noodle you like. Make the sauce while the noodles are drying.

For the sauce

Bring a large pot of salted water to a rolling boil.

Heat the olive oil in a large sauté pan over moderate heat. Add the onion and cook for a few minutes. When the onion begins to wilt, add the pancetta and cook for another 5 minutes. Add the peas and a small ladleful (about ¼ cup) of the boiling pasta water and cook for a few minutes, until the peas turn bright green and most of the water has evaporated.

At this point, add the pasta to the boiling water—it will be cooked in about 3 minutes. In the meantime, add the cream to the sauce and simmer. Season with salt and pepper. Drain the pasta and add to the sauce. Toss to combine and then simmer briefly, just to give the flavors a chance to meld. Serve garnished with the fresh mint and pass the cheese at the table.

La Petraia Chestnut Pasta with Wild Mint and Pistachio Pesto

La Petraia is famous for its *marrone*, a type of chestnut especially good to eat, and people turn up here from all over Tuscany in the fall to collect them. Our friend Alessandro, who lives in the Val d'Arno just over the mountain from us, says in days gone by his ancestors moved their animals here in the fall to graze on chestnuts and mountain herbs. The growth in the forest beneath the ancient *marrone* trees would be mowed down so much by these animals that it resembled a golf course.

Today it is wild boar that live here, and rather than graze, they root, leaving the landscape more like a minefield at the end of chestnut season. Local hunters say if it is a plentiful year for chestnuts, there will be a lot of boar.

Chestnut flour is used to make gnocchi and fresh pasta, breads, cakes, cookies and many other sweet and savory dishes. It is made from chestnuts that have been dried by being smoked over a wood fire. This gives the flour a smoky taste absent in the fresh nut. The best Italian chestnut flour is still produced today in small mills; at some of them the chestnuts are ground using a water-powered stone mill. Chestnut flour is available in the late fall in Italy, flying off the shelves and not seen again for another year. In North America it is found in specialty grocers. Check the "best before" date before you buy it. It has a short shelf life and should be stored in the refrigerator.

Pestare is the Italian verb meaning "to grind, crush or pound." In Italy a *pesto* refers to any condiment that has been pounded by hand in a mortar. The most famous is the Ligurian basil pesto. The traditional way to serve it is with fresh pasta cooked in the same water as a few potatoes and, in season, fresh green beans. While purists insist that pesto is best made with a mortar and pestle, for the busy cook a food processor or hand blender does quite nicely.

SERVES 4

For the pasta
100 g (3.5 oz) (¾ cup) chestnut flour
100 g (3.5 oz) (scant ¾ cup) all-purpose flour
2 eggs
1 tsp extra virgin olive oil

I use the wild mints called *mentuccia* and *nepitella* that grow in our fields, and often include a few leaves of the spicy cress I pick from the bed of the Pesa River, which starts its life on our property. To these I add a few herbs from my herb garden—thyme, parsley, rosemary, sage, oregano or marjoram.

For the pesto

¼ cup pistachio nuts

1 cup loosely packed fresh herb leaves, mostly mint (See note at left)

A few flakes of hot chili pepper

1 garlic clove

About ½ cup extra virgin olive oil

A pinch of salt

To finish

2 or 3 small potatoes, cubed

A handful of fresh green beans in season (optional)

To garnish

A handful of cherry tomatoes, halved (optional)

Fresh basil leaves (optional)

Grated Parmesan cheese to pass at the table

For the pasta

Make the pasta and cut pappardelle as described on pages 168 to 173.

For the pesto

Toast the pistachio nuts on a baking sheet in a 300°F/150°C oven for 8 to 10 minutes. Place the herbs, chili flakes, garlic and nuts in the bowl of your food processor, and, while pulsing, drizzle the oil in bit by bit until you have a fairly thick sauce. Season with salt.

To finish

Bring a large pot of water to a rolling boil. Add 1 tbsp salt, and then throw in the potatoes. Let them cook for about 5 minutes before adding the green beans. After another minute or two, add the pasta and cook for 4 to 5 minutes, until the pasta is done.

To serve

Heat a large serving bowl or individual pasta plates. Drain the pasta-vegetable mixture, reserving some cooking water, and put the pasta mixture in the bowl. Dilute the pesto with a bit of the cooking water and add to the pasta. Toss to mix. Serve immediately, making sure each person gets some potato and green beans with their pasta. The plates can be garnished with a few of the cherry tomatoes and a couple of basil leaves. Pass the Parmesan cheese at the table.

Pizzoccheri ◆ Buckwheat Pasta with Cabbage, Potatoes and Cheese from the Valtellina

Pizzoccheri is a substantial first course that comes from the Valtellina in northern Lombardy. The valley begins at the northeast tip of Lake Como and climbs gently towards the high Alps and the Swiss border. An area known for the production of award-winning red wines, apples and mountain cheeses, this is an interesting place for the food-motivated traveler. *Pizzoccheri* is a dish made using a noodle of the same name, Italy's equivalent to the revered Japanese soba. Handmade buckwheat noodles cooked with cabbage, loaded with garlic-and-sage-seasoned butter and layered with lots of cheese are this valley's pride and joy, and one that has achieved national acclaim. Mention this remote alpine valley to almost any Italian and they will tell you about *pizzoccheri*. That speaks volumes about how delicious this pasta is.

Up until the beginning of the last century, buckwheat was an important staple in the diet of the peasants who lived in this region. Grown in the summer on mountain terraces, as part of a crop rotation that included barley, potatoes and rye, it was a hearty crop that could withstand the cooler alpine climate while adding nutrients to the soil. It was used to make pasta, polenta and bread. During the green revolution of the last century, buckwheat fell out of fashion. It was a grain that recalled poverty and hard times. As well, it required a lot of manual labor and did not adapt well to industrialization. Today much of Italy's buckwheat flour is imported, but happily in recent years there has been a renewed interest in its culinary use. Fortunately, some farmers in the Valtellina are still cultivating the grain, and if you visit the area in the summer you may even see it growing here and there on the odd mountainside.

The traditional cheese used for *pizzoccheri* is called Bitto. It is a large wheel made from cow's and goat's milk and is named after the Bitto River, which flows through the Bitto Valley. Made only in the summer, when the cows are grazing on the high pastures, it has extraordinary longevity and can be aged for up to ten years.

It is unlikely you will find Bitto when you set out to make this pasta, but no matter. A fontina or a Swiss Gruyère will not disappoint. Traditionally, the dish is made with enough butter to clog an artery, some recipes calling for a pound for four servings. I have tasted these heavy versions of *pizzoccheri* in the Valtellina, and find that unless you have a ravenous mountain appetite, it's simply too rich for modern tastes. My version is lighter than most, but it is still a substantial meal and should be served either in very small portions or as a main course.

If you don't want to make the pasta, look for dried *pizzoccheri* noodles in a specialty Italian grocer, or use plain dried pasta. Choose a wide noodle such as pappardelle or tagliatelle. You will need ¾ pound.

For the pasta

100 g (3.5 oz) (⅔ cup) buckwheat flour

75 g (2.75 oz) (½ cup) bread flour

½ cup water

1 tsp extra virgin olive oil

To finish

1 small Savoy cabbage (about 1 lb)

2 medium potatoes, scrubbed and cut into 8 wedges

½ cup (1 stick) butter

1 large garlic clove, thinly sliced

3 to 5 large fresh sage leaves, stacked, rolled up and finely sliced
  into a *chiffonade*

1½ cups (about 5 oz) (140 g) grated cheese (Bitto, fontina or
  Gruyère)

Salt and freshly ground black pepper

For the pasta

Make the pasta and cut pappardelle as described on pages 168 to 173.
Cut each noodle crosswise into pieces 2 to 3 inches long. Because this
pasta is made with buckwheat flour and does not contain eggs, it is not
as strong as egg-based pasta, and you'll find it a bit more delicate to work
with. But don't be discouraged if the noodles tear or break. This is a rustic dish and the noodles are not meant to be perfect. Commercially made
pizzoccheri noodles are sold in odd-sized bits to emulate the homemade,
roughly shaped noodle.

If you are using store-bought pasta, cook according to package directions. The potatoes need about 8 minutes to cook, the cabbage about 2, so add the pasta accordingly.

To finish

Before you start cooking, warm a large serving bowl. Bring a large pot of salted water to a rolling boil. Wash the cabbage leaves and remove their tough inner ribs. Coarsely shred the cabbage. This is easily done by rolling the leaves up into a cigar shape and cutting them in ½-inch slices.

If you have made the pasta yourself, add the potatoes to the boiling water and cook them for about 2 minutes after the water returns to a full boil. Then add the pasta, let the water return to a boil and cook for another 3 minutes. (If you are using dried pasta, see the note at left.) Add the cabbage and, when the water returns to a boil, cook for another 2 to 3 minutes or until tender.

While the pasta cooks, melt the butter over moderately high heat and sauté the garlic for about 2 minutes—don't let it color. Stir in the sage and remove from the heat.

Drain the pasta and vegetables and turn into the serving bowl. Add the seasoned butter, stir well and then add the cheese. Stir. The cheese will melt into the hot pasta and vegetables. Season with salt and pepper and serve immediately.

Cjalzons ◆ Stuffed Pasta from Friuli

In the Friulian dialect, *cjalzons* (or sometimes *cjalson, cialzon, cjarcons* or *cjarsons!*) means a stuffed pasta of the ravioli variety. But here it is the stuffing that intrigues and delights. How about cocoa, raisins, spinach, candied fruit and smoked ricotta? Or maybe fresh ricotta with dried figs, prunes and cinnamon? Apricot jam, pine nuts and the local montasio cheese? Wild berries, honey, pine nuts and rum? Grappa, rye bread, grated pears and boiled potatoes?

The many variations on the name, along with the variety of bizarre fillings, suggest this dish comes from an isolated alpine region dotted with important trading routes, a place through which precious ingredients passed and where dialects changed from one valley to the next. And so it does. Once citizens of "La Serenissima"—the Republic of Venice—residents of Friuli were no strangers to the spices and exotic ingredients the Venetians imported from all over the world. It was through their high mountain passes that those treasures were transported for sale in the markets of central and eastern Europe.

I've been to Friuli many times, and have eaten countless plates of *cjalzons*. I have yet to taste the same dish twice. There seem to be a few ground rules, however. The savory-sweet ravioli traditionally do not contain meat. Cinnamon, dried fruit, fresh and smoked ricotta cheese, pine nuts and herbs are common ingredients. They are usually served as a first course, simply dressed with melted butter and some grated smoked ricotta, montasio or Parmesan cheese. Sometimes the list of ingredients in the filling can be exhaustive. I've heard of recipes that contain up to forty, but more often than not one encounters a simpler version, like the one below.

SERVES 4

For the filling
  2 small potatoes, boiled and riced or mashed
  56 g (2 oz) (⅔ cup) grated smoked ricotta cheese
  1 small pear, peeled, cored and grated
  3 tbsp finely chopped mixed herbs, including basil, parsley and mint
  1 tbsp cocoa

MAKE-AHEAD NOTE

Cjalzons can be made ahead and frozen, uncooked, for several days. There is no need to thaw them before boiling. They will take a minute or two longer to cook.

1 tbsp candied fruit (orange or citron peel)

1 tbsp apricot jam

4 amaretti cookies, finely crushed

A pinch each of cinnamon and ground cloves

Salt and pepper to taste

For the pasta

280 g (10 oz) (2 cups) all-purpose flour

2 large eggs

For the topping

Melted butter

Grated cheese (Parmesan, smoked ricotta or montasio)

For the filling

Mix all of the filling ingredients together.

For the pasta

Make the pasta as described on pages 168 to 170. Roll out all the dough into one large sheet. Using a 2-inch round cookie cutter, cut the dough into as many rounds as you can. Place 1 tsp of the filling in the center of half the rounds, and cover each of these with the other half of the rounds. Gently pat the filling to distribute it evenly, being careful not to push it too close to the edge. Press the edges of the pasta rounds together to seal well. Place them on a clean tea towel while you shape the remaining *cjalzons*.

Bring a large pot of water to a rolling boil and add 1 tbsp salt. Cook the *cjalzons* for about 5 minutes or until they rise to the surface. Drain and serve immediately, topped with the melted butter and grated cheese.

Ravioli al Cacao con Selvaggina
◆ Chocolate Ravioli with a Game Filling

Chocolate and game are often combined to make a *dolce amaro,* or "sweet and sour" savory dish dating back to the Renaissance. These special ravioli make the perfect meal for a cold winter evening and go well with a hearty red wine such as a Chianti Classico. For the filling you can use the leftovers from any braised meat dish (such as the wild boar *ragù* on page 180 or *Cinghiale in Dolce e Forte* on page 251). Simply remove the meat from the braising liquid and purée it in your food processor along with the pine nuts and Parmesan cheese. Season to taste and use it to stuff these lovely chocolate ravioli.

SERVES 4

For the filling

About 1 cup leftover braised meat

⅓ cup grated Parmesan cheese

3 tbsp pine nuts

Salt and pepper to taste (optional)

For the pasta

112 g (4 oz) (¾ cup plus 4 tsp) all-purpose flour

15 g (3 tbsp) cocoa

1 large egg

1 egg yolk

1 tsp olive oil

To finish

1 cup hot meat-braising liquid

Grated Parmesan cheese to pass at the table

For the filling

Pulse the meat along with the cheese and pine nuts in your food processor until the mixture is just combined. Taste and season with salt and pepper if needed.

For the pasta

MAKE-AHEAD NOTE
The ravioli can be made several days ahead and frozen, uncooked. They do not need to be thawed before boiling. Simply drop them frozen into the boiling water. They may take an extra minute or two to cook. If you make the ravioli on the day you plan to serve it, it is best made just before serving time, to avoid having the pasta dry out.

Make the pasta as described on pages 168 to 170. Roll out all the dough into one large sheet. Using a 2-inch round cookie cutter, cut the dough into as many rounds as you can. Place 1 tsp of the filling in the center of half the rounds, and cover each of these with the other half of the rounds. Gently pat the filling to distribute it evenly, being careful not to push it too close to the edge. Press the edges of the dough rounds together to seal well. Place them on a clean tea towel while you shape the remaining ravioli.

Bring a large pot of water to a rolling boil and add 1 tbsp salt. Cook the ravioli for about 5 minutes, until they rise to the surface. Drain. Serve in heated soup plates, drizzled with the braising liquid. Pass grated Parmesan at the table.

Variations

You can serve these ravioli dressed simply with melted butter and chopped fresh sage. Or you can make chocolate and chestnut ravioli by stuffing half of the filling in the chestnut pasta on page 188.

Tortelloni con Sorpresa
◆ Tortelloni with a Surprise Filling

In the dog days of summer, my hens are busy producing an egg a day. Always on the lookout for new ways to showcase their superb taste, I came across a version of this recipe in an Italian food magazine, *La Cucina di Casamia*. It produces one large tortelloni per person. Inside each is a ring of spinach filling and inside that is the surprise—a soft-boiled egg yolk! The pasta will cook in about 3 minutes, the same amount of time it takes to soft-boil the yolk. When your guests strike their fork into the center, out will stream the delightful yellow surprise. The dish is a sort of deconstructed version of the classic Italian spinach and cheese tortelloni. Normally the spinach filling is bound with an egg. In this case, the egg has been left out of the filling but comes to the party anyway, on its own and unannounced.

Since it is the egg that is the star here, it is worth seeking out the best quality, freshest ones you can find. Look for free-range organic eggs with a deep yellow yolk. These tortelloni are also perfect for brunch.

SERVES 4

For the pasta
　　100 g (3.5 oz) (¾ cup) all-purpose flour
　　2 large eggs
　　1 tsp extra virgin olive oil

For the spinach filling
　　300 g (10.5 oz) steamed spinach or chard*
　　100 g (3.5 oz) (approx. ½ cup) mascarpone cheese
　　100 g (3.5 oz) (1 cup) grated Parmesan cheese
　　A pinch of freshly grated nutmeg
　　Salt and pepper to taste
　See note on page 165 for cooking greens.

MAKE-AHEAD NOTE
You can make the spinach filling a day ahead.

To finish

4 small egg yolks (see note at left)

Extra virgin olive oil

Grated Parmesan cheese to pass at the table

Don't throw out the egg whites! They keep beautifully in the freezer and can be used to make *amaretti* (page 369), *cavallucci* (page 360) or *ricciarelli* (page 362).

For the pasta

Make the pasta as described on pages 168 to 170. Roll out all the dough into one thin sheet, and let it dry briefly while you make the filling.

For the spinach filling

Squeeze the spinach dry and place it in a blender with the mascarpone, Parmesan, nutmeg and salt and pepper. Process until you have a smooth mixture.

To assemble the pasta

Bring a large pot of water to a rolling boil. Add 1 tbsp salt.

Using a 4-inch cookie cutter, cut 8 rounds out of the dough. With the spinach filling, form a ring inside 4 rounds, leaving enough of an edge (no more than ½ inch) to seal the pasta. Inside each of your spinach rings, place 1 egg yolk, being careful not to break it. Cover with the remaining pasta rounds. Seal the edges well. The pasta should be cooked immediately after it is stuffed.

Using a slotted spoon, gently transfer the tortelloni to the boiling water and cook for exactly 3 minutes. Drain and transfer to warmed pasta plates. Drizzle with olive oil and serve immediately. Pass the cheese at the table.

Panzarotti al Sugo di Noce ✦ Pasta Stuffed with Greens and Herbs in a Walnut Sauce

In ancient times the Celts are said to have traded with Liguria, eventually settling there. The Ligurians are sometimes referred to as the Scots of Italy. They have a reputation for being a bit on the frugal side, and when you visit the area it is clear how geography has helped shape a proud sense of economy. This slender province is rugged and mountainous. Eking out a living from the steep mountain terraces must have been anything but easy. Like most places in Italy, where a sense of thrift governed what was put into the pot, what came out of it was often remarkable.

In this recipe, most of the ingredients would have been foraged. The nuts and herbs grew wild on the mountain hillsides, and if you were lucky you might own a hen to provide an egg for the pasta.

Like most food with humble and honest beginnings, these pretty packages of stuffed pasta sitting in a pool of savory walnut sauce will please and delight even the most sophisticated gourmand. Ligurians stuff *panzarotti* (or *pansoti, panzerotti* and *pansotti* as they are also called) with a variety of greens and herbs called *preboggion,* some of which still grow wild on Ligurian hillsides. When my husband and I stayed in Santa Margherita Liguria, I would often buy bundles of these ugly greens from a local farmer who had a small stall in the daily market on the town's main square. She usually also had a few eggs from her hens for the pasta. You can make a poor man's *preboggion* by adding a few fresh herbs to as many different types of greens as you can find. These might include chicory, beet greens, kale, chard, sorrel and spinach.

Ligurian recipes for fresh pasta often include a glass of their local white wine in place of all or part of the eggs normally called for.

MAKES ABOUT 40 PANZAROTTI, ENOUGH FOR 6

MAKE-AHEAD NOTE

The filling can be made
up to a day ahead.

For the filling

500 g (18 oz) mixed fresh greens (chard, spinach, borage, kale, etc.)

100 g (3.5 oz) ricotta cheese

⅔ cup grated Parmesan cheese

½ cup loosely packed mixed fresh herb leaves (marjoram, mint, basil, parsley, thyme and oregano)

1½ tbsp extra virgin olive oil

1 tsp butter, at room temperature

1 egg

A pinch of freshly grated nutmeg

Salt and pepper to taste

For the pasta

200 g (7 oz) (1½ scant cups) all-purpose flour

1 large egg

¼ cup white wine

2 tsp extra virgin olive oil

For the walnut sauce

100 g (3.5 oz) drained ricotta cheese (see page 152)

¼ cup extra virgin olive oil

1 cup walnuts

1 tbsp pine nuts

1 tbsp dry bread crumbs

½ tsp chopped fresh marjoram

1 garlic clove, chopped

Leaves from a few sprigs of fresh parsley

Salt to taste

To garnish
   Finely chopped fresh parsley

For the filling
Wash, stem and cook the greens in boiling salted water until tender. If you are using a mixture of greens, start with the tougher ones (like kale) before adding the more delicate and quicker-cooking ones like spinach and Swiss chard. When the greens are tender, drain them, run them under cold water and then squeeze very dry. This takes a strong arm— you want to eliminate as much water as possible from the greens.

   Roughly chop the greens and place them in the work bowl of your food processor. Add the rest of the filling ingredients. Process briefly to combine. Refrigerate the mixture for at least half an hour before using.

For the pasta
Make the pasta as described on pages 168 to 170. Roll out all the dough into one large rectangular sheet and use a pastry wheel to cut it into 2½-inch squares. You will need at least 40 squares.

For the sauce
Traditionally the sauce is made using a mortar and pestle, but I make it with a hand blender. Process all the ingredients together to a smooth paste. Add salt and set aside. The mixture will be very thick—like a butter. It will be diluted with some of the pasta cooking water later.

To cook
Place about ½ tsp of the filling in the center of each square of pasta. Fold up the bottom right-hand corner of each square to meet the top left-hand corner, forming a triangle. Gently pat the filling to distribute

it evenly, being careful not to push it too close to the edge, and seal the edges well with your fingers. If necessary, use a pastry wheel or cookie cutter to trim any uneven edges. If you are not planning on cooking the *panzarotti* immediately, arrange them on a baking sheet lined with parchment paper and sifted with flour, cover them with a clean tea towel and refrigerate for several hours. They can also be frozen, and do not need to be thawed before cooking.

Bring a large pot of salted water to a boil. Add the pasta and cook for 5 minutes or until they are done. In the meantime, place the sauce in a small saucepan over very low heat and dilute it with a little of the pasta cooking water. Drain the *panzarotti* and divide them among heated pasta plates. Pour some of the walnut sauce over them. Serve immediately, garnished with the parsley.

Agnolotti con Fonduta ◆ Agnolotti Filled with Fonduta

Fonduta is the Italian version of fondue. It is made with fontina cheese from the Val d'Aosta, a cheese famous for its melting qualities. (For more on fontina, see page 273.)

Agnolotti is the name given to ravioli in the northern Italian regions of Piedmont and parts of Lombardy. *Fonduta* is traditionally served as a first course, ladled over a piece of toasted dark bread and, if you're lucky, topped with some shavings of fresh white truffle. It is also used to thicken flans, as a sauce for vegetables and, as in this recipe, as the filling for stuffed pasta.

MAKES ABOUT 20 AGNOLOTTI, ENOUGH FOR 4

1 recipe pasta dough (page 168)
1 recipe *fonduta* (page 273), refrigerated until firm

To finish

Melted butter

Grated Parmesan cheese

Several leaves of fresh sage, stacked, rolled up and finely sliced into a *chiffonade*

Roll out the pasta dough into one large sheet. Use a 2-inch cookie cutter (or the rim of a glass) to cut the dough into rounds. You will need at least 20 rounds. Place a teaspoon of the *fonduta* in the center of each pasta round. Fold the round in half and gently pat the filling to even it out, being careful not to push it too close to the edge. Press the edges of the half-moon shape together. If the edges are messy, trim them with your cookie cutter or use a serrated pastry wheel to make a neat (and pretty) edge.

Leave the agnolotti to dry on a well-floured surface in a cool place until you are ready to cook them.

Bring a large pot of water to a rolling boil. Add 1 tbsp salt, then the agnolotti. Cook until the water returns to a boil and the pasta has risen to the surface, about 5 minutes.

Drain and transfer to warmed serving plates. Drizzle with the melted butter and sprinkle with the cheese. Serve garnished with the sage.

In late fall in Piedmont, when the famed white truffles found around the town of Alba are in season, they are shaved over this dish. I sometimes add a spoonful of white truffle butter to the melted butter topping to get a hint of truffle flavor.

Pastasciutta ✦ Dried Pasta

I've limited the dried pasta recipes in this section to six, and they are described as much by means of a narrative as they are as a list of ingredients. Dried pasta, to the Italian cook, is a staple. The sauce, or *condimento*, the word used to describe what goes on top, is made up of whatever the chef has available. It is parsimoniously ladled on top of the pasta and is meant to compliment its flavor, not drown it.

There are a million different *condimenti* for dried pasta. The ones I've provided are my favorites, a starting point for your own ideas. To come up with your own sauce for pasta, consider what you have on hand, the season, where you live and what you like to eat. And don't forget the golden rule when making dried pasta. You should be able to whip up the sauce in about the time it takes the pasta to cook.

You may find it a useful exercise, as I did, when learning to cook like an Italian, to think about the pasta condiment as something you can put together quickly and easily from your pantry (and garden if you have one), rather than having to go to the store to buy. You may be surprised at the results. Not only should it taste divine, it will be effortless.

Finally, pasta should be served up the minute it is *al dente*. Up and down the Italian peninsula, home cooks put the pasta water on to boil at midday. As soon as the last member of the family arrives home (or comes into view from the kitchen window), in goes the pasta, and the cook shouts, "*Ho buttato la pasta!*" Although this translates as "I've thrown in the pasta," in reality it is an order from the high command meaning, "To the table, everyone, right now!" This is Italian fast food, and it waits for nobody.

Most quality brands of Italian pasta provide precise cooking times for perfectly cooked *al dente* pasta.

Salsa di Pomodoro Crudo con la Mozzarella
◆ A Sauce of Raw Tomatoes and Mozzarella for Easy Summertime Pasta

In the summertime, when cherry tomatoes are at their best, I love to make this quick sauce for pasta. I use the long, hollow noodle called *candele* (candles), but you may have trouble finding them in North America.

Bucatini or spaghetti will do, and 1 lb will serve 6 as a *primo* or 4 as a main course.

Take about ½ lb of perfectly ripe and sweet cherry tomatoes and chop them up into quarters. Mince a clove of garlic and toss it into the tomatoes with ¼ cup of extra virgin olive oil. Season with salt and pepper and toss in some shredded leaves of fresh basil. Leave this mixture to sit at room temperature for a half hour or longer. The tomatoes will sweat some of their juice, providing you with a raw sauce (which can also be used as a topping for *bruschetta*). Take a ball of fresh mozzarella cheese weighing 225 g (8 oz) and cut it into small cubes. Put a large pot of water on to boil and cook the pasta until *al dente*. Drain and toss with the tomatoes and cheese. The mozzarella will melt a little into the hot pasta. Serve warm, topped with more leaves of fresh basil.

Spaghetti ai Cinque Sapori ✦ Spaghetti with Five Flavors

Many towns in our part of Tuscany have an annual *festa* held in the late summer called the *Festa del Perdono*, or the Festival of Forgiveness. Radda's is held late each August and always includes a town dinner. At this feast our neighbor Marcello is often asked to make a huge cauldron of his signature *spaghetti ai cinque sapori*. I was a little astonished when he described the recipe to me. It is a summertime tomato sauce, yet it contains sage and rosemary. I had never heard of a tomato sauce using those herbs. Oregano, basil, parsley, marjoram, yes . . . but sage and rosemary? But when I tasted it I found the combination so successful, it is now one of my unflappable standards. For years I assumed this was a local Raddese specialty, but when I asked around, I found that this recipe is Marcello's own invention. You know how good it is when the whole town elects him to cook it for them on their special day.

I sometimes use whole wheat spaghetti for added color and texture. This is a lovely dish to serve at summer's height, when cherry tomatoes are at their sweetest. It is an easy first course for an outdoor dinner, perhaps the perfect dish to precede a piece of meat grilled over a wood fire, like the famous Tuscan *bistecca* (page 263). And to quench the thirst, it prefers a glass of Chianti Classico.

SERVES 6 AS A FIRST COURSE OR 4 AS A MAIN COURSE

For the soffritto
> 1 small onion, chopped
> 1 garlic clove, minced
> A few flakes of hot chili pepper
> 1 tbsp extra virgin olive oil

For the five flavors
> 1 oz pancetta or bacon, finely diced
> Leaves from a sprig of rosemary, finely chopped
> A sage leaf or two, finely chopped
> A dozen cherry tomatoes, quartered
> 1 lb whole wheat spaghetti
> A touch of cream to finish (optional)
> Grated Parmesan cheese to pass at the table

Bring a large pot of water to a rolling boil and add 1 tbsp of salt.

In the meantime, in a large saucepan over moderate heat, cook the onion, garlic and chili flakes in the olive oil for about 5 minutes, until the onion is transparent. Add the pancetta and cook for a few minutes until it begins to release its fat, and then add the rosemary, sage and tomatoes.

Reduce the heat and let the mixture simmer while you cook the spaghetti according to package directions. The tomatoes should release all of their liquid, and the sauce should begin to thicken. If the mixture looks like it is getting too dry, add a small ladleful of the pasta water. If you're using the cream, add it in the last minute or two of cooking.

Drain the pasta and toss it into the saucepan. Mix using a pair of kitchen tongs. Serve immediately, passing the cheese at the table.

Spaghetti alla Carrettiera ✦ Cart Driver's Spaghetti

This interesting dish comes from southern Italy, where tradition often calls for bread crumbs as a garnish the way grated cheese is used in the north. Although some superb grating cheeses are made in the south, this was a poor region and a little bit had to go a long way. Once you've tried this pasta, I think you will understand the logic. The bread crumbs add the same textural juxtaposition as grated cheese, providing satisfaction from a frugal meal that probably would not have included a second course.

Researching recipes for *spaghetti alla carrettiera*, I found countless incarnations. Some came from Lazio, the region around Rome, and called for tomatoes and *guanciale* (cured pig's cheek that is used like bacon). In this case it seems the cart drivers referred to were the ones who used to haul wine and oil into the ancient city from the surrounding countryside.

In the end, I decided that tracking down the authentic *spaghetti alla carrettiera* was rather like pinning jelly to the wall. The thing to do was to choose the version I liked best and stick to it. This version, apparently of Calabrian origin, does not contain tomatoes. Cart drivers (truck drivers today) have been employed in Italy since Roman times, long before anyone had ever heard tell of a tomato.

MAKE YOUR OWN BREAD CRUMBS

To make your own bread crumbs, toast cubes of day-old bread on a baking sheet in a 350°F/175°C oven until completely dry—10 to 15 minutes. Transfer to a food processor and process to a fine meal. Alternatively, you can roll the toasted bread cubes between two sheets of wax paper using a rolling pin. If you happen to have any leftover Sicilian-style bread from the recipe on page 55, it is perfect to use for the bread crumbs.

This simple, delicious dish comes together in a flash—the sauce is made while the pasta cooks—so it is food for an easy weeknight pantry supper, when time is short and the grocery shopping has yet to be done. Serve it with a crisp green salad and a glass of chilled white wine. If you want more, I suggest a can of sardines with a little lemon juice squeezed over them. Ideally, you should make your own bread crumbs from an artisanal loaf.

SERVES 4 TO 6

1 lb spaghetti (whole wheat can be used)
⅓ cup extra virgin olive oil
2 garlic cloves, minced
Hot chili pepper flakes to taste
½ cup toasted bread crumbs (see note at left)
Salt and pepper to taste
Finely chopped fresh parsley to garnish

Bring a large pot of water to a rolling boil and add 1 tbsp of salt. Cook the spaghetti until *al dente*.

In the meantime, heat the oil in a sauté pan over moderate heat with the garlic and the chili flakes. Cook, stirring, for a few minutes until the garlic begins to give off its scent but is not turning brown. Drain the spaghetti, pouring the hot water into your serving bowl. Add the pasta to the sauté pan along with a small ladleful (scant ¼ cup) of the hot pasta water and cook for another minute or two—just until the water is absorbed. Discard the hot water in your serving bowl and turn the pasta mixture into it. Toss with the bread crumbs. Season with salt and pepper. Garnish with the parsley and serve immediately.

Bigoi in Salsa

✦ Spaghetti with Onions and Anchovies, Venetian Style

Bigoi, as it is called in Venetian dialect, or *bigoli* in Italian, is a thick spaghetti-like noodle that is common in the Veneto region. *Bigoi in salsa* is rather a tough recipe to nail down. Here, too, I have found many different interpretations. Some call for tuna instead of anchovies, some for chicken or duck offal, some for the pasta to be cooked in chicken stock, and so on. I wouldn't be surprised if there were as many recipes as there are Venetians, each one claiming to be more authentic than the next. The name of the recipe simply means *"bigoi* in sauce," so I suppose this gives the cook a certain discretionary allowance.

A common version, and my favorite, is a sauce made from melted onions and anchovies. By the time the sauce has cooked, the anchovies have disappeared and the onions have almost turned into jam. It is an ideal combination, and in my experience even those who claim to dislike the humble anchovy love this spaghetti. In Venice, *bigoi in salsa* is prepared along with *sarde in saor* (page 107) for the Festa del Redentore, one of the town's most important annual celebrations. It makes a quick and easy pantry dinner, and is washed down nicely with a glass of white wine from the Veneto, such as a Soave. Here at Petraia, I make it in the late winter, when my *orto* is having its annual siesta and last year's onions are one of the few fresh vegetables left in my *cantina*.

Unless you happen to have a particularly well-stocked Italian grocer, you will not likely find the *bigoli* noodles, but whole wheat spaghetti makes a nice substitute.

2 tbsp olive oil (or oil from the preserved anchovies)

1 lb white onions, thinly sliced

112 g (4 oz) anchovies preserved in olive oil

1 lb spaghetti

Salt and pepper to taste

Finely chopped fresh parsley

¼ tsp cinnamon

Heat the oil in a large sauté pan over moderate heat. Add the onions and reduce the heat to low. Cover and cook gently, stirring occasionally, for about 30 minutes. The onions will wilt and become translucent. Remove the cover and turn the heat to moderate, add the anchovies and cook for another 10 to 15 minutes, stirring frequently, until the anchovies dissolve into the onion mixture and the onions have begun to turn golden.

In the meantime, bring a large pot of water to a rolling boil. Salt the water and add the spaghetti. Cook until *al dente*. Drain the pasta, reserving some of the cooking water. Transfer the spaghetti to the sauté pan along with a scant ¼ cup of the water. Mix everything well and cook for a minute or two until the water is absorbed. Season with pepper and taste for salt. Sprinkle with the parsley and cinnamon. Serve immediately.

Rimasti di Pasta con Salsa di Cetriolo, Speck e Finocchio Selvatico • Pasta Odds and Ends with a Cucumber, Smoked Ham and Wild Fennel Sauce

If I time things just right at La Petraia, and if Mother Nature is willing, I might harvest a cucumber in late September, just as the wild fennel that grows in our fields goes to seed. This may be a rare occurrence, I'll admit, but this recipe celebrates the possibility. This is a dish that I surprised myself with one evening when I was feeling discouraged. We'd just endured one of the hottest and driest summers on recent record in Europe. Then, in September, the weather turned cold, damp and miserable. It was a disastrous year for the farm. No grain, no fruit, no olives, no grapes, no wine, no oil. *Niente*.

The week I was to take the exam for my Italian driver's license, I found myself in Siena late one afternoon. I was a bit dispirited; the first of three requisite pre-exam driving tests had not gone very well. The test had involved driving in an ancient walled city, normally closed to traffic, whose cobblestone streets were packed wall to wall with tourists. I was worried—failing the upcoming exam would mean not being able to drive in Italy. And I live on a remote farm, by myself for much of the time, at the end of a long, steep dirt road. I really needed to pass this test.

As I sulked towards the Porta Camollia and the car park that evening, I happened to spot a crate of gorgeous English cucumbers in a small fruit and vegetable shop. My own cucumber plants had long since been fermenting on the compost heap, so I bought one as a sort of farewell gesture to summer.

I was in need of consolation that unseasonably cold and wet night, and when I arrived home I realized a raw cucumber wasn't going to do the trick. So into the pan went enough olive oil to cover the bottom, along with a few flakes of hot chili pepper. Once the oil was hot, I sliced a small red onion into rings and added it to the mix. A couple of minutes later, once the onions had wilted, I added an ounce or two of finely chopped *speck* (smoked ham) I'd found perishing in the back of the fridge. Along with this went a scant flourish of the wild fennel seeds I'd collected that morning in our fields.

Finally, I placed my mandoline over the pan and sliced that lusty peeled cucumber into the mixture. (If your cuke is full of seeds, I'd recommend also seeding it.) After a minute I threw in a generous amount of heavy cream and salt and pepper, and then let it bubble away until it looked perfect. In the meantime, I found enough bits and pieces of leftover dried pasta in my pantry to make a meal and threw them into a pot of boiling water.

A few days later I passed the driving test.

La Petraia Whole Wheat Pasta in a Winter Sauce of Cabbage, Pancetta, Shrimp and Sage

This recipe makes use of the wrinkly Savoy cabbage I always plant lots of to see me through the winter. I am always amazed by how much my garden slows down then. A cabbage that seemed to grow overnight in the summer takes months to come to term in winter. Along with my fennel, leeks, kale and cardoons, the cabbage is one of the few inhabitants of my *orto* that will confront a Tuscan winter. I am thankful to have them, and reminded by the nearby camellia bush, already covered in buds in mid-December, that spring is not so far away either.

This meal comes together easily. The sauce is made while the pasta cooks. I usually have a few shrimp squirreled away in the freezer and a bit of pancetta in the fridge. I steal a couple of cabbage leaves from the garden. If you happen to find a nice Terlaner or Pinot Grigio from Italy's Alto Adige region, they will make a lovely accompaniment, but any crisp dry white makes the dish sing.

1 lb whole wheat penne

2 tbsp extra virgin olive oil

2 slices pancetta (or bacon), chopped

1 onion, minced

1 garlic clove, minced

¼ Savoy cabbage, thick ribs removed and the leaves shredded

4 large shrimp, peeled, deveined and chopped

¼ cup heavy cream

2 or 3 fresh sage leaves, rolled together and cut into a *chiffonade*

Salt and pepper to taste

Bring a large pot of salted water to a rolling boil. Add the penne and cook for about a minute less than the package directions say.

In the meantime, heat the oil in a sauté pan over moderate heat and add the pancetta. When it starts to give up its fat, add the onion and cook until it begins to turn transparent. Add the garlic and cook for a minute before adding the cabbage. Add a ladle of the hot water from the pasta pot and cook for a few minutes, until the cabbage is tender. Add the shrimp and, as soon as it has turned pink, the cream and salt and pepper.

Drain the penne, reserving a ladleful or two of cooking water. Turn the pasta into the pan containing the sauce. Ladle a bit of the water into the pan and stir to combine. Cook for another minute or until the water has been absorbed by the pasta. Serve immediately in a large heated pasta bowl.

Variation

I sometimes add a bit of thinly sliced butternut squash along with the cabbage for extra color.

Grain-based First Courses

Orzotto con Pane Integrale e Fontina

✦ **Barley Risotto with Toasted Brown Bread and Fontina**

I often use pearl barley or *farro* in place of rice to make a risotto-type first course. Pearl barley will cook in about 20 to 25 minutes and lends itself nicely to most risotto recipes. I like the character whole pearled grains bring to the table. Unlike white rice, they demand some notice with their chewy texture and nutty flavor.

This recipe features fontina cheese, which is known for how it melts. This is a rich dish—wonderful for a late-fall evening. It pairs well with a sprightly young red wine such as an Italian Vino Novello, or a Beaujolais Nouveau.

Serves 4

    Extra virgin olive oil

    1 onion, minced

    1 cup pearl barley

    ½ cup white wine

    4 cups hot chicken or vegetable broth

    100 g (3.5 oz) fontina cheese, cut into small dice

    1 potato, boiled in its skin and diced

    2 egg yolks

    2 slices whole wheat bread, cut into small cubes and toasted in
        a 300°F/150°C oven

    Chopped fresh parsley to garnish

In a saucepan suitable for making risotto, add enough olive oil to cover the bottom. Heat over moderately high heat. Sauté the onion until it is transparent. Add the barley and stir for a couple of minutes. Add the white wine and stir until the barley has absorbed the wine.

Add the hot broth, 1 cup at a time, stirring until most of the liquid is absorbed before adding more. Continue to stir until the barley is tender, about 20 minutes. In the last few minutes of cooking, add the cheese and the potato and stir until the cheese has melted into the dish. Remove from the heat and stir in the egg yolks.

Serve in warmed soup plates. Top each serving with a scattering of the croutons and parsley.

Farro Risotto with Pears and Gorgonzola

This is a combination I discovered late one day when I was traveling in the mountains of northern Italy in a camper van. A small camper is a great asset for the research I do, which leads me into the agricultural hinterland of Italy's more rugged and isolated areas. A little house on wheels, it affords the luxury of travel without fixing a plan. I can venture into some of the obscure and out-of-the-way places where Italy's best raw  materials are produced to track down mountain cheeses, polenta flour, cured meats, special breads, game and much more. The drawback to traveling in some of these remote areas is that overnight accommodation can be hard to find, especially off-season. The camper is the perfect solution and was my constant companion while I was researching this book.

This particular day ended late, and I was too tired to think about finding a place to eat. Having secured a parking spot in a pretty mountain village alongside a couple of other overnight campers, I looked in my tiny pantry to find a pear, a bouillon cube, a hunk of gorgonzola cheese and a handful of *farro.* "I'll do something with this," I thought to myself. So successful was the result, the dish has become a signature one at Petraia, where I serve it in a *frico* basket (see page 79). It never fails to get applause.

The pear should not be rock hard, but nor should it be soft and over-ripe. Look for something *almost* ripe—that might be ready to eat out of your hand by tomorrow or the next day. If you want to make this a dish to remember, serve it with a light fizzy red wine, such as an Oltrepò Pavese, or, to be radical, a glass of *spumante* or a sparkling sweet wine such as a Moscato d'Asti.

SERVES 4

2 tbsp extra virgin olive oil
1 onion, minced
1 tsp finely chopped fresh sage
A few flakes of hot chili pepper (optional)
1 large almost ripe pear, peeled, cored and diced
1 cup pearled *farro*
A glass of white wine
2 cups hot chicken broth (or use a bouillon cube dissolved in
    2 cups boiling water)
About 100 g (3.5 oz) gorgonzola cheese
Salt and pepper to taste
Finely chopped fresh parsley to garnish

Heat the oil in a saucepan over moderate heat. Add the onion, sage and chili flakes, if using, and cook, stirring occasionally, for about 5 minutes or until the onion wilts and becomes transparent. Add the pear, cook for a few minutes, then add the *farro*. Stirring constantly, cook for another minute or two. Add the glass of wine. Continue to stir until the wine has been absorbed. Start to add the hot broth, one ladleful at a time, while continuing to stir. The broth should be almost completely absorbed by the *farro* before you add more. When the *farro* is tender, after about 20 minutes, add the gorgonzola and stir until it has melted into the mixture. Season with salt and pepper.

Serve immediately, garnished with the parsley, in a *frico* basket if you wish (see page 79).

Variation

If you can't find pearled *farro*, use pearl barley or an Italian rice suitable for risotto, such as Carnaroli or Arborio.

Chapter 4 I Secondi ✤ The Second Course

The *secondo* in an Italian meal is composed of meat, fish, poultry or game. Sometimes a vegetarian option of asparagus or mushrooms is offered, considered a rare treat when these delicacies are in season. While North Americans think of this part of the meal as "the main course," in Italy this is not the case. There is no main course. A formal Italian dinner is like a play in several acts—each one as essential as the next, critical to the unveiling of the plot. Portion sizes in the *secondo* are modest compared to a typical continental meal, consideration given to the fact this is one of a series of dishes. In restaurants, the *secondo* usually arrives with no adornment. If a vegetable side, or *contorno*, is desired, it is ordered separately.

At a formal dinner or a special occasion there may be two or even three *secondi*. As the number of plates increases, portion sizes diminish, and this is one of the secrets to the Italian slender figures and healthy hearts. Everything, but everything in moderation.

This chapter starts off, appropriately, with fish. The long, slender boot of Italy is surrounded by the sea, and you are hard pressed anywhere to find yourself more than three hours away from *il mare*. This close proximity means seafood plays a prominent role in the Italian diet; the variety and above all the emphasis on its freshness is almost unfathomable. A drive to a coastal town to eat fresh fish is usually preferred over an attempt to source it inland. That way you are certain of both freshness and quality. But declining fish stocks in the Mediterranean mean seafood today is increasingly becoming an expensive commodity, reserved for special occasions. Many seafood restaurants tend to be rather formal places where innovative chefs turn out some of the country's most enlightened food, as illustrated in the first two recipes in this chapter. When a drive to the coast is not feasible, there is the omnipresent and much loved *baccalà*, or salt cod, along with a wide range of high-quality olive-oil- or salt-preserved fish such as tuna, mackerel, herring, anchovies and sardines. Each region of the country has its own traditional *baccalà* specialties, and I've included two of my favorites.

The remainder of the chapter is dedicated to what meat and game I have available on our property or can source locally. Having been a vegetarian for almost half my life, I once found this part of the meal my biggest challenge. But when I moved to Petraia, with its abundance of game and the custom of hunters sharing their catch with the owners of the land, I became interested in what this place had to offer. Now I enjoy cooking and serving the boar, venison, pigeon and pheasant hunted on our property as well as the pigs, rabbits, geese, guinea hens, turkeys, ducks and chickens I raise. I have happily become an omnivore. But the meat I eat is from animals who share our home with us. There is a relationship between us, and this makes sense to me. The quality of their life needs to be optimum, because it has a direct influence on the quality of my own.

These creatures wander freely and graze on a diet of grass, herbs, fruit, chestnuts, acorns, vegetables and grain. Their meat, while full of flavor, is lean and tough and takes kindly to low flames and ovens, slow braises and stews.

These recipes lend themselves easily to entertaining. There is little or no work to be done *à la minute*, which means you can enjoy your *primo* while the next course simmers away, ready for service when you are.

Zuppa di Pesce di Roccia e Agrumi
✦ Rockfish and Citrus Soup

In Italy and all over the Mediterranean, fish soup is esteemed. Originally it was made by tired and hungry fishermen as a way to use up the tiny fish that got caught in their nets but that customers didn't want because they were small and full of bones. Today, these fish have become fashionable as chefs discover that this food of the Mediterranean's poorer kitchen is packed with flavor.

Of the 550 varieties of fish that call the Mediterranean home, only about 60 have been commercialized and are eaten regularly. Faced with the depletion of these popular fish stocks, chefs are increasingly turning their attention to the plethora of other species once known only to the fishermen who ate them. Because they're often small and bony, they are perfect for soup. They've become so popular they have spawned a movement in Italy. They are called the *pesce dimenticato* or sometimes *pesce ritrovato*—the forgotten or rediscovered fish of the Mediterranean.

This is a wonderful soup inspired by a Michelin-starred chef and one of France's leading spice experts, Gérard Vives. Vives is not Italian, but his delicious tribute to the ubiquitous fish soup made all over the Mediterranean could easily be. It evokes the *bouillabaisse* of Marseille, *brodetto* from Genoa,

Fish from the Mediterranean may be hard to find in North America. Red snapper, sea bream or porgy make good substitutes. Since these fish are larger than red mullet, you will likely need to have more than one-quarter of your fish filleted and skinned. If this is the case, ask the fishmonger for the skin, head and bones and add them to the soup.

cacciucco from Livorno and the Sicilian dish called *triglie alla Siciliana*. This version is more sophisticated than most, playing as it does with the use of cooked and raw fish and combining sweet and savory flavors.

Gérard Vives has a restaurant in Provence but spends much of his time traveling the world in search of high-quality peppers and other spices. I watched him demonstrate this soup at Slow Fish, a sustainable seafood fair held in Genoa a few years ago. He was using it as a way to showcase the saffron and one of the many black peppers he imports. He insisted that pepper and saffron should not be added until just before the soup is served. When I tasted it, it was easy to see why. The combination of really fresh fish, citrus, saffron and exceptional black pepper was divine.

Vives used only one kind of fish for his preparation, one of the most appreciated fish in the Mediterranean—the red mullet, known as *triglia* in Italy and *rouget* in France. This recipe involves some preparation the day before. Nonetheless, it is surprisingly simple and does away with the notion that making a good fish soup is complicated and time consuming. It is worth seeking out good-quality saffron threads, salt and black pepper to finish this dish.

SERVES 4 TO 6

For the marinade
> A dash of white wine vinegar
> Juice from ½ orange, ½ lime and ½ lemon

For the soup
> 1 kg (2¼ lb) red mullet (have your fishmonger clean ¾ of the fish, leaving the heads and tails on, and fillet and skin the remainder)

1 onion, minced

¼ cup extra virgin olive oil

The fronds from 1 fennel bulb, roughly chopped

3 plum tomatoes, chopped

1 carrot, chopped

1 tbsp chopped fresh parsley

1 bay leaf

½ cup white wine

A few freshly ground coriander and anise seeds

Leaves from a sprig of fresh thyme, chopped

Juice of 2 oranges

Several threads of saffron

Fleur de sel or sea salt and freshly ground black pepper to garnish

MAKE-AHEAD NOTE

The soup can be made one day ahead, but don't add the saffron until just before you serve it.

THE EVENING BEFORE YOU PLAN TO EAT THE SOUP:

Remove all the tiny bones from the fish fillets. Tweezers are the best tool to use. These are bony fish, so this may take you a little time. Marinate the fillets in the vinegar and citrus juices, covered and refrigerated, overnight.

THE NEXT DAY:

In a large saucepan over moderate heat, cook the onion for a minute or two in the olive oil until it is soft and then add the fennel fronds, tomatoes, carrot, parsley and bay leaf. Continue to cook for 15 minutes, stirring occasionally, and then deglaze your pan by adding the wine and scraping up any browned bits from the bottom of the pan. Add the coriander and anise seeds, thyme and the cleaned whole fish. Pour enough hot water into the pan to just cover the fish and simmer, covered, over low heat for 1 hour.

While the soup cooks, bring the marinated fillets to room temperature.

Remove the bay leaf and pass the soup through the finest disk of a food mill, or press it through a fine sieve, and add the orange juice. Rinse the pan and pour the resulting purée back into it. Bring to a boil and boil over moderately high heat for 15 minutes to reduce the liquid and intensify the flavors.

Let the soup cool a bit and then stir in the saffron threads.

To finish

Ladle into soup plates and then add one of the marinated fillets to each serving. Top with some fleur de sel or sea salt and freshly ground pepper.

Triglie con Pomodoro e Olive Candite e Salsa di Acciughe ✦ Red Mullet with Candied Olives and Tomatoes in an Anchovy Sauce

This recipe is inspired by Filippo Volpi, of the Hotel Casa Volpi in Arezzo. The olives to use are the small black or very dark green ones that are sold in jars and preserved in brine. In Italy these are called *olive in salamoia*, and the best ones come from Liguria. You can also make your own if you have access to fresh olives—I have provided a recipe on page 398. Plum tomatoes work best for this recipe. As they are baked in a low oven to bring out their sugars, use firm fruit that will hold its shape when baked.

You will need 4 individual ovenproof molds that hold about ½ cup.

SERVES 4

6 to 8 anchovy fillets preserved in olive oil
½ cup olive oil
4 small firm plum tomatoes

1 garlic clove, minced

A selection of fresh aromatic herbs (such as thyme, oregano, marjoram), finely chopped

½ cup sugar

Half a dozen olives per person

500 g (18 oz) red mullet fillets (approx. 8 small red mullets or 16 fillets)

To finish

1 firm plum tomato

Fresh basil leaves to garnish

Process the anchovies and oil together in a blender. Set aside.

Preheat the oven to 250°F/120°C. Drop the tomatoes in boiling water for a minute and then remove. Peel, seed and cut into halves lengthwise. Place them cut side up on a parchment-lined baking sheet and cover with the garlic and herbs. Sprinkle a pinch of the sugar over each tomato and bake for about 45 minutes. They will have shriveled somewhat but will still retain their shape and be soft and malleable. Remove from the oven and increase the heat to 400°F/200°C.

Make a syrup by adding ¼ cup of water to the remaining sugar and bringing it to a rolling boil. Boil until the syrup starts to turn a light caramel color. Add the olives, return the syrup to a rolling boil and remove the olives to a piece of parchment paper. Let them cool.

Carefully bone the fish fillets using a pair of tweezers. Oil the molds and line each one with 3 or 4 fillets. Place 1 or 2 pieces (depending on their size) of the candied tomato in the center of each mold. Cover each mold with foil and place in a pan large enough to hold all the molds. Make a *bain-marie* by pouring enough boiling water into the pan to come halfway up the sides of the molds. Bake for 15 minutes. Remove the foil and place under the grill for 2 minutes.

While the fish is baking, peel and seed the remaining tomato and cut it into small dice for the garnish.

To serve

Remove the molds from the oven and dip each mold into a bowl of ice water to loosen its contents. Invert onto your serving plates. Drizzle some of the anchovy sauce over the fish and arrange the candied olives and the diced tomato on the plate. Top with fresh basil leaves.

Variation

I have made this dish successfully using Pacific sole, ocean perch and salmon trout. Alternatively, look for small, mild and firm-fleshed fish. You will need 500 g (18 oz) of skinned fillets to serve 4 people.

Stockfischgrostl ✦ Salt Cod and Potato Skillet Dinner

In the South Tyrol, or Alto Adige as the region is known in Italian, when you see the word *grostl* at the end of a recipe it usually means that sliced boiled potatoes are involved in a dish of boiled meat or, as in this case, fish. Fried together in a pan with lots of onions, it is a hearty one-dish meal that goes nicely with a side of sauerkraut. In Italy, salt cod is usually available already "bathed" and ready to cook. If you visit an Italian or Portuguese market in North America, you may be able to find presoaked cod. Otherwise, you will need to plan ahead a few days and do the soaking yourself.

The best way to determine how long the fish needs to soak is to buy it from a reputable vendor and ask them. They should know best. I usually find the better the quality of the salt cod, the shorter the time it needs to soak. It is important to change the soaking water as often as possible. Better still, if you have a spare sink in the house, leave the cod soaking in a bowl of water under a very slowly running tap. Be diligent and patient with this step—if the fish has not been soaked long enough to remove the salt, the dish will be inedible.

SERVES 4

500 g (18 oz) best-quality salt cod, soaked (see note at right)

500 g (18 oz) (2 large) waxy potatoes

2 tbsp butter

1 onion, minced

1 garlic clove, minced

½ cup heavy cream

Pepper to taste

A pinch of grated nutmeg

1 tbsp finely chopped fresh parsley to garnish

Skin the cod and remove any bones. Cut into 1-inch pieces.

Clean and halve the potatoes—do not peel. Bring a pot of water to a boil. Add 1 tsp salt and the potatoes. Parboil the potatoes until they begin to lose their firmness but are not completely cooked—about 15 minutes. Drain the potatoes and peel them while they are still warm. Let cool. Slice fairly thinly.

Melt the butter in a large saucepan over moderate heat and cook the onion until it starts to become transparent—about 5 minutes. Add the potatoes and garlic and cook until the potatoes are tender—about 10 minutes. Add the cod, stir well to mix and cook for 10 to 15 minutes. The cod will lose its translucency and become opaque.

SOAKING SALT COD

Place the fish in a basin and let it sit under a slowly running faucet for at least 24 hours. Taste it after 24 hours; if it is still very salty, then you will need to continue soaking it. If you prefer not to leave your tap running, then soak the cod in a basin of water, changing the water every few hours. When you are ready to cook, drain the cod and remove the skin and any bones.

Stir in the cream and cook for a minute or two. Season with pepper and nutmeg and taste for salt. Remove from the heat. Serve garnished with the parsley.

For the sauerkraut
If you want to serve this dish with a traditional Tyrolean side, take a few slices of bacon (smoked if you can find it) and cut into 1-inch pieces. Cook them in a nonstick frying pan over moderate heat until the bacon has released most of its fat and has just started to brown. Add 450 g (1 lb) of drained sauerkraut. Stir well and cook until the sauerkraut is hot.

Baccalà con la Bietola
✦ Braised Salt Cod with Swiss Chard

This recipe comes from the area around Lucca and is one of my favorite ways to use salt cod. Serve this stew on a slice of grilled bread that has been rubbed with a clove of garlic or over a bed of creamy polenta. This is a hearty, healthy dish.

SERVES 4

750 g (1⅔ lb) best-quality salt cod, soaked (see page 229)
⅓ cup extra virgin olive oil
1 onion, thinly sliced
2 carrots, finely diced
1 leek, white part only, thinly sliced
3 garlic cloves, minced
2 tbsp finely chopped fresh parsley

750 g (1⅔ lb) fresh Swiss chard or spinach*

½ cup white wine

Freshly ground black pepper

A few basil leaves, finely chopped, to garnish

*Frozen spinach or chard can be substituted for the fresh. You will need about 225 g (½ lb).

Skin the cod and remove any bones. Cut into 1-inch pieces.

Heat the oil in a large sauté pan over low heat and add the onion, carrots and leek. Cook, stirring occasionally, until the onions begin to wilt but do not color, about 15 minutes. Add the garlic and the parsley and cook for another 4 minutes. In the meantime, wash the chard and remove the thick stems. Chop the leaves but do not dry them. Add them to the vegetables and cook briefly until they begin to wilt. Add the cod and the wine.

Partially cover the pan and cook over fairly low heat for 25 to 30 minutes, stirring occasionally. The liquid will evaporate and the greens and fish will almost melt into each other, forming a thick stew. Season with the pepper and taste for salt. Serve topped with the basil.

Fricassea di Animali di Cortile
◆ Courtyard Animal Fricassee

Although we usually associate a fricassee with the French, it is said that this method of cooking has Italian origins. Recipes for *fricassea* appear in many Italian cookbooks. The method usually involves creating a white stew by cooking pieces of meat (rabbit, chicken, lamb and veal are common) in broth or wine on top of the stove and then thickening the pan

juices with egg yolks, cream or flour to create a rich white sauce. A hint of lemon juice completes the picture, and the result is a silky smooth sauce with a delicate and sophisticated flavor. The following recipe works well with rabbit, guinea hen or chicken.

I choose to cook our hens in a *fricassea* because they are often tough, having spent their lives roaming freely. They require a long cooking time for their meat to become tender. I usually make this dish in the springtime, after we've culled our flock for the year, getting rid of the older hens and poor layers. I serve it with steamed new potatoes and asparagus from the garden.

SERVES 4

1 onion, finely chopped
¼ cup extra virgin olive oil
1 chicken or rabbit, cut into 8 to 12 pieces
1 carrot
1 celery stalk
Several sprigs of fresh parsley
A sprig of fresh rosemary
1 bay leaf
About 2 cups hot chicken broth
Salt and pepper to taste
Chopped fresh parsley to garnish

For the sauce
3 egg yolks
Juice of 1 lemon

In a large sauté pan or enameled cast-iron Dutch oven, cook the onion in the oil over moderate heat for several minutes, until it becomes transparent but does not brown. Add the chicken or rabbit and brown lightly on all sides. Tie the carrot, celery and herbs together with a piece of string and add them to the pan along with 1 cup of the hot broth. Reduce the heat to low and simmer, partially covered, until the meat is tender and falling from the bone. This time will vary, depending on the meat, and could be anywhere from ½ hour to 1½ hours.

Transfer the meat to a warmed platter and discard the vegetable bundle. Remove all but 1 cup of the liquid from the pan. (If there is not 1 cup left, add more of the hot broth.) Whisk the yolks into the liquid in the pan, then whisk in the lemon juice. Return the meat to the pan, turning to coat it in the sauce. Heat, stirring constantly, just until the sauce thickens. Season with salt and pepper and serve immediately, garnished with the parsley.

Nature or Nurture? La Petraia's Turkey Mom

I'd been raising chickens for a while before I decided it was time to see if we couldn't produce our own turkey for Christmas dinner. Early one July morning a couple of years ago, I made my way down the mountain to the Saturday market in San Giovanni Val d'Arno, our nearest town of any size, to visit Stefano, the poultry man. He always has local breeds, *nostrano* (ours) he calls them. Generally, whether they are chickens, ducks, geese or turkeys, they are smaller and, by all accounts, tastier than the larger, more commercial breeds he also sells.

I chose a pair of tiny poults, male and female, of the black *nostrano* variety. They would mature at a weight of four to five kilograms,

Stefano said, a good ten kilograms less than the commercial breed of white turkey he had. He encouraged me to buy them by holding up his thumb and index finger, pressing them together and kissing them in the typical Italian gesture. These birds will be "*squisiti*," he said.

Home I went with a pair of ugly-looking baby turkeys in a cardboard box, planning on fattening them up in time for the holidays. I introduced them to my *pollaio*, and slowly they grew large and stupid. They hardly seemed to know how to peck for food or where to find it, and I worried whether they would survive. My chickens seemed like Einsteins in comparison to this pair. Neighbors who stopped by would take one look at them, draw in a breath and raise their shoulders and eyebrows. Waving an index finger in front of me, they would tell me, "*Sono molto fragili*"— they are very fragile. It seemed I had gotten myself into a tricky business with these turkeys. Apparently they were a delicate bird, prone to illness when they are young. In short, not so easy to raise.

Slowly, however, they grew. By the early fall the male had turned into a rare beauty, boasting a splendid tail of colored feathers and spending half his time puffing himself up and parading around the chicken coop to impress his young wife, who was homely by comparison and about half his size. These two also turned out to be much wilder and braver than our chickens, flying up into the trees at night to roost instead of huddling inside the henhouse as the chickens do the minute the sun begins to fade from the evening sky.

In early December the female started laying an egg every day. These were twice the size of my chickens' eggs, very useful for the holiday baking I was caught up in just then. As Christmas approached, I asked around to find out which bird would be best to eat—the male or the female? She won hands down, so we set the date, December 23, to butcher her. But on that day, when we went to retrieve her, she was sitting on top of the egg she'd laid that morning, refusing to budge. She spat at us nastily when we tried to grab her. "*Sta covando*"—she's gone broody—said our friend Franco. She's not so dumb after all, I thought.

As I had used all of her eggs, I gathered up a dozen from our hens for her nest. Next we proceeded to track down her tom, who, as it turned out, made an exceptional Christmas dinner.

For the next three weeks the young widow sat proudly on her nest of chickens' eggs, hardly moving to eat or to drink. In mid-January, twenty-one days after she'd saved herself from the pot, she hatched a flock of tiny chicks and turned into the most vigilant, fierce and competent mother imaginable. Hissing at anyone who came close to her brood, she was always on the lookout for predators, continually clucking away and calling her chicks to take cover under her ample wings whenever she sensed danger lurking. She patiently taught them how to eat and drink.

Over the weeks I learned what a great mother a turkey is, even when her offspring are chickens. Somehow she didn't seem to notice or care that these babies of hers were midgets. She raised them as turkeys, a little on the wild side like her. She taught them to fly out of the coop and into the trees to roost all night long, instead of gathering together inside the henhouse. Sadly, I lost a few of them to the local fox as a result.

When the five chicks that remained were four months old and more than able to fend for themselves, she began to lay eggs again. Sensing how much I coveted these, she hid them from me, burying them and then moving them several times a day to a new location. I played along with her antics, curious to see what her plan was. When she had amassed a collection of eight or nine, she unearthed them, rolled them into a nest and gently settled on them. Her chicks, now a good size, all climbed on top of her, keeping Mom company while learning the important facts of life.

Sadly, I didn't have a male turkey anymore, so her eggs were not fertile. The next day, when I was sure she was determined to brood, I swapped them for twenty hens' eggs. Once again unbeknownst to her, my favorite turkey had become a mother of chickens, all of whom think they are turkeys, and all of whom spend their nights roosting in the trees. It was her second flock, and she was not yet a year old.

Most hens today are hatched in incubators, and it is not always easy to find a breed of chicken that will brood on a clutch of eggs. Even the rare breeds that I keep at Petraia don't make very good mothers—either they simply refuse to brood or they lose interest halfway through the process. Without having had a mother, they seem useless at being one. I consider myself fortunate to have this great turkey that has solved the problem for me. Determined to mother, she's teaching my flock of chickens to reclaim their ancient instincts, to procreate naturally without human intervention. I suppose she has also given me my own rare breed of chickens—ones who think they are turkeys.

Coniglio al Gorgonzola
◆ Rabbit in a Gorgonzola Cream Sauce

Our friend Franco got us started raising rabbits with a birthday gift to my husband of a handsome *marito e moglie* (husband and wife) several years ago. Our rabbits are not caged, but roam freely in a large fenced-in area in the woods where they can graze on wild herbs and plants. They are easy to look after and are pleasant animals to have around. After several years now of keeping them, I have learned that it is true what they say. Our male bunny has matured into a big, handsome great-grandfather, and we keep a spare yard for him and his male progeny. Every so often, when the population looks like it is about to explode, we send them there for a holiday. They "bach it" for a few months while the girls get a well-deserved rest.

This is the nicest way I know to cook rabbit. If the idea of eating Flopsy is not appealing, you can substitute chicken or pheasant. In Italy, rabbit is often braised in white wine with olives or in a tomato sauce. Because it is a lean, muscular animal, the meat is dry, and braising is the key to preserving as much flavor and moisture as possible.

This method, using cream and stock as the braising liquid, produces a moist, flavorful and elegant dish that perfectly complements the subtle taste of the rabbit. Look for a plump, organically raised rabbit. I like serving this in the spring when the first *primizie*, or spring vegetables, start appearing in the market. I accompany it with steamed new potatoes, new red onions and green peas.

SERVES 4

1 rabbit, cut into 8 pieces

1 carrot

1 onion

1 garlic clove

A few leaves of fresh sage

2 tbsp olive oil

1 bay leaf

140 g (5 oz) gorgonzola cheese, broken into large pieces

⅔ cup chicken broth

Salt and pepper to taste

MAKE-AHEAD NOTE
This dish can be made several hours ahead and reheated.

Place the rabbit pieces in a large bowl and let it sit under a tap of running water for half an hour. If this is impractical, you can let the pieces soak, changing the water three or four times.

Finely chop the carrot, onion, garlic and sage and place in a casserole with the oil and bay leaf. Drain the rabbit pieces and place them on top of the vegetables. Cover and cook over medium-low heat for about 40 minutes, turning the rabbit pieces once at the halfway point. (The cooking time can vary considerably, depending on how the rabbit was raised, its age and what it was fed. You may find you need more or less time for this recipe. When done, the meat should be very tender, falling from the bone.)

Rabbit sometimes gives off a lot of water as it cooks. If this is the case, you may find you don't need to add all—or even any—of the broth. You want to have enough liquid in the pan to make a thick, creamy sauce when the gorgonzola is added. Add the gorgonzola and the broth, if using, and stir until the cheese has melted. Simmer, covered, for another 20 minutes, stirring from time to time. Season with salt and pepper. Remove the bay leaf.

If you'd like, you can pass the sauce through a food mill to purée it, but it is also nice left chunky.

Variation

For *coniglio alla crema*, substitute an equal amount of heavy cream for the gorgonzola.

Petto d'Anatra con Chianti Caldo
✦ Duck Breast with Hot Chianti Jelly

I usually have a few fuzzy yellow ducklings quacking away amongst my courtyard animals. They are very timid creatures when they are young but seem to grow quite attached to their human caretakers as they mature. Greedy eaters, they grow quickly and begin to produce eggs when they are about five or six months old. I am always torn whether to keep the females in the hope they will decide to start a family or to put them in the pot because they are so good to eat.

SERVES 4

4 whole cloves

2 allspice berries

2 juniper berries

2 garlic cloves

½ tsp peppercorns

½ tsp salt

A pinch of freshly grated nutmeg

2 tbsp liquid honey

2 large duck breasts

⅓ cup *Chianti Caldo* (page 403) or store-bought red-wine jelly*

1 or 2 tbsp water

If using store-bought jelly, heat it gently and add a few flakes of hot chili pepper. Let it steep while the duck cooks and then strain out the chili flakes before serving.

In a mortar or a spice grinder, grind the cloves, allspice, juniper, garlic and peppercorns with the salt. Stir in the nutmeg and honey and rub all over the duck breasts. Refrigerate, tightly covered with plastic wrap, for several hours or overnight.

Heat a frying pan over high heat and place the duck breasts skin side down. Cook for about 5 minutes, until the skin is crispy and most of the fat has been rendered. Remove all but a teaspoon of the fat. (The fat can be used to roast potatoes to accompany the duck—see page 316—or frozen for future use.) Turn the breasts and cook on the other side for about 5 minutes. The juice from the breast should run clear when it is done. Remove the duck to a platter and let it sit for a minute before slicing.

In the meantime, make the sauce by heating the jelly with a little water. Slice the duck thinly and serve with a drizzle of the sauce around the plate.

Salsicce con Polenta Rossa
◆ Grilled Sausages on a Bed of Red Polenta
Polenta stained red with beetroot provides a colorful and delicious backdrop and adds more than a bit of style to an Italian sausage. This is humble food that satisfies and sticks to the ribs, perfect for a winter weeknight.

Serves 4

1 beet
2 tbsp extra virgin olive oil
⅓ cup heavy cream
1 cup coarsely ground cornmeal
Salt to taste
4 Italian sausages
2 tbsp minced Italian parsley to garnish

Preheat the oven to 350°F/175°C. Scrub the beet clean but do not peel it. Prick it several times with a knife and wrap in foil. Bake until tender, about 30 minutes. Let cool to room temperature, then peel and purée with the olive oil and the cream.

Make polenta according to the instructions on page 148, adding the puréed beets after the first 25 minutes. Cook for another 15 to 20 minutes, until the polenta is done. Taste for salt.

Grill or broil the sausages and serve them on top of the polenta. Garnish with a scattering of the parsley.

Piccione alla Brace con Frutti di Bosco
✦ Grilled Pigeon with Wild Berries

Although I don't keep pigeons at Petraia, we have no shortage of wild ones. In the summertime they often land in my chicken coop for a free lunch, eating the corn and grains I leave out for the poultry, so I consider it a fair trade when once in a while these freeloaders mysteriously find their way into my kitchen.

Count on about one pigeon, or squab as they are sometimes called, per person. To be authentic, the meat should be cooked over the coals of a wood fire. Here at Petraia, like most Tuscan farmhouses, we have an iron grill in the fireplace where in the winter we grill meat and bread for *crostini*. In the summer, the grill is transferred outdoors.

SERVES 4

4 pigeons

For the spice rub
12 sage leaves
Leaves from a sprig of fresh rosemary
2 juniper berries
2 allspice berries

¼ cup extra virgin olive oil

2 garlic cloves, minced

Salt and pepper to taste

For the sauce

1 cup fresh or frozen blackberries or elderberries

¼ cup sweet wine such as Marsala or Vin Santo

¼ cup extra virgin olive oil

1 onion, minced

½ cup chicken broth

1 tbsp liquid honey

2 tbsp butter to finish

Salt and pepper to taste

For the spice rub

Finely chop the sage and rosemary. Crush the juniper and allspice berries in a mortar or a spice grinder. Combine the herbs and spices with the olive oil and garlic. Season with salt and pepper. Cut the pigeons in half along the backbone and press on them so they will lie flat. Rub them all over with the spice rub. Refrigerate for several hours, tightly covered.

For the sauce

Soak the berries in the sweet wine for 30 minutes to an hour.

Heat the olive oil in a sauté pan over moderate heat and add the onion. Cook until it begins to wilt but does not color, about 5 minutes. Drain the wine from the berries, reserving the berries, and add the wine to the pan. Increase the heat to high. When the wine has evaporated, add the broth and the berries. Reduce the heat to moderately high and cook for 5 minutes to reduce the sauce. Add the honey and swirl in the butter. Season.

To grill

Cook the pigeons on a grill over hot coals, turning several times. Or, if you have a rotisserie on your grill, use it. Baste the birds occasionally with some of the sauce. The pigeon is done when the juices run clear. The cooking time will depend on your heat source, but count on at least 30 minutes. Serve the pigeon with the remaining sauce.

Agnello al Forno ◆ Roasted Lamb

Here in Tuscany, lamb is eaten in the early spring. Where I live, in the heavily forested Chianti Mountains, it is not lamb country and, even at Easter, lamb is not easy to find in Radda. I have to go to another nearby town, Gaiole in Chianti, where the excellent Chini Brothers' butcher shop always has lovely spring lamb. Gaiole, while only fifteen minutes away, is a little closer to the famous Crete Senesi, the starkly barren hills around Siena that are littered with herds of sheep. It is their milk that is used to produce the pecorino cheese for which the region is famous.

Sometimes as a special treat, I order lamb from Zeri, a tiny mountain village high up in the Tuscan hinterland called the Lunigiana. Zeri is known all over Italy for the quality of its lamb. Going to Zeri for lamb is really just an excuse to drive up into this lovely remote part of Tuscany near the border with Liguria and Emilia-Romagna. Although it's a good three-hour drive from La Petraia, I make a day trip out of it, stopping in a favorite restaurant in Ponteremoli for a traditional Luni lunch of *testaroli* (page 158) and *farinata* (page 128). Thus fortified, I can tackle the hairpin mountain turns on the road to Zeri. After twenty minutes of white-knuckling it, I breathe a huge sigh of relief as the dark narrow mountain valley I've been climbing opens up to reveal a paradise lost. Above bucolic pastures littered with little white lambs and pretty alpine flowers, the road ends and the picturesque village of Zeri sits under a crown of snow-covered Apennine peaks.

Lamb in Italy is butchered much younger than it is in North America. Chops are so tiny I find them hardly worth buying. Instead I ask for a shoulder to roast in the oven.

This is the simple roasted lamb one encounters all over Tuscany at Easter.

SERVES 4 TO 6

¼ cup extra virgin olive oil
3 garlic cloves, minced
Leaves from 2 sprigs fresh rosemary, finely chopped
Salt and pepper
1 kg (2¼ lb) bone-in lamb shoulder (or small leg)
¼ cup white wine

Mix together the olive oil, garlic, rosemary, salt and pepper. Rub this all over the lamb. Cover the lamb with plastic wrap and refrigerate for at least 6 hours or overnight.

Preheat the oven to 450°F/230°C. Place the lamb in a roasting pan and roast for 15 minutes. Turn the heat down to 350°F/175°C. Add the wine to the pan and baste the lamb. Continue to roast until the lamb is done to an internal temperature of 140°F/60°C for medium-rare. Count on 10 to 15 minutes per pound for a medium-rare roast, approximately 45 minutes. Let the roast sit, loosely covered with foil, for about 15 minutes after it is removed from the oven before it is sliced.

page 163

page 290

page 295

page 158

page 184

page 140

page 84

245

page 151

page 198

page 350

page 366

page 323

page 340

page 336

pages 36, 48

page 31

page 55

pages 48, 49

pages 384

pages 386

es 385

pages 385

Cesti di Polpettine ◆ Spinach Meatballs Served in a
Frico Basket with a Cucumber and a Tomato Sauce

This recipe turns the meatballs in the antipasto chapter (page 77) into a
secondo by placing them in a *frico* basket and drizzling two pretty sauces
over them—one of fresh tomatoes and the other of cucumbers. This
visually stunning dish, which gives the simple meatball a well-deserved
turn at elegance, never fails to get raves. The meatballs can be made ahead,
as can the two sauces, so the only last-minute task is baking the meatballs.
This leaves you lots of time to enjoy your guests rather than fussing in the
kitchen. I serve this in the summer when tomatoes and cucumbers are
both at their peak. A plain white dinner plate is the perfect backdrop.

SERVES 4 TO 6

1 recipe *polpettine* (page 77)
1 recipe *frico,* shaped into baskets (page 79)
Fresh basil leaves or rosemary sprigs to garnish (optional)

For the tomato sauce
3 large tomatoes, peeled and seeded
2 tbsp butter
Salt and pepper to taste

For the cucumber sauce
2 large cucumbers, peeled, seeded and finely diced
2 tsp salt
1 tbsp extra virgin olive oil

⅓ cup finely chopped onion

1 tbsp all-purpose flour

1 cup hot milk

1 tbsp chopped fresh mint

Salt and pepper to taste

For the tomato sauce

Purée the tomatoes in your food processor and cook them over moderate heat until they have reduced enough to make a thick sauce. Stir in the butter and season with salt and pepper. Set aside until you are ready to serve.

For the cucumber sauce

If you did not dice your cucumbers small enough, or if you prefer a smoother sauce, you can purée it using your hand blender. You may have to reduce it slightly afterwards, as you will have released more water from the cucumbers.

Put the cucumbers in a colander, sprinkle with the salt and mix with your hands to spread the salt, then let stand at room temperature for half an hour. Rinse the cucumbers and pat them dry with paper towels.

In a small saucepan, heat the oil over moderate heat. Add the onion and cook, stirring occasionally, for about 10 minutes, until it is transparent. Add the flour and cook, stirring constantly, until it turns golden—do not let it burn. Pour in the hot milk and, stirring constantly, bring just to the boil. Reduce the heat to low and keep stirring until the sauce starts to thicken. Add the cucumbers and simmer, uncovered, for 15 minutes or until the cucumber is tender. Remove from the heat and season with the mint, salt and pepper. Set aside until you are ready to serve.

To assemble

Half an hour before you plan to serve them, bake the meatballs according to the instructions on page 79.

Meanwhile, reheat both sauces if they have been made in advance.

Put 2 or 3 meatballs in each *frico* basket. Drizzle some of the tomato sauce over the meatballs and then some of the cucumber sauce. Drizzle some of both sauces around the outside of the plate. Garnish the plate with a few leaves of fresh basil or a sprig of rosemary, if desired.

Uccellini Scappati ✦ Little Birds That Escaped (Rolled Veal Scaloppini with Prosciutto)

The daughter of an avid Canadian sportsman, I am familiar with numerous stories of "the one that got away." It turns out that is not just a Canadian phenomenon. In Italy, it appears, a remarkable number of little birds get away, and hunters return home empty-handed. Veal scallops, pounded thin, stuffed with prosciutto and sage and cooked like a small bird is the dinner that awaits those unlucky hunters.

The dish is found in many parts of northern Italy, with slight variations. The Romans make something similar, with the equally amusing name of *saltimbocca* (jump in your mouth). The name makes sense once you taste these succulent morsels—they really do jump into your mouth, they are so good.

Veal is common in Italy. The selection of veal in butcher shops is often much larger than that of beef. Much of the country is rugged and mountainous, not well suited for raising beef cattle, but in the past farmers often had a bit of land on which they could keep one or two milking cows whose offspring could be used for veal.

We've come to know veal in North America fairly recently, and all too often the stories of how it is raised are discouraging. But veal has a history in Italy that is both humane and sensible. Fortunately, it is not so hard to find organically raised, hormone-free veal. In some areas, grass-fed (free-range) veal is also available.

This is an elegant, easy dish that lends itself nicely to entertaining. It is also simple enough to put together on a busy weeknight when time is short and the gourmands are famished.

SERVES 4

Have your butcher flatten the veal slices for you into *scaloppine* about ¼ inch thick. Or, if you wish to do this yourself, place a veal scallop between two sheets of plastic wrap and pound it using a meat pounder.

4 veal scallops (approx. 450 g) (1 lb), flattened into *scaloppine*

4 slices prosciutto

1 or 2 sage leaves per veal slice

Flour for dredging

4 tbsp (½ stick) butter

½ cup Marsala or other sweet wine

¾ cup chicken or beef broth

Salt and pepper to taste

Lemon wedges and parsley sprigs to garnish

Lay a slice of prosciutto and a sage leaf or two on top of each slice of veal. Roll up into a log. Cut each log into two or three pieces. If they seem loose, you can secure them with a toothpick. Dredge in the flour and shake off any excess.

In a large sauté pan, melt 3 tbsp of the butter over moderately high heat. Add the veal and brown on all sides. This will just take a few minutes. Remove the "birds" from the pan and add the Marsala. Cook quickly over high heat, scraping up any brown bits in the pan, until reduced by about half. Add the broth and reduce by about half. Stir in the remaining tbsp of butter, then return the veal to the pan to reheat briefly—1 to 2 minutes—turning the meat once or twice. Season with salt and pepper. Serve immediately, drizzled with the pan sauce and garnished with a lemon wedge and a sprig of parsley.

Peposo dell'Impruneta
◆ Peppery Beef Stew from Impruneta

This spicy beef stew is a Tuscan classic that hails from the famous pottery-making town of Impruneta. The town is just a few miles from Florence along the scenic route through the hills of Chianti. For centuries its furnaces have supplied Florentines with the beautiful terra-cotta urns traditionally used to store wine and oil. Today one finds *peposo* on the menus of restaurants all over the region, but it is said that its origins lie with the workers of the ovens of Impruneta. As the kilns had to be kept watch over and never allowed to cool down, the work in them was nonstop, so this simple but substantial slow-cooked meal was put on the fire to simmer while the work was done.

Today you are hard pressed to find a recipe for *peposo* that does not include tomatoes. But purists argue that *peposo* was eaten in Impruneta long before the tomato plant found its way to Italy. So this recipe contains no tomatoes. The result is a dark, winey stew with a peppery kick that contains only five ingredients—beef, wine, garlic, salt and lots of pepper. It is cooked very slowly for a long time. The result is a dish with a depth and purity of flavor that belies its simple preparation. This recipe is based on one I found by Nanni Ricci of Florence, in *Ricette di Osterie di Firenze e Chianti*, published by Slow Food Editore.

Here at Petraia I like to make *peposo* on a lazy Sunday or holiday. It can be put together in an instant and then placed in a slow oven. In the meantime, my husband and I and our two canine companions have time for a long afternoon walk through the Chianti hills to work up the appetite this zesty dish demands. By the time I return home, ravenous from these adventures, the amazing smells wafting out of my kitchen sometimes give me a start. If I didn't know better, I'd think someone had been slaving away all day in there!

Traditionally, *peposo* is served over a thick slice of grilled Tuscan bread, but I find it is also nice—and very pretty—when ladled on top of a bed of polenta. Alternatively, you can serve it over pasta, but I would choose dried pasta over fresh to complement the rustic and hearty nature of the stew.

SERVES 4 TO 6

1 kg (2¼ lb) stewing beef, any visible fat trimmed, cut into
　2-inch pieces
6 to 8 large garlic cloves, unpeeled
2 tbsp coarsely ground black pepper
1 bottle red wine (preferably a young Chianti)
Salt to taste

Place the beef in a Dutch oven (enameled cast iron or terra-cotta work well) large enough to hold all the meat tightly in a single layer. Add the garlic cloves, pepper and enough red wine to totally cover the meat. Cover the pot and place it in a cold oven, then turn the oven to 250°F/120°C. Alternatively, place the pot over the lowest possible heat on top of the stove.

The *peposo* will need to cook for 4 to 5 hours. During the last hour, partially uncover the pot, to allow the liquids to reduce and to concentrate their flavor. When the stew is done, the meat should be very tender and fall apart when pierced with a fork. The stew should be almost black in color, the sauce reduced so that it is very thick, and the garlic cloves should still be visibly whole.

Taste for salt and ladle over toasted Tuscan bread, making sure each person gets one garlic clove. Encourage your guests to mash up the garlic into their sauce.

Variation

I often make *peposo* using our wild boar or venison in place of beef.

Cinghiale in Dolce e Forte
✦ Sweet and Strong Wild Boar

I always have a freezer full of wild boar, which I prepare in all kinds of ways, but this recipe is always the winner. The unusual preparation includes chocolate, raisins, candied fruit and pine nuts and is a Tuscan specialty, albeit an uncommon one these days.

Sweet-and-sour preparations were once used to mask flavors of meat and game that had been hung too long. Chocolate, a New World discovery, was introduced to Europe in the late Renaissance.

A dish like this would have been found only on the best tables, for the expensive and exotic ingredients it contained put it quite out of reach of ordinary folk. Traditionally, some sugar was included, but I find the chocolate and the fruit contribute sufficient sweetness.

Wild boar is increasingly easy to find these days in butcher shops that specialize in game, but you can also use pork shoulder. In Tuscany hare is also prepared in this way.

I serve this stew over creamy polenta, but you could also use the sauce as a condiment for a *primo* of fresh pasta and serve the meat as the *secondo*, as is often the tradition in Tuscany. Leftovers are wonderful tossed in a blender with some Parmesan cheese and used to make the ravioli on page 197.

I like to make this recipe a day ahead to let the flavors develop. Serve it with a red wine made from the Sangiovese grape, such as a Brunello di Montalcino, Vino Nobile di Montepulciano, Morellino di Scansano or Chianti Classico.

For the marinade

    1 kg (2¼ lb) wild boar or pork shoulder, cut into 2-inch pieces

    1 carrot, cut into 2 or 3 pieces

    1 onion, peeled and halved

    1 garlic clove, smashed

    Enough red wine to cover the meat (about 1 bottle)

    1 tbsp red wine vinegar

For the dolce e forte

    ¼ cup extra virgin olive oil

    1 onion, minced

    1 garlic clove, minced

    1 carrot, sliced

    1 celery stalk, chopped

    Several juniper berries, crushed

    3 whole cloves

    1 bay leaf

    A sprig of fresh rosemary

    ¼ cup large raisins

    2 tbsp mixed candied peel

To finish

    15 g (½ oz) dark chocolate

    Scant 2 tbsp pine nuts

    Salt and pepper to taste

For the marinade

Put the meat in a glass or other nonreactive bowl and add the remaining marinade ingredients. Cover and let sit overnight in the refrigerator.

For the dolce e forte

Drain the meat from the marinade, reserving the marinade, and pat the meat dry. Strain the marinade.

In a casserole large enough to hold all the meat, heat the olive oil over moderately high heat. Add the meat to the pan and brown it on all sides. Remove the meat to a platter and lower the heat to moderate. Add the onion, garlic, carrot and celery and cook, stirring from time to time, for 10 to 15 minutes, until the onions wilt and the vegetables begin to give off their delicate aroma. Meanwhile, wrap the juniper berries, cloves, bay leaf and rosemary in a piece of cheesecloth tied with a string, or place them in a tea ball. Return the meat and any juices to the casserole along with the spice packet, raisins, candied peel and enough of the strained marinade to cover. Simmer over the lowest possible heat, partially covered, for 2 to 3 hours or until the meat is very tender. Add more of the marinade if required.

Add the chocolate and the pine nuts about 15 minutes before serving. Season with salt and pepper and remove the spice packet. If you like, you can purée some or all of the sauce.

The La Petraia Variations

In the late fall, when our chestnut harvest begins, I throw in a handful of peeled fresh chestnuts along with the raisins and candied peel. (See page 121 for more about chestnuts.) At this time of year I usually offer a chestnut-themed dinner, which might include the following:

- Chestnut soup from page 119
- Chestnut pasta from page 188
- *Dolce e forte* with chestnuts added
- Chestnut bread from page 51
- Chestnut soufflé from page 356

Daino al Forno con le Mele Cotogne
+ Roast Haunch of Venison with Quince

In late August and early September the hunting season opens with a limited deer hunt in our part of Tuscany. Following that, our woods are full of hunters until the end of January with the progressive seasons of hare, pheasant and finally wild boar opening in November. We have grown used to the hunters who roam our property during these months. In Italy, hunters are allowed to hunt almost anywhere—private property or not.

We have no shortage of game, and our woods are considered prime hunting ground. My early-morning *passeggiata* with our dogs, Olive and Hockley, at this time of year is restricted to the main trails that crisscross our forest, and I always have a whistle around my neck, which I blow constantly to alert any hunters hidden in blinds or up a tree of our presence. Each year in Italy many people die from hunting accidents, and I'm not interested in being one of them.

Three different kinds of deer call Petraia their home: tiny playful herds of *caprioli* (roebuck), larger *daini* (fallow deer) and the handsome *cervi* (stags). While boar, whose population is soaring out of control in parts of Tuscany, are hunted by large teams of men in an open hunting season, deer are more carefully controlled by the local forestry officials. From time to time a limited deer hunt will be allowed, but there is never an open season, so it is a great privilege to get a bit of venison from one of the local hunters.

The quince come from one of the old trees I have on the property. A late-fall fruit, they marry beautifully with the venison.

SERVES 4

For the marinade
   1 venison roast, about 900 g (2 lb)
   1 bottle red wine
   ¼ cup olive oil
   1 tbsp good-quality balsamic vinegar
   1 tbsp liquid honey
   A sprig of fresh rosemary

For the quince
   2 quince (see note at right)
   ½ cup liquid honey
   1 cinnamon stick
   2 whole cloves

For the roast
   Salt and freshly ground black pepper
   2 tbsp butter

Pears and apples make a good substitute for quince. Substitute 1 large pear and 1 large apple for the 2 quince. Choose a pear that is a tad on the hard side, something that will be ready to eat out of hand in a few days.

For the marinade
Combine the venison with the remaining marinade ingredients. Cover and let sit overnight in the refrigerator.

For the quince

Peel and core the quince and cut into large chunks. Place in a saucepan with the honey, cinnamon and cloves and simmer over moderately low heat, stirring occasionally, until the quince are cooked. They will turn a pretty pink color and should be very tender. This will take a good half-hour. Remove from the heat and discard the cinnamon stick and the cloves. You can leave the sauce chunky or purée it in a food processor. It can be served warm or at room temperature.

For the roast

Preheat the oven to 450°F/230°C. Remove the venison from the marinade, reserving the liquid, and pat the meat dry. Place the meat in a roasting pan, season with salt and pepper and rub all over with half of the butter. Roast the venison for 15 minutes, then reduce the heat to 400°F/200°C. Add about ½ cup of the marinade and roast for another 30 minutes or until the meat is done, basting from time to time and adding more of the marinade if needed. An internal temperature of 140°F/60°C is medium-rare.

Remove the meat to a platter and let it sit, loosely covered with foil, while you make the sauce. Add ½ cup of the marinade to the roasting pan and cook over high heat, scraping up the bits from the bottom as you go. Swirl in the remaining tablespoon of butter. Season with salt and pepper. Slice the roast and serve with the pan sauce and the quince sauce.

Fegato di Vitello con Cipolle ◆ Liver and Melting Onions in a Balsamic Vinegar Reduction

Wild boar in Tuscany is hunted in large groups—by teams of up to forty men. On a good day, several boar are killed and the lots get divided up between the hunters. The liver is awarded as a prize to the hunter whose shot actually kills the boar. Our friend Alessandro, who is an excellent shot but not fond of liver, often arrives in hunting season bearing the gift of fresh boar liver. It is stronger than calves' liver, a real liver lover's treat, and I always look forward to getting some. It is unlikely you will find wild boar liver in North America, but calves' liver works just as well in this recipe. I also offer this up in a very small serving as an antipasto.

SERVES 4

450 g (1 lb) calves' liver
1 tbsp butter
1 tbsp olive oil
2 large red onions, very thinly sliced
3 tbsp good-quality balsamic vinegar
Salt and pepper to taste
Finely chopped fresh parsley to garnish

Cut the liver into ½-inch cubes. Heat the butter and oil together in a sauté pan over low heat. Add the onions and cook, partially covered and stirring from time to time, for about 20 minutes, until they have wilted. Add the balsamic vinegar and ¼ cup hot water. Increase the heat to moderate and continue to cook for another 10 to 15 minutes, until the liquid has evaporated. Add the liver and cook, tossing to cook all sides, for just a minute or two, until it just loses its color but is still tender. Season with salt and pepper.

Place a dollop of polenta (or mashed potatoes) on each plate and top with the liver and onions. Garnish with the parsley and serve.

Cuestis di Mont (*Costicine di Maiale alla Montanara*)
♦ Mountain-style Braised Pork with Polenta

Braised pork ribs with polenta are found in various parts of northern Italy, including Emilia, Lombardy, the Veneto and Friuli. Sometimes the braising liquid includes tomatoes and red wine, but this recipe comes from the mountain region of Friuli and white wine is called for. This makes sense, since Friuli produces much of Italy's best white wine.

Traditionally, *cuestis di mont* is made with spareribs that have been lightly smoked. You may be able to find lightly smoked ribs if you have access to an Eastern European butcher or deli (see note on page 259). Here in Tuscany they are almost impossible to find, so I use smoked salt in the spice rub. But don't worry; the dish will also be good without any smoke. The ribs marinate in a dry rub for several hours before being browned and are then cooked in a soupy polenta until the meat falls from the bone.

A delicious, simple and economical meal, this is perfect for a winter's night. It can be made a day ahead and reheated. Serve it with a glass of white wine, from Friuli if possible.

SERVES 4 TO 6

For the spice rub
    1 garlic clove
    2 juniper berries
    Smoked or plain sea salt
    Coarsely ground black pepper
    Leaves from a sprig of fresh rosemary or thyme

For the braise

1.5 to 2 kg (3⅓ to 4 lb) lean country-style pork ribs (have your butcher trim away any excess fat and cut the ribs into 2-inch pieces)

1 tbsp extra virgin olive oil

1 cup white wine

About 6 cups boiling water

⅔ cup cornmeal

Salt and pepper to taste

If you use smoked ribs, you will not need to marinate them in the spice rub overnight. Instead, add the spices to the pan when you return the browned ribs after deglazing.

For the spice rub

Finely grind the spice rub ingredients in a spice grinder or using a mortar and pestle. Rub over the ribs. Refrigerate for 6 hours or overnight, tightly covered in plastic wrap.

For the braise

In a casserole large enough to hold all the ribs, heat the oil over moderately high heat. Brown the ribs in two batches on all sides. This will take 20 to 25 minutes. Remove the ribs to a platter. Deglaze the casserole by adding the wine and scraping up any browned bits from the bottom of the pan. Return the ribs to the pan and add enough of the boiling water to cover. Reduce the heat to low and begin to add the cornmeal, a little bit at a time, stirring constantly. Once all of the cornmeal has been added, continue to stir for about 10 minutes, until the mixture begins to thicken. Cover the pot and cook, stirring occasionally, until the ribs are falling from the bone, 45 minutes to an hour. Season with salt and pepper.

Scottiglia ✦ A Mixed Braise of Meat and Poultry

"Chi ha il mestolo in mano, fa la minestra a modo suo"—Who has the ladle in his hand makes the soup the way he likes it. Perhaps the author of this old Tuscan proverb had *scottiglia* in mind, because this dish, made from whatever bits of meat you fancy or have on hand, will be different every time you make it depending on what you use.

I often have bits of rabbit or chicken, duck or some game in the freezer—not enough for a meal on their own, but thrown into this easy one-pot supper, a feast is possible. *Scottiglia* is a mixed meat stew said to have Etruscan origins in the Maremma region of southwestern Tuscany. But then legend also has it that it belongs to the Casentino, the beautiful mountain range south of Florence close to Italy's central spinal Apennine column and Tuscany's border with Romagna. Quite a long way from the Maremma, even by today's standards. But there is perhaps truth to both claims, for the ancients are said to have had an important transhumant route through the Maremma to the Casentino, along which they led their animals to higher ground each year to graze throughout the summer months.

I have also heard the dish called *cacciucco di carne. Cacciucco* is a fish soup, versions of which are made both in Livorno and Viareggio, containing several different kinds of fish. Traditionally, the soup was made by fishermen and used the smaller, less noble fish that would come up in their nets with the more valuable, larger fish. And so, in the nearby Maremma, one finds the cousin of *cacciucco* that uses meat instead of fish and was the way to use up *avanzi*—meat that was about to go bad.

Whatever the name, the principle is the same: several kinds of meat are cooked together with *odori* and wine. Today, tomatoes are almost always added to *scottiglia*, but, like much traditional Italian cooking, this ancient dish remembers the days before the Italian love affair with the nightshade began.

Use as many different kinds of meat as you like. Traditionally, bits of chicken, duck, rabbit, pigeon, lamb, veal and beef might be found in a *scottiglia*. You can add them all at once, since the dish cooks very slowly for several hours. You don't need to get carried away, though—this dish is good even when you use only one kind of meat.

I prefer to make this stew a day ahead and reheat it so that the flavors have a chance to mingle. If you refrigerate the dish overnight, the fat will congeal at the surface and can be skimmed off easily before the stew is reheated.

This is a noble Tuscan stew and deserves a noble Tuscan wine as accompaniment. Choose a robust Brunello di Montalcino, Chianti Classico or Morellino di Scansano and you won't be disappointed.

SERVES 4 TO 6

For the marinade

    1 kg (2¼ lb) mixed cuts of meat (such as chicken, duck, rabbit, veal, beef, venison or boar)

    Enough red wine to cover the meat (about 1 bottle)

For the braise

    2 tbsp extra virgin olive oil

    1 onion, minced

    2 garlic cloves, smashed

    1 celery stalk, diced

    1 carrot, diced

    Leaves from a few sprigs of basil and parsley, finely chopped

    Leaves from a sprig of fresh rosemary, finely chopped

    A few flakes of hot chili pepper

    Zest of 1 lemon

280 g (10 oz) tomato purée
Salt and pepper to taste

For the marinade

Trim away any excess fat and chop the meat small enough so that each person can have a piece of everything. I prefer not to bone the meat, as the bones add flavor. However, if you're using fowl or rabbit, then you may want to remove all those small bones for an easier time at the table.

Place the meat in a large bowl and add the wine. Cover and refrigerate overnight.

For the braise

The next day, when you are ready to cook, drain the meat, reserving the marinade. Pat the meat dry.

In a casserole large enough to hold the meat, add the oil and turn the heat to moderately high. Cook the meat in two batches until it has given up any remaining absorbed marinade and has browned well on all sides. Remove to a platter. Add the *aromi*—the onion, garlic, celery, carrot, basil, parsley and rosemary. Cook for several minutes, stirring frequently, until the onion becomes transparent, then return the meat and any juices to the pan along with the chili flakes, lemon zest and 2 cups of the marinade.

Continue to cook over moderately high heat until most of the wine has evaporated, then add the tomato purée. Reduce the heat to low, partially cover, and cook at the lowest simmer possible for about 3 hours. When it is done, the meat should be very tender and fall from the bone. Check the liquid in the pot from time to time and add more water or red wine if it gets too low. Season with salt and pepper.

Ladle the meat and a bit of the sauce over grilled bread rubbed with a clove of garlic, or over polenta or pasta.

Grilled Meat in Tuscany

I would be remiss in this chapter if I did not to say a word about the Tuscan love affair with the grill. I used to think grilling meat outdoors over a wood fire was a strictly North American obsession. Then I moved here and discovered what an important role it plays in the local kitchen. A Tuscan mixed grill often includes a bit of sausage; some spareribs rubbed with some salt, pepper, finely chopped rosemary and sometimes some lemon zest; pork chops; chicken and, most famously, the *bistecca*.

Often at Petraia there are long days spent working outside. The property buzzes with activity. People seem to be busy everywhere, restoring fields, ancient terraces and their stone walls, and the out-buildings. When lunchtime rolls around, it's not a quick sandwich from a paper bag that is produced. Far from it. Someone usually lights a fire in the front yard, and a short while later on goes an enormous pile of meat that seems to materialize from nowhere: ribs and sausage, huge slabs of homemade pancetta, and chops of veal and pork. A flask of Chianti and a loaf of Tuscan bread are always passed around. This is a meal that is divine in its simplicity, standard fare for the lucky Tuscan worker. I always wonder how anyone can face an afternoon of heavy labor afterwards, but that is inevitably what happens next. Unless, of course, it starts to rain.

One thing I have learned living here is that Tuscan men know how to grill meat. The other thing is that to taste a glass of homemade wine is quite a different thing here than it is in North America. Some of the best Chianti is that poured for you from an unlabeled bottle by the people who made it themselves—wine made at home with great care and expertise. It is as different from the supermarket table wine sold by the gallon and drunk by many Italians every day as a frozen apple pie is from one made at home by a skilled home baker. It is a special treat, one money simply cannot buy.

The most famous grilled meat in Tuscany is the *bistecca*, a thick slab of steak usually weighing about two pounds and similar to a T-bone or porterhouse cut. The most famous of these (the only real one, if you ask a Tuscan) comes from the Chianina Classica, one of the oldest breeds of cattle in Italy. These cows were originally raised in the Val di Chiana, south of Arezzo, where they were used for farm labor. Now they are bred in other parts of Tuscany also, and it is their meat that is prized. They are a large and very magnificent white cow that produces tender meat perfect for *bistecca*. Cooked over a hot grill, these steaks are always served *al sangue* (very rare). Forget it if you don't like rare meat, for Tuscans consider it a sin to eat or to cook these steaks any other way.

My husband and I tried our first *bistecca* more than twelve years ago, when we stumbled into a little *osteria* in the town of Sinalunga, south of Arezzo, the heart of the region famous for breeding Chianina cattle. That evening, as we came to appreciate is always the case, the place was packed. The cook shuffled out from the kitchen when we arrived and escorted us to the only empty table. She had on an attractive hairnet, bedroom slippers and a white lab coat snugly buttoned over an ample figure. I knew the minute I saw her that this was a serious cook and we were in for a good meal.

There was no printed menu, and we understood little Italian in those days. Trusting her judgment as she reeled off the menu, we nodded, and she shuffled off. We had no idea what was coming.

Soon a family-size steaming bowl of *acquacotta*, or cooked water (see the recipe on page 135), was placed before me and an equally large platter of *pici* (thick Tuscan noodles) with tomato sauce for Michael. We were famished, the food was good, and we wolfed it down. Assuming we were done, we were preparing to settle the bill when out came the cook again, this time balancing a huge *bistecca* sizzling away on top of a hot piece of *pietra ollara,* the gray-green soapstone of the Valtellina often used for cooking meat. The steak was huge, a good two inches thick, and easily a couple of pounds. It was charred black on the outside but still blue inside. Seasoned with salt, pepper and some Tuscan extra virgin olive oil, it was covered with a toss of arugula leaves. A couple of lemon wedges accompanied it.

I was well past full by this time, and besides, I was a vegetarian in those days. So was Michael. But I could tell by the look in his eyes when he saw the steak what his intentions were. He ate it. Every last bite, till he got to the bone, which he picked up and gnawed bare.

When we left the restaurant, I asked him how he felt after all the meat he'd consumed. His reply came in the form of a proposal that we pay a return visit the following evening. Now this is a man who, although he does not lack a healthy appetite, never plans his life around the next food event, unlike his wife. I was worried. He was not. He was *dead serious.* In the end I managed to talk him out of the repeat performance, but those turned out to be the last days of vegetarianism for Michael.

That is my story of how good a Tuscan *bistecca* is. I know that every Tuscan visitor who tastes the real thing here has a tale like mine. I don't know how many times since we've taken friends and relatives out for *bistecca* and heard them announce at the end of their meal, "I think that was the best steak I've ever had." I smile when I hear this, thinking of the great story they will be telling about steak in Tuscany when they get back home.

Chapter 5 · Piatti Unici · One-Dish Meals

The *piatto unico* can be a heavier casserole-type preparation before which no pasta course is required, such as the *timballo* on page 268, or a simply put together light evening supper like the *frittata* on page 278, taken after a large Sunday or holiday lunch, when appetites are faint. Either way, it is a relief to know that not every Italian meal requires multiple courses. Sometimes just one is okay, and there is no need to worry about what should come before or what should follow. A green salad, a glass of wine and maybe a piece of fruit for dessert, and you're good to go.

Alongside the examples of traditional Italian dishes in this chapter, the one course meal today often serves as the place where foreign dishes are introduced to the Italian table. For example, I have seen things like paella, bakmi goreng, sushi and curry described as *piatti unici*. It is also a label sometimes used by creative chefs to describe a novel dish of their own invention.

Timballo di Fagiano ✦ Pheasant Pie

Like all Tuscan men, our friend Alessandro has a nickname. His is Stioppo, a Tuscan slang word suggesting he is not only a hunter but a famous shot. Whenever I have a special meal to prepare, I depend on him to furnish the showstopper ingredient, be it fresh hare, pigeon, wild boar, deer or pheasant. "Now don't go buying meat at the butcher," he instructs, when he hears I have guests coming. *"I'll* bring whatever you need. Tell me, what do you want? Some boar? Pigeons? How about a nice leg of venison? *Dimmi*, Susan." Although I love all the game he brings us, perhaps my favorite is one of his freshly caught pheasants, which I prepare in a *timballo*.

Each year we host a dinner for all of the people who've helped us over the course of the year. Alessandro usually dictates the menu for this big event, which is the highlight of our summer. We'll muse over the details for several weeks in advance. I mentioned to him one day that if he brought me a pheasant I could make a *timballo*, thinking this might be an impressive main course. I got his famous look, which I translated (correctly) to mean, "Real men don't eat *timballo*." Instead, he brought me rabbits, boar, a few plump chickens from his mother's flock, pigeons, a whole flock of *uccellini*, or "little birds," caught on his annual hunting trip to Calabria and a gorgeous leg of venison. Needless to say, it was a busy day in the kitchen.

Anyone who has seen the movie *Big Night* has probably dreamt of making, or at least tasting, a *timballo*. This special dish may sound like a lot of trouble, but the beauty is that the various elements—the pheasant, the sauce, the noodles and the pastry—can be prepared ahead of time and easily assembled and baked at the last minute. This way you can impress your guests while at the same time serving a casserole-type meal.

This dish is very special when made with a freshly caught pheasant, but if you can't find a pheasant you can use a rabbit or even chicken.

SERVES 4

For the pheasant

2 tsp butter

¼ cup olive oil

1 onion, finely chopped

1 carrot, finely chopped

1 garlic clove, minced

A sprig of fresh rosemary

A few fresh sage leaves, finely chopped

1 bay leaf

2 juniper berries, crushed

A few flakes of hot chili pepper

1 pheasant, cut into 6 pieces

For the sauce

28 g (1 oz) dried mushrooms (porcini or shiitake work well)

1 cup hot chicken broth

2 tbsp all-purpose flour

1 cup white wine, preferably a Riesling

2 tbsp butter

1 tbsp liquid honey

Salt and pepper to taste

For the pasta

Pappardelle noodles, made with 1 large egg and 140 g (5 oz)
(1 cup) all-purpose flour, following the instructions on pages
168 to 173 (or ½ lb store-bought fresh or dried egg noodles)

For the pastry

280 g (10 oz) puff pastry (see page 390 or use store-bought)

For the pheasant

Heat the butter and oil together in a casserole over moderate heat and add all the ingredients except the pheasant. Lay the pheasant pieces on top. Cover and simmer for 15 minutes. Turn the pheasant pieces over, cover and cook for another 15 minutes. In the meantime, for the sauce, soak the mushrooms in the broth for half an hour.

Remove the pheasant to a platter. Leave the vegetables in the casserole to make the sauce.

For the sauce

MAKE-AHEAD NOTE
The pheasant and the sauce can be cooked ahead and will keep well in the fridge for one day.

Remove the mushrooms from the broth. Strain the broth through a coffee filter and rinse the mushrooms to remove any dirt. Gently pat them dry. Cut them into small pieces if they seem too large.

Put the casserole with the vegetables over moderate heat. Stir in the flour and let it cook for a couple of minutes. Add the mushrooms and their soaking liquid, then add the rest of the sauce ingredients. Simmer, uncovered, for 20 minutes or until the mushrooms are tender and the sauce has reduced somewhat. Remove the bay leaf. Increase the heat and reduce the sauce by half. Remove from the heat and let cool.

For the noodles

Cook the noodles for 3 minutes in boiling salted water until partly done. Drain under warm water, mix with a little butter and let cool.

To assemble and bake

Preheat the oven to 375°F/190°C.

In a buttered deep baking dish (a large soufflé dish works well), place half the noodles. Lay the pheasant pieces on top of the noodles, then cover them with the mushroom sauce. Top with the remaining noodles.

On a lightly floured surface, roll out the pastry to a thickness of about ¼ inch. It should be wide enough to cover your baking dish with at least an inch to spare. Cut a disk from the dough wide enough to fit over your baking dish. Gather the trimmings and roll them into a long rope about ½ inch wide. (If at any point you find your pastry is getting too warm and limp, place it on a parchment-lined baking sheet and transfer to the freezer for 5 to 10 minutes to firm up before proceeding.) Insert the rope around the inside edge of the baking dish, on top of the pheasant. Place the pastry disk on top of the rope. Cut a chimney in the middle of the pie for the steam to escape.

Bake for half an hour or until the pastry is golden brown.

Il Tortino di Verza, Patate e Mozzarella
◆ A Potato, Cabbage and Cheese Pie

Again and again these three elements—potatoes, cabbage and cheese—appear center stage in the Alpine menus of Italy, France, Switzerland and Austria. This pie is a wonderful celebration of these ingredients and makes a satisfying one-dish winter meal. It is also a great way to introduce cooked cabbage to those members of your family who claim not to like it. There is a good chance they will change their minds after they taste this delicious pie.

If you don't feel like making the pizza dough from scratch, you can use store-bought pizza dough.

SERVES 4

For the dough

1 recipe pizza dough (page 68)

For the filling

2 large potatoes (any kind will do)

6 Savoy cabbage leaves

2 tbsp extra virgin olive oil, plus extra for coating pan

1 garlic clove

A few flakes of hot chili pepper (optional)

140 g (5 oz) mozzarella, fontina or any other good melting cheese,
thinly sliced or grated

½ cup grated Parmesan cheese

1 tsp poppy seeds or ¼ tsp cumin seeds (optional)

Preheat the oven to 500°F/260°C.

Boil the potatoes in salted water until they are tender. Reserve the water. Peel and cube the potatoes.

Return the potato water to a boil and blanch the cabbage leaves for 1 to 2 minutes. Drain them and refresh under cold water to stop the cooking. Dry the leaves well and cut out the thick center rib from each leaf.

Heat the olive oil in a large frying pan over moderately high heat. Sauté the garlic with the chili flakes, if using, until the garlic starts to turn golden. Remove the garlic. Add the cabbage leaves and cook them until tender—about 2 minutes.

Coat a large pie plate or pizza pan with a thin layer of olive oil. Using your hands, stretch the pizza dough into a disk large enough to cover the bottom and sides of your pan (see instructions for stretching pizza dough on page 69). Place the dough over the bottom of the pan and up the sides. Spread the cabbage leaves on top and arrange the potatoes over them. Spread the mozzarella over the potatoes and top with the grated Parmesan. Sprinkle the seeds over the top if using.

Bake for 10 minutes, then reduce the heat to 450°F/230°C. Bake for another 20 minutes. The cheese should start to bubble and turn golden, and any visible dough should be nicely browned.

Fonduta Valdostana ✦ Fondue from the Val d'Aosta

Like its French and Swiss cousins Comté and Gruyère, fontina is a cheese with exceptional melting qualities. The name of this classic Valdotain melted-cheese specialty—*fonduta*—is derived from the verb that is similar in both Italian and French (*fondere* in Italian, *fondre* in French) meaning "to melt."

Like its French and Swiss neighbors on the other side of the Alps, Italy's smallest region, the Val d'Aosta, has its own version of fondue. Made with the region's fontina cheese, it is a melted-cheese dish that, unlike most French and Swiss versions, is enriched with egg yolks. The yolks give it a creamier texture and a beautiful golden color that is appropriate for a recipe that comes from the sunny side of the Alps.

Fonduta is wonderfully versatile and forms a staple of the Aosta kitchen. It has become so popular throughout Italy that it is canned and sold in almost every supermarket. It is eaten the way you would a traditional fondue: as a one-dish meal along with some crusty bread and steamed potatoes. But ingenious and resourceful Italian cooks also use it to produce a wide variety of other dishes, and it has a versatility in the kitchen not dissimilar to béchamel, hollandaise or Mornay sauce. You can ladle it over asparagus, fish, steamed vegetables, gnocchi, poached eggs or grilled meat. You name it; the sky seems to be the limit. Once you master the art of making it, I am sure you will find many ways to enjoy it.

I've provided a few ideas for using *fonduta* on page 275, but if you are interested in finding more, you might want to visit the fontina cheese producers' website, at **www.fontinacoop.com**, where there are many more mouth-watering recipes. They will mail you a booklet in English if you ask.

SERVES 4

2 tbsp butter

3 tbsp all-purpose flour

1¾ cup hot milk

400 g (14 oz) young fontina, cut into small dice

4 egg yolks, lightly beaten

In a heavy-bottomed saucepan, glazed terra-cotta pot or enameled cast-iron fondue pan, over moderate heat, melt the butter. Whisk in the flour and cook for a few minutes, stirring constantly. Do not let the flour brown. Add the hot milk and the diced cheese. Reduce the heat to low and stir constantly with a wooden spoon until the cheese has melted. Remove the pan from the heat and rapidly whisk in the egg yolks. Return to low heat and cook for just a couple of minutes, while continuing to stir, just long enough that the *fonduta* thickens a little bit more as the yolks cook and becomes shiny. If you overcook it and the cheese coagulates into a gluey mass, you can correct it by stirring in a little more hot milk.

I take *fonduta* to the table in the same pan it was made in, along with a bowl of new potatoes steamed in their skins (page 315) and lots of crusty white bread (page 31). I use a tea light burner to keep it warm while guests help themselves by dipping bread and potatoes into it.

Variation

If you own a jar of truffle butter, stir a dab into your *fonduta* just before serving.

Other Uses for Fonduta

- Use it as a filling for agnolotti (page 204).
- Ladle it over steamed asparagus or cauliflower.
- Thin it with a little milk and ladle over polenta. Bake in a 450°F/230°C oven until golden and bubbly.
- Ladle it over *Spinaci alla Fiorentina* (page 305).
- Drain a jar of roasted Italian red peppers preserved in oil, or a can of roasted Spanish *piquillo* peppers. Place the peppers in a single layer in a baking dish and top with *fonduta*. Bake in a 350°F/175°C oven until the *fonduta* is golden and beginning to bubble.

Polenta con Baccalà ✦ Polenta with Salt Cod and Cream

I first ate a version of this dish in Ollomont, at the Locanda Della Vecchia Miniera. Ollomont is a small village about halfway up the Valpelline, nestled amidst the highest peaks of Europe not far from the San Bernardo pass. Definitely off the beaten track, but like so many isolated villages up and down the Italian peninsula, it boasts an exquisite restaurant. Here you eat carefully prepared dishes made using strictly local ingredients. This is the kind of food you'd pay a small fortune for in many of the world's capitals. My three-course lunch that day, accompanied by one of the excellent local white wines, cost less than 25 euros.

I arrived late on a weekday, hungry and unannounced. Only one other table was occupied, by an elegant elderly couple who were halfway into what looked and smelled like a feast from out of this world.

I knew I'd come to the right place. All the signs were there: an out-of-the-way location but an up-to-date room, good smells wafting out of a modern kitchen visible from the dining room, a friendly welcome from the owner and a pair of blissfully happy customers. The chef's wife was the waitress. Their young daughter returned home from nursery school shortly after I arrived and immediately began to help out *la mamma* in the dining room. I wondered as I watched if I might find her running the place were I to come back in twenty years' time. My guess would be yes.

The highlight of the meal was a plate of two divine yellow dumplings containing bits of salt cod. These were served on a bed of the local acidified cream called *brossa*. *Brossa* is a by-product of the making of fontina cheese and is similar to a light *crème fraîche*. After the first bite, I realized that salt cod and polenta were a match made in heaven.

SERVES 4

450 g (1 lb) salt cod, soaked (see page 229)
1 onion, minced
2 tbsp olive oil
1 garlic clove, minced
1 tsp finely chopped fresh rosemary
4 cups hot water
1 cup cornmeal
1 cup *crème fraîche* or heavy cream

To finish

Very small sprigs of fresh rosemary or finely chopped fresh parsley
Extra virgin olive oil

Skin the cod and remove any bones. Cut into 1-inch chunks. Set aside.

In a large, heavy-bottomed saucepan, sauté the onion in the olive oil over moderate heat for several minutes, stirring a few times, until the onion begins to wilt. Add the garlic and rosemary and cook for another minute or two. Add the hot water and bring to a boil. Turn the heat down and begin to stir in the cornmeal, a bit at a time, stirring all the while. Cook, stirring constantly, for about 10 minutes, until the polenta begins to thicken. Add the cod and continue to stir until the polenta is quite thick, 25 to 30 more minutes.

To assemble

Warm 4 serving dishes. Gently heat the *crème fraîche* or cream, being careful not to allow it to boil. Spoon a serving of the polenta into each dish. Drizzle some cream over top of it. Garnish with a small sprig of fresh rosemary or some finely chopped parsley. Drizzle with extra virgin olive oil and serve.

Uova con Salsa di Pomodoro
✦ Eggs Poached in Tomato Sauce

This recipe is perfect for a simple weeknight supper for two or a lazy-weekend brunch. It is a breeze to make, especially if you have some homemade tomato sauce in your pantry.

SERVES 2

For the tomato sauce
    2 tbsp extra virgin olive oil
    ½ onion, minced

1 carrot, finely diced

1 celery stalk, finely chopped

1 garlic clove, minced

2 tbsp finely chopped fresh parsley

450 g (1 lb) ripe plum tomatoes, peeled, seeded and diced

Salt and pepper to taste

To finish

2 free-range organic eggs

2 thick slices crusty bread, grilled and rubbed with a clove of garlic

Several leaves of fresh basil to garnish

In a sauté pan, heat the oil over moderate heat. Add the onion, carrot, celery, garlic and parsley. Cook, stirring from time to time, until the onion begins to wilt, about 10 minutes. Add the tomatoes and simmer for 20 minutes. Season with salt and pepper.

Crack the eggs over the tomato sauce and cover the pan. Cook over moderate heat until the eggs are soft-poached, 4 to 5 minutes. Place a piece of toast on each plate and top with some tomato sauce and a poached egg. Top with a leaf of basil.

Frittata con Fiore di Cavolo Nero
◆ Frittata with Cavolo Nero Flowers

Early spring can be deceptive at La Petraia. Sunny skies and high temperatures often prevail. Winter coats and sweaters are traded in almost overnight for short sleeves and sandals, and our forest is finally silenced of hunters' shots. The lizards emerge from their winter slumber to bathe on hot, dry terraces, and the families of *rondini* (swallows) return, as they do every year, to nest in the beams above my summer kitchen. How many generations of this family have called Petraia home? Thousands? Have they been nesting here since Etruscan times?

Along with the *rondini* comes the annual *invasione*, the onslaught of tourists, and our year begins in earnest. The quiet little town of Radda fills up with German, Dutch, Swiss, English and North American visitors. Wine shops, restaurants and bars, the kind of places that have been closed all winter (no respectable local would be caught dead in them), throw open their doors and fill up with customers. It gets hard to find a parking spot outside the town's medieval walls, and our little Co-op grocery store has a half-hour lineup at the cash register. The winding country roads are more hazardous now, crowded by late-model foreign-plated convertibles and SUVs, groups of walkers, cyclists and even scooters. Their fuel, more often than not, is a local Chianti Classico.

I am always challenged to make splendid what I have in this, our most frugal of seasons. Last year's winter stores of squash, potatoes, beets, onions and garlic are dwindling if not gone. While local markets are full of late-spring and summer vegetables from southern Italy—deep purple Sicilian eggplants, fava beans, the sweetest cherry tomatoes, artichokes, cucumbers and zucchini—the Tuscan *orto*, especially one like mine that lives on top of a mountain, is still recovering from a long, hard winter. My potatoes, peas, favas, onions, artichokes, asparagus and garlic are barely beginning to sprout. All that is edible is what managed to survive in the ground over the winter, at times covered in a few feet of snow. It is that brief corner of the year when eating seasonally and locally doesn't feel so instinctive. I have to exert more than a bit of control, seduced by that lovely-looking stuff coming up from the south and hungry for it after a long winter. But my own garden is really just around the corner, so I wait it out, in the meantime consoling myself with what I have.

When I stop to think about it, what I do have now is quite astonishing. Wild asparagus grows just over the hill, and wild greens (*insalata di campo*), in season only briefly, sprout in the fields. Our streams are bursting with spicy watercress and mint, and the blossoms of the acacia trees are coming out, a seasonal delicacy when lightly battered and fried. Last year's *cavolo nero* is going to seed in my *orto*, producing brilliant yellow florets. Although Tuscans turn up their nose at them in favor of their beloved *porcini*, *champignons* are popping up fresh each morning in the fields. I have a wealth of bitter but good winter lettuce, not to mention the jars of bright red tomato sauce lining my shelves, last summer's sun in a bottle. Things are not so sad after all.

Our guests often prefer to dine *al fresco* at this time of year as the sun rises and sets a little later each day. The outdoor tables and umbrellas are retrieved from winter storage and arranged on the stone piazza in front of the house. Here is the view that originally sold Petraia to us: Chianti's forested hillsides, interrupted only here and there by neatly tended vineyards, the picture-perfect hill towns of Radda and Volpaia, medieval castle towers and Siena's *campanile* in the distance. From here I have heard more than one guest pronounce, "I feel like I'm in a movie sitting here." Our fields are brilliant green, not yet parched by summer's heat, and lined with bright yellow *ginestre* (broom) that grows wild along their perimeters. The wisteria that climbs willy-nilly over the old stone house is in full bloom and perfume, as are countless other blossoms and spring flowers in the old stone terraces.

I make this frittata using those yellow flowers of last year's *cavolo nero*, or Tuscan black kale. I blanch a large handful of them, attached to about an inch of their green stems, for just a minute in boiling salted water before stopping their cooking in ice cold water. In the meantime I beat together 4 or 5 fresh eggs, seasoned with sea salt and freshly ground pepper. To the eggs I stir in the kale flowers, carefully drained and dried in a clean kitchen towel.

I heat some oil in a large nonstick frying pan and sauté a minced onion and clove of garlic briefly. I pour the egg and flower mixture in and cook over moderate heat for about 10 minutes or until the egg has set. I place a large serving plate on top of the pan and invert the frittata onto it. I slide it back into the pan to briefly cook the other side before serving.

A slice of frittata topped with a dollop of homemade tomato sauce (see previous recipe, page 277) and a sprig of fresh mint alongside a basket of crusty bread and a salad of winter greens makes an easy lunch or supper dish. Because I am so proud of the flavor of the eggs my hens produce, I always try to offer guests a frittata at some point during their stay. Sometimes it appears as a small cube, skewered by a piece of whole wheat spaghetti as part of an antipasto platter. Or it is served in a fat wedge, smothered in tomato sauce and fresh herbs for breakfast. While you may be hard pressed to find the flowers of Tuscan *cavolo nero*, there are plenty of good substitutes. Try broccoli florets, fava beans, spring onions or asparagus.

Chapter 6 Contorni e Intermezzi ✤ Vegetable Sides and Salads

One of the things I enjoy most about living where I do is the ability, year-round, to go to the garden to see what dinner will be. In the absence of guests, our meals are largely vegetarian. We save our game, pork, poultry and rabbit to share with visitors. My husband and I were vegetarians in previous lives and appreciate a respite from a meal where an animal has been sacrificed. Instead, we slaughter a plant or two. For the lover of animals and plants it is hard to say which is worse.

As a Canadian, I'm accustomed to a limited growing season, so the ability to grow food in the dead of winter is a miracle to me. In mid-November I pull up the last of my tomatoes, eggplants and peppers, but the winter garden is just getting started. I have leeks, onions, lettuces, cabbages, broccoli, beets, kohlrabi, turnips, fennel, celery, parsnips, carrots, cardoons and Brussels sprouts to keep us going until early spring, when fava beans, potatoes, peas and asparagus begin to appear.

There is always an *orto* to adore in Italy, no matter where you are. If you take the fast train from Florence to Rome, as it begins its creep into that ancient city, you can see, amidst the ruins alongside the tracks, lovingly tended vegetable plots. How, you might wonder, can anything grow here? The pollution must be enough to squelch any vitality this primal dirt might have. Apparently not. Even in a big old city like this, where gorgeous *primizie* (the first and best vegetables of the season) are found year-round in shops on almost every street corner, people still stubbornly grow their own. Most people I know have at least one, usually two or three bits of land somewhere. Communal vegetable gardens are common, and seeds are saved and exchanged amongst avid gardeners, local varieties being preferred over modern hybrids. My own *orto* is full of heirloom plants that I have grown from seeds and seedlings given to me to me by friends—a lemon tree from Sorrento and a loquat from Salerno, caper plants, peppers, gourds, tomatoes, melons, flowers, all growing more gifts.

Thankfully, the vegetable in Italy, like the child, is adored and worshipped in a thousand and one ways. My own love affair with this country began in her markets. Long before I came here to live, I was a frequent visitor, dreaming of what it would be like to live here, to buy, cook and eat such amazing vegetables. This is a country that begins in the highest Alps of Europe and stretches a long reach south to within just a few miles of the African coast. There is little call for imported produce. Most shoppers look for the vegetables grown close to home, labeled *nostrano* ("ours" or "local"). These are always the freshest, cheapest and most trusted. "Are your melons any good?" a shopper asks the beautiful elderly woman, an organic grower with a stall at the market I frequent most Saturdays. "Well, they're small still, a bit early maybe," responds the vendor with a troubled brow and a sigh. But her face lights up when she points to a crate of tomatoes. "But try these—they're perfect. These ones here, the pink ones." Her husband, who up until this point has been occupied with another customer, provides a recipe. "Slice them thin and have them with a sprinkle of salt, a slice of fresh mozzarella, some basil and a drizzle of our olive oil." Like most Tuscan men, he comes with a good recipe attached and will happily provide excellent ingredients, be they game, foraged mushrooms or lovingly tended vegetables from his plot. Buying locally here brings trust, an honest exchange in return for satisfied and loyal customers.

"L'orto mi fa morto."

In the late fall the first citrus fruit from Sicily begins to appear in our Chianti markets, a sweet, sun-filled joy for the shortest days of the year. They are soon followed by fava beans, peas, potatoes, strawberries and asparagus, preceding our own Tuscan spring. Then come the stone fruit and summer parade of nightshades, melons and summer squash. Peppers soon follow, and shortly after come the squash, pumpkins, cabbages, apples, pears, fennel, grapes, quince and winter lettuce. All too soon the citrus begins to arrive from the south and the season starts again in earnest.

So why grow your own? Why be bothered to plant a garden? The answer to these questions every gardener knows. Best gets better when you grow your own. Now that I own some land here and have my own *orto*, I go to the market only to buy seedlings to plant or some young birds for my *pollaio*. Only occasionally do I need some fruit or a few vegetables—especially in the leaner months of the year. Then, as I examine the produce with the critical eye of a grower, I think how lucky I am to have my own garden. You see how one becomes an Italian vegetable snob. The time from the plot to the pot is critical to the taste of a vegetable.

I have arranged this chapter on a seasonal basis—starting at Easter, the beginning of the *orto* year, and following the flow of produce through the next twelve months.

Insalata di Campo Germinata ✦ Sprouted Field Salad

MARCH

As Easter approaches, my winter *orto* is laid to rest—the last of the leeks, *cavolo nero*, carrots, turnips and other winter vegetables are dug up or plowed under. The earth is turned, allowed a brief respite to rejuvenate for a spring planting in a few weeks. In a separate plot, *fave* (which the Tuscans refer to as *baccelli*), peas, potatoes, asparagus, rhubarb, garlic and onions are sprouting. But pickings are still slim, so I join the throngs of Italians who take to abandoned pastureland and forests in search of wild greens and asparagus.

In our own fields, varieties of wild mustard, cabbage, peas, mint, fennel, onions and garlic sprout at this time of year. Wild asparagus grows in the forest near a quarry not far away. Sometimes, at the crack of dawn (the early bird getting the worm), I load the dogs in the car and go asparagus hunting. The asparagus that grows wild in Tuscany is quite different from the kind my father taught us about as children, the kind that grew wild near Ontario side roads. There, wild asparagus looked and tasted pretty much the same as the kind grown at home in the vegetable garden or bought in the store. Here, it is a long, spindly purple shoot with a very mild taste. It is a highly prized delicacy, and it takes a lot of work to collect enough of the slender stalks to make a meal. But it is relaxing and enjoyable to be out with the dogs early on a beautiful spring morning.

Asparagus picking is an activity women in Tuscany take to with as much passion and determination as their men take to hunting. I'd seen them for years along country roads with plastic shopping bags, walking sticks and high rubber boots. The sticks and boots I understood were the prescribed anti-viper apparatus. But I couldn't figure out what was going into those shopping bags. Now I have joined them and I know. This is no longer a sport reserved for the hunched elderly widow dressed in black.

The passion for gathering wild greens is growing and is shared by young and old alike, although largely reserved for women. Ask a Tuscan man where the *asparagi* grow and you'll usually be told to ask his better half.

Apart from the wild greens I use in this salad, I toss in some sprouted legumes along with a little fresh green garlic from my garden. This is the time of year I use up any dried mung beans, lentils or chick peas from the last harvest by sprouting them. Some of these sprouts are destined for my *orto*, to be planted for next year's crop. I make this early-spring salad out of what I have left after the garden has been looked after.

You'll need to start the legumes a day or two in advance, so some planning is required to make this recipe. I usually have a sheet of sprouts going in my pantry at this time of year and reach for a handful at almost every meal to toss into a salad like this one or to add to a sauté that will dress a pasta.

To make this salad using domestically grown greens, it's best to use baby greens of a sturdy variety that will hold their own against the legumes. Baby black cabbage, broccoli, spinach, arugula and radicchio work well. Here in Tuscany one finds mixtures of these rough-looking (but delicious) greens in the markets in late winter. They are called *insalata di campo* and are a sure sign spring is on the way.

SERVES 4

½ cup dried lentils, mung beans or chick peas
A mix of baby salad greens, such as baby black cabbage, radicchio,
    arugula, fennel, spinach
A few asparagus spears, steamed until tender and cut into
    1-inch pieces
1 small red onion, thinly sliced

Finely chopped fresh green garlic to taste (or ½ garlic clove,
    finely chopped)
Finely chopped fresh mint leaves
Extra virgin olive oil
White or red wine vinegar
Salt and pepper to taste

To sprout the legumes, soak them overnight in enough water to barely cover. By the next morning, they should have soaked up all the water and feel dry. Cover them again with water and drain immediately. Place a damp tea towel on a baking sheet and lay the legumes on top of it in a single layer. Cover with another damp towel and leave in a cool, dark place until they start to sprout—usually 24 hours. Check periodically, and spray the towel covering them with water if it has dried out. Use the legumes as soon as they have sprouted.

Add the sprouts to the greens, asparagus and onion in a bowl. Toss with the garlic, mint, oil and vinegar to taste and season with salt and pepper. If you run across some, a few cherry tomatoes are nice in this salad.

Baccelli e Pancetta ◆ Stewed Fava Beans with Pancetta
APRIL

The appearance of fresh fava beans in the market marks the beginning of the spectacle of spring vegetables and is a great cause for celebration amongst Italians. At this time of year you can find fresh pecorino made with the milk of those lucky ewes that graze on spring herbs and grasses. Fresh pecorino and fava beans are considered a match made in heaven, and huge piles of favas are unceremoniously dumped onto dining tables alongside a wheel of young pecorino to make a feast. If you happen to visit an

Italian market at this time of year, look around towards midday at the outdoor tables of local bars. You're likely to spot a shopper or two who can't wait to get home chomping down on a few freshly shelled beans and some new pecorino cheese while nursing an *aperitivo*. Simplicity at its best.

As the bean plants mature, the favas lose their sweet tenderness and develop a thicker inner skin. Then they are stewed with a little prosciutto and some broth rather than eaten raw.

SERVES 4

1 kg (2¼ lb) fresh unshelled fava beans

1 tbsp extra virgin olive oil

56 g (2 oz) pancetta, cubed

1 onion, minced

A few flakes of hot chili pepper

A pinch of sugar

Salt and pepper to taste

½ cup chicken broth

1 head iceberg lettuce, chopped (optional)

Shell the fava beans. If your beans are still young, the inner skin will not yet have developed and you can use them as they are. If they are a bit older, as is usually the case, you will also need to remove the thin inner skin surrounding each bean. This skin slips off easily when gently rubbed.

Heat the oil in a sauté pan over moderate heat and add the pancetta, onion and chili flakes. Cook for about 10 minutes, stirring now and then, until the onions wilt and become transparent and the pancetta starts to brown. Add the shelled beans with the sugar and season with salt and pepper. Cook until the beans are tender—about 10 minutes. Add some of the broth from time to time if the pan seems too dry. At the end of the cooking time, throw in the chopped lettuce, if using, and cook for a few seconds, just to wilt.

Variation
Replace the fava beans with freshly shelled spring peas, or combine the two.

Sformatini di Piselli ◆ Individual Spring Pea Flans
MAY THROUGH JUNE

A *sformato*, an elegant molded vegetable dish, is often served as a *piatto di mezzo*—a course to act as a bridge between other more substantial courses in a formal meal. It can also stand alone, making a stylish luncheon dish or brunch alongside a crispy green salad or cheese plate.

Sformati are made out of just about every vegetable imaginable, but in the spring I love to use fresh green peas. This recipe is based on one I found in Lorenza de' Medici's wonderful book *The Villa Table*. Lorenza is our nearest neighbor to the southeast, and there is nothing we like better on a sunny Sunday than to strap on the hiking boots and trek along the top of the Chianti mountain range, working up an appetite as we go, to arrive famished at her family's splendid estate, Badia a Coltibuono. There we enjoy a wonderful lunch at their *osteria*, run by her son. As far as we are concerned, this is one of the best places to taste a real Tuscan steak—the famous *bistecca*. Of course we take our dogs with us on these marvelous walks. Curled up exhausted in the shade outside the restaurant with a bowl of fresh water, they rest up. But before the hike back home they get to enjoy their own fabulous Sunday lunch as they make light work of the awesome bones from our steak. The last time I was there, I noticed two pretty white cows grazing on a lush mountain slope outside the restaurant. Inquiring as to their future, I was told to come back in a few months, when I would find them on the menu.

SERVES 4 TO 6

2 tbsp extra virgin olive oil
450 g (1 lb) shelled peas, blanched, cooled in ice water and drained
1 tsp sugar
Salt and pepper to taste
3 eggs, lightly beaten

For the tomato sauce
2 tbsp butter
4 plum tomatoes, peeled, seeded and chopped (or 4 canned
    tomatoes, seeded and chopped)
A pinch of sugar
Salt and pepper to taste
Fresh basil leaves to garnish

Preheat the oven to 350°F/175°C. Butter 4 to 6 individual soufflé or crème caramel molds. Put a kettle of water on to boil.

Heat the oil in a pan over low heat and add the peas. Season with the sugar, salt and pepper. Cook until the peas are tender, about 10 minutes, then purée in a blender. Pass the purée through the fine disk of a food mill or a fine sieve. Whisk in the eggs.

Pour into the buttered molds and place in a roasting pan. Add enough hot water to come halfway up the sides of the molds. Bake for 20 to 25 minutes, until the flan is set and a piece of spaghetti or a cake tester inserted in the center comes out clean. Remove the molds from the roasting pan.

While the *sformati* are baking, make the tomato sauce. Melt the butter in a pan over moderately low heat. Add the chopped tomatoes and sugar and cook for 20 minutes, stirring occasionally. Season with salt and pepper. Transfer to a food mill or blender and purée.

Loosen the *sformati* from the molds by dipping them in a bowl of ice water. Turn out onto serving plates. Ladle the tomato sauce over the top and garnish with the basil.

Patate, Cipolle e Piselli al Vapore
+ Oven-steamed New Potatoes, Onions and Peas

May through June

Peas are one of my first crops, and I keenly monitor every move they make after I plant in February. First the seeds burst forth from the earth and a bit of green graces a soil that not so long ago had several feet of snow cover. Next shoots appear, eager to climb, so we cut trellises from branches in the woods for them to scale. Then come the delicate white-and-purple blossoms, and when they've matured and been blown offstage by the wind, the pods finally present themselves. The peas inside take a few weeks to fatten up before they are ready to harvest in early June.

After all this time, the right moment to pick peas seems to come and go in a minute. In just a couple of weeks they are finished. Fortunately, this is a vegetable that takes well to freezing, so I plant lots. I freeze them in small packages and use them almost year-round. A few succulent green peas can make a pantry supper sing (see the pasta on page 177) or, thrown on top a mound of *ragù*-laden homemade noodles, add splendid color and flavor. The pea flans on page 290 are always showstoppers. Topped with a dab of our sweet homemade tomato sauce and a basil leaf, they are as vibrant in color as they are in flavor.

I plant several kinds—sugar snaps for salads, lots of the traditional shell peas that are suitable for freezing and a lovely French variety that produces tiny peas that are bursting with flavor. These jewels always disappear before I manage to turn around. And because I save seeds, the best-looking specimens never end up on my table. Dried in the sun and put away in the *cantina*, they are responsible for next year's crop.

This is how I like to use our fresh young peas: a combination of new potatoes, spring peas and spring onions tossed with a drizzle of extra virgin olive oil, a pinch of sea salt and freshly ground pepper. Wrapped in foil and steamed in the oven, they are a simple, quick and delicious accompaniment to spring rabbit (see page 236 for rabbit with gorgonzola cheese), chicken or lamb.

Use only the freshest peas and try before you buy. They should be bright green, tender to the bite and sweet to taste. The pods should not be too swollen, nor should they be too thin. The perfect pea pod is pleasingly plump, but still on the slender side of bursting.

There is not much need for precise measures in this recipe. Just mix enough of everything to suit your pleasure.

New potatoes
1 or 2 spring onions or baby leeks per person
Extra virgin olive oil
Salt and pepper to taste
Shelled fresh peas

Preheat the oven to 350°F/175°C.

Wash the potatoes but don't peel them. Clean the onions or leeks well, removing any tough outer leaves, and leaving an inch or two of the green stem. Dry well with a clean towel. Place the potatoes and onions in a bowl.

Drizzle with enough olive oil to coat the vegetables, season with salt and pepper and, using clean hands, mix everything together. Prick each potato in two or three places with a skewer and transfer the lot to a sheet of foil. Wrap loosely, making sure the package is closed securely but has room to expand. Place in a baking dish and bake for 20 minutes or until the potatoes and onions are verging on tenderness (the exact time will depend on the size of your vegetables). Remove from the oven, undo the package and add the peas. Wrap up again and bake for another 5 minutes or so. The potatoes and onions should be tender and the peas cooked.

Zucchine Bollite ◆ Boiled Zucchini

SUMMER

Boiling vegetables has fallen from grace in the past few decades, but this method of cooking is still appreciated in Italy. I am often surprised by what a popular choice the boiled vegetable course is in restaurants. At lunch, especially, people often will base an entire meal around a platter of boiled vegetables—potatoes, green beans, carrots and zucchini being the usual choices. There may be a bit of tuna preserved in olive oil, a boiled egg or a thin slice of roast meat as well, but the meal is about the vegetable.

This is the way I like to eat zucchini. It's something that grows like a weed all summer, and I never seemed to find any good use for it until I discovered the Italian genius of simply boiling it. Many zucchini recipes call for stuffing them with meat or cheese, deep-frying them or grating them into something or other—in other words, doing anything to disguise a prolific vegetable using time-consuming and complicated procedures. This recipe lets them stand on their own.

The preparation seems to want a rather decadent amount of butter, but don't skimp here—the butter is a big part of the secret. And don't throw away the broth. Use it to make one of the whole wheat loaves in the bread chapter and you won't have to add any fat to the recipe. The broth can also be used for risotto.

SERVES 4

4 medium zucchini
½ cup (1 stick) butter
1 tbsp baking soda
Salt to taste
Olive oil, sea salt and chopped fresh mint to garnish

Cut the zucchini into slices about ½ inch thick. Place them in a saucepan with enough water to cover them by an inch. Remove the zucchini. Add the butter, baking soda and salt to the water and bring it to a boil. Put the zucchini back in the water and cook for about 5 minutes or until very tender (see note at right). Drain, reserving the butter-rich broth for another use. Serve on a platter, drizzled with the best-quality extra virgin olive oil and garnished with the sea salt and fresh mint.

Cooking time will depend both on the freshness and size of your zucchini. A freshly picked or smaller vegetable will need less time to cook. The baking soda helps the vegetable retain its color.

Verdure alla Griglia ⋄ Grilled Summer Vegetables

SUMMER

Zucchini, eggplants and peppers are the usual suspects for grilling. A gas, wood or charcoal barbecue, stovetop grill or grill pan can all be used. Zucchini and eggplant should be cleaned and sliced about ¼ inch thick. A mandoline makes this job easy if you own one. Peppers should be cut in half (or quarters if they are huge), and the white pith and seeds removed.

Toss the vegetables together in enough olive oil to coat, and season with salt. Leave them to marinate while the grill gets hot. Brush some more oil over the grill and lay on the vegetables. Cook for several minutes, until they are tender, turning once at the halfway point. Zucchini and eggplant will be cooked first, peppers will take a bit longer. Serve with a sprinkle of finely chopped fresh herbs—I like mint with zucchini and basil with peppers. Eggplant loves basil, mint or oregano. A few drops of balsamic vinegar are nice to finish.

Verdure Ripiene ◆ Stuffed Vegetables (Eggplant, Zucchini, Tomatoes and Onions)

SUMMER AND FALL

Brutte ma buone—ugly but good—stuffed vegetables are deceptive. They are for sale in almost every *gastronomia* in Italy and often look withered, leaden and not very appetizing. I ignored them for years. But when I started to grow my own vegetables, I rapidly found myself facing the dilemma of an overabundant plot. So I gave away the surplus—things like eggplants, onions, zucchini and tomatoes. I was often told by the recipients of these gifts that their plan was to stuff them, and I realized that stuffed vegetables must taste good, despite their appearance. So I started asking for recipes. Each reply was unique, nothing precise or measured, just a bit of this, a handful of that. Some used ground meat, others grains such as rice and *farro*, still others bread crumbs. This was obviously not brain surgery. I was inspired.

Stuffing vegetables is something done off the cuff by most Italians, using whatever is at hand, the main ingredient being common sense. Like stuffing a turkey, everyone has their own family way, but there are always a few simple rules.

How to stuff a vegetable

This stuffing contains no meat but tastes like it does for those vegetarians hankering after the taste and texture of meat. Choose the best small to medium-sized vegetables. In Italy, large eggplants and zucchini are considered over the hill—*avanzi*, not fit for human consumption, reserved for the livestock or left to go to seed for next year's crop.

Cut the vegetable in half. If you have a long zucchini or long eggplant, cut it in half lengthwise, like a boat. If it's an onion, tomato or round eggplant or zucchini, cut it in half crosswise. Scoop out the inside using a spoon. Leave enough of a shell—⅛ to ¼ of an inch, depending on the size of your vegetable—to create a hull that is sturdy enough to hold your filling.

Chop the flesh into small pieces, add some minced onion and garlic and sauté in olive oil—enough to coat the bottom of your pan—until tender.

Combine the sautéed flesh with some dry bread crumbs, an egg, some grated Parmesan cheese, finely chopped fresh herbs (basil, mint, sage, rosemary or what have you) and salt and pepper. I do this step in my food processor. (Alternatively, you can use cooked rice or *farro* instead of the bread crumbs, but don't process the rice—mix it in afterwards.) Don't worry too much about quantity—I usually find that one egg and ¼ cup of bread crumbs and another of cheese added to the flesh of 3 or 4 medium-sized vegetables will produce the right consistency. You are looking for a thick but not firm texture (think thick porridge)—it will firm up as it bakes. If your filling is too stiff (that is, if you've added too many bread crumbs or too much grain), the end result will be too dry.

Fill the hollowed-out vegetable with the filling and top with a generous dollop of tomato sauce and cheese (grated Parmesan or pecorino or a slice of mozzarella).

Bake in a 350°F/175°C oven until the vegetable is tender.

For the tomato sauce, you can use the recipe on page 245.

At the height of summer I stuff tomatoes, onions, zucchini and eggplant together, combining their scooped-out flesh to make the filling. I stuff them with this homogenous mixture and bake them in separate gratin dishes so I can remove each vegetable separately when it is perfectly cooked. They can be reheated before serving. The cooking time will vary depending on the size of the vegetable, but generally speaking, tomatoes will be ready first, then zucchini, eggplant and finally onion.

Fagioli al Fiasco ✦ White Beans in a Flask

YEAR-ROUND

The Tuscans are often referred to as *mangiafagioli,* or bean eaters. The dried bean is an adored staple, and countless varieties are available, many of which cost a small fortune to acquire. There is the sulfur-colored *zolfino* from a small area in the Pratomagno and the *sorana* from the area around the town of Sorana, northeast of Lucca. These beans are precious, costing as much per kilogram as the best Tuscan *bistecca.* Other varieties include the *garfagnina, schiacciona, aquila, borlotto, cannellino, burro, cappone, occhio, coco nano, diecimino, giallorino, malato* and *pievarino,* to name just a few. Here you come to know the attributes of a good dried bean.

This is an excellent pantry side dish to make for a meal when you are puzzling about what to serve for a vegetable. There is always the humble white bean.

One of the most traditional ways to cook beans in Tuscany was in a Chianti wine flask buried in the embers of the hearth. Today they are rarely done this way, but are cooked instead on top of the stove or in a low oven in a terra-cotta bean pot. It is a simple preparation, and its goodness will depend on the quality of the beans you use. Good beans should be no more than a year old, so buy from a reputable source. A farmers' market is the perfect place to find good-quality beans. If you don't own a bean pot, use a heavy saucepan or an enameled cast-iron casserole.

SERVES 4

1 cup dried white beans, such as cannellini
4 fresh sage leaves
2 garlic cloves, unpeeled

¼ cup extra virgin olive oil, plus extra for drizzling

Sea salt and freshly ground black pepper to taste

Soak the beans in water overnight, using enough water to cover them by several inches. The next day, drain them and place them in a pot with enough water to cover by an inch. Add the sage, garlic and olive oil, cover the pot and place it over very low heat. Cooking time will vary depending on the type and age of your beans, but count on at least 1 hour. Check the beans from time to time to make sure they are still covered, adding more water if necessary. Serve the beans with salt, pepper and a drizzle of extra virgin olive oil.

Variation

The beans can also be served on top of grilled slices of Tuscan bread and drizzled with the oil to make bean *crostini*.

Fagioli e Pomodori

✦ Romano Wax Beans Stewed in Tomatoes

SUMMER

The long, flat *romano* bean is my favorite variety of green (or yellow) bean. I grow both colors and cook them in tomatoes to produce this luscious stew. They are also good boiled and served with new spring potatoes, a drizzle of extra virgin olive oil and a sprinkle of sea salt. If you can't get a *romano* bean, use any kind of seasonal green bean.

SERVES 4

450 g (1 lb) *romano* beans, cleaned, tipped and tailed

2 tbsp extra virgin olive oil

1 onion, thinly sliced

1 garlic clove, minced

4 ripe tomatoes, peeled and seeded (or 4 canned tomatoes, seeded)

Salt and pepper to taste

Several leaves of basil

Blanch the beans briefly in a large pot of boiling salted water. Drain the beans in a colander and place them under cold running water to stop the cooking. Let the beans drain while you cook the onion and garlic. Heat the oil in a frying pan large enough to hold all of the beans and cook the onion over moderate heat for about 5 minutes, until it begins to wilt and turn transparent. Add the garlic and continue to cook, stirring constantly, for a few more minutes, until the garlic begins to smell but does not brown. Add the blanched beans, tomatoes and a pinch of salt. Reduce the heat to low. Partially cover the pan and simmer for 15 minutes or until the beans are tender. Check for salt and season with pepper. Transfer to a warm serving dish and tear the basil leaves over the beans.

Panzanella di Farro
◆ Farro, Cucumber and Tomato Salad

JULY THROUGH AUGUST

Panzanella is a popular Tuscan salad made with day-old saltless bread. The bread is soaked, squeezed dry and dressed with tomatoes, red onions and cucumbers. It is a delicious summertime treat, but unless you bake your own unsalted bread (see page 31), it is hard to reproduce with a regular salted loaf. There is something about the cardboard-like texture of saltless Tuscan bread that lets it be soaked and squeezed dry without turning into a glutinous mass.

Traditionally, this salad was made with whole wheat Tuscan bread, but I have found that *farro* makes a wonderful substitute. *Farro* is sometimes hard to come by in North American markets. When you can find it, it tends to be a bit pricey, as it will have been imported from Italy. If you can't find it or don't want to pay the price, you can substitute pearl barley.

SERVES 4

1 cup pearled *farro*
1 large English cucumber, peeled, seeded and sliced
1 sweet red onion, thinly sliced (use a mandoline if you have one)
A generous handful of vine-ripened cherry tomatoes, halved or
    quartered
¼ cup extra virgin olive oil
1 tbsp red wine vinegar
Salt and pepper to taste
A generous bunch of fresh basil leaves to garnish

Bring 2 cups of salted water to a boil and add the *farro*. Reduce the heat to low and simmer, partially covered, for about 20 minutes, until the *farro* fluffs up, is tender and has absorbed most of the water. Turn the *farro* into a sieve, run cold water over it and drain it well.

Add the *farro* to a bowl with the cucumber, onion and tomatoes, dress with the oil and vinegar and toss. Season with salt and pepper. Tear the basil over the salad just before serving.

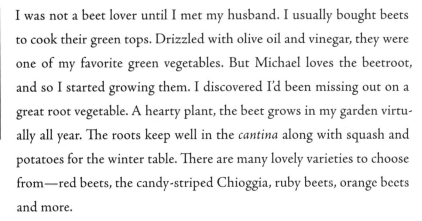

Insalata di Barbabietole
✦ Roasted Beet Salad with Mint and Red Onions

Year-round

I was not a beet lover until I met my husband. I usually bought beets to cook their green tops. Drizzled with olive oil and vinegar, they were one of my favorite green vegetables. But Michael loves the beetroot, and so I started growing them. I discovered I'd been missing out on a great root vegetable. A hearty plant, the beet grows in my garden virtually all year. The roots keep well in the *cantina* along with squash and potatoes for the winter table. There are many lovely varieties to choose from—red beets, the candy-striped Chioggia, ruby beets, orange beets and more.

I make this colorful salad almost any time. It is served at room temperature so can be made ahead. It adds a very pretty touch to the table, never mind how easy it is to make. If you want to, you can also blanch the beet stems and greens in equal parts water and vinegar and toss them into the salad.

Serves 4

4 medium beets
1 red onion, thinly sliced
¼ cup extra virgin olive oil
1 tbsp balsamic vinegar
Salt and pepper to taste
Several fresh mint leaves

Preheat the oven to 350°F/175°C.

Scrub the beets but don't peel them. Prick them several times with a fork and wrap them together in a sheet of foil. Place in an ovenproof dish and bake for about half an hour, until tender. Remove from the foil and let the beets sit for a few minutes. When cool enough to handle, slip off their skins by rubbing the beets with your fingers. Dice the beets and toss them in a bowl with the onion, olive oil and vinegar. Season with salt and pepper. Garnish with the fresh mint before serving.

Variation

In the summer, when I don't like to turn my oven on, I make a raw version of this salad. Scrub the beets clean and peel them. Cut them into a very fine matchstick using a mandoline (or you can grate them). Omit the onions and dress the salad as above.

Insalata di Cavolo Cappuccio con Speck
✦ Green Cabbage Salad with Speck

SUMMER AND FALL

Speck is the excellent lightly smoked raw ham made in Italy's Alto Adige or South Tyrol, and it turns up in this popular salad made with cabbage, which is a common vegetable in this northern region. This crunchy raw salad, enlivened by good-quality red wine vinegar and dotted with crispy bits of fried *speck*, is the ideal foil to the region's rich cuisine. It is a good match for the *stockfischgrostl* on page 228.

Traditionally, this salad is made with a type of cabbage called *cavolo cappuccio*, a light green cabbage whose head grows in an oval shape and is named after the hoods of the same shape worn by Capuchin monks. It is a perfect cabbage for salad because its leaves are plump and tender and provide good crunch. But you can use any firm green cabbage. Avoid leafy varieties like the Savoy.

The region once belonged to Austria, and this history is reflected in the traditional use of caraway. *Speck* can be found in Eastern European delis; otherwise, smoked bacon or pancetta can be substituted.

SERVES 4

1 small head green cabbage
1 tbsp olive oil
Salt and pepper to taste
A pinch of caraway seeds (optional)
56 g (2 oz) thinly sliced *speck*
Good-quality white wine vinegar to taste

Quarter the cabbage, cut out and discard the core and slice the leaves finely. (Use a mandoline if you have one.) Place in a serving bowl and add the oil, salt, pepper and caraway, if using. Mix together using clean hands. Roll the *speck* slices up into a tight log and cut them into thin shreds.

Heat a small frying pan over low heat and cook the *speck* until it gives off its fat and crisps. Deglaze the pan with a splash of the wine vinegar, scraping the bottom with a wooden spoon. Pour the hot sauce over the salad, toss and taste. Add more vinegar and olive oil if needed. Serve.

Spinaci Saltati ✦ Sautéed Spinach

YEAR-ROUND

Tuscans are big spinach eaters. Spinach is found all year in almost every eating place, from the fanciest restaurant to the simplest *osteria*. If it is not on the menu, it can often be had for the asking. A plate of spinach and another of white beans (see page 298) are the traditional accompaniments to a

Tuscan meal. This recipe can be adapted to any kind of green, such as chard, kale or beet tops. Tougher greens will need to be cooked a bit longer.

It is important to cook the spinach well, in lots of olive oil, so that each bite is luxuriously coated and cooked enough to almost melt in the mouth.

SERVES 4 TO 6

1 kg (2¼ lb) fresh spinach leaves, washed well and thick stems
   removed
½ cup extra virgin olive oil
2 garlic cloves, minced
Salt and pepper to taste

Bring a large pot of salted water to a rolling boil. Add the spinach and blanch the leaves briefly—about a minute. Remove to a colander to drain, reserving a cup of the cooking water. Run cold water over the spinach until it is cool enough to handle. Gently squeeze most of the water out of the spinach (you don't need to squeeze it completely dry—it should still have some water clinging to its leaves). Transfer the spinach to a cutting board and roughly chop.

Heat the oil over moderate heat in a sauté pan large enough to hold all the spinach. Cook the garlic for a few minutes, being careful not to let it brown. Add the spinach and cook, stirring constantly, until it is very tender, about 10 minutes. You can add some of the cooking water from time to time if the spinach looks too dry. Season with salt and pepper.

Variation

For *Spinaci alla Fiorentina*, preheat the oven to 350°F/175°C. Prepare the sautéed spinach as described above and combine the spinach with

1 recipe béchamel sauce (page 312). Transfer to an ovenproof gratin dish. Top with ½ cup of grated Parmesan cheese or 2 tbsp of dry bread crumbs. Bake for 25 to 30 minutes, until the top is golden and bubbly.

Peperonata ✦ Yellow and Red Pepper Stew

LATE SUMMER THROUGH FALL

Peppers love our red Siena soil, and I plant lots of different kinds: several hot varieties to dry or to be preserved in oil or vinegar, as well as the traditional large sweet kind, which are wonderful roasted, grilled or made into this easy Tuscan standard.

This traditional late-summer side dish is especially attractive made with a mix of red and yellow peppers. *Peperonata* can be served warm or at room temperature and can be made a day ahead.

SERVES 4

3 tbsp extra virgin olive oil

1 red onion, thinly sliced

1 large garlic clove, roughly chopped

4 large yellow and/or red sweet peppers, cored, seeded, white pith removed, and cut into 1-inch chunks

2 fresh or canned tomatoes, peeled, seeded and diced

Salt and pepper to taste

Fresh basil leaves to garnish

Heat the oil over low heat in a sauté pan large enough to hold all the vegetables. Add the onion and cook, stirring once in a while, for about 5 minutes, until it begins to wilt. Add the garlic, peppers and tomatoes, cover and simmer for 15 minutes. Remove the lid and cook, stirring occasionally, for another 15 minutes, until the peppers are tender. You may need to add a little water from time to time if it looks too dry. Season with salt and pepper and serve garnished with the basil.

Variation

I make a meal out of leftover *peperonata* by puréeing it and reheating it gently while poaching an egg for each person on top of the purée. I serve it on a piece of grilled Tuscan bread rubbed with garlic and drizzled with some extra virgin olive oil.

Insalata di Finocchio ◆ Fennel Salad

SEPTEMBER THROUGH NOVEMBER

If you have good-quality extra virgin olive oil, a fresh fennel bulb and some *fleur de sel* or good-quality sea salt, you can make this salad. It is my favorite way to eat fennel. A lot of Italian preparations call for fennel to be braised, but I enjoy the crunch and the slight licorice taste of the raw vegetable. Look for small, young fennel bulbs.

Reserve some feathery fennel fronds for the garnish. Trim a thin slice off the root end of the fennel and remove the outer layer or two. If you have a large bulb, cut it in half lengthwise and remove the core. Slice the bulb finely—use a mandoline if you have one. Toss with the best-quality extra virgin olive oil you can afford and a pinch of sea salt. Finely chop the reserved fronds and use them as garnish. The salad is delicious as is. If you want to gild the lily, you can add a few drops of red wine vinegar, a few wrinkly black olives that have been preserved in olive oil, and a thinly sliced red onion.

In the late fall, when the blood oranges begin to appear in the markets from Sicily, I sometimes add a few thin slices to this salad.

Finocchi Gratinati ✦ Fennel Gratin

The fennel plant is a hearty vegetable that can take a fair bit of winter before it gives up the ghost. I plant lots of fennel seeds around the middle of June to see me through the spare months of the year. My fennel bulbs never get very big, but what they lack in size they make up for in flavor. Unlike the pure white monster bulbs one finds in most markets, mine are small, slender and a fresh lime green color that fades to white near the bottom of the plant. The delicate flavor of fennel, with its suggestion of anise or licorice, always brings welcome zest to the winter table. When used as the base for a gratin, it sticks to the ribs as well.

This recipe is straightforward and uncomplicated. It goes well with roasted meat and game, and makes a nice partner for the venison and quince recipe on page 254. It's also substantial enough to stand on its own as a vegetarian main course, perhaps alongside a beet salad (page 302) and a plate of Tuscan white beans (page 298) drizzled with some peppery new Tuscan olive oil (see page 309).

Serves 4

2 to 3 large fennel bulbs (or twice as many small ones)
3 tbsp butter
½ cup milk
Salt and pepper to taste
A pinch of freshly grated nutmeg
56 g (2 oz) (⅔ cup) grated Parmesan cheese
¼ cup dry bread crumbs

Preheat the oven to 350°F/175°C.

Cut the green stalks away from the fennel bulb. Remove any tough outer layers and trim the root end by removing a thin slice from the bottom of the bulb. Cut the bulb in half vertically. Cut out and discard the hard core from both halves; wash the fennel and cut crosswise into ¼-inch slices.

Over moderate heat, melt 2 tbsp of the butter in a sauté pan large enough to hold all of the sliced fennel. Add the fennel and cook, stirring from time to time, for about 5 minutes. Add the milk and season with the salt, pepper and nutmeg. Lower the heat and cook for another 10 minutes. Transfer to an ovenproof gratin dish and sprinkle the grated cheese over the top, followed by the bread crumbs. Dot with the remaining 1 tbsp of butter. Bake for about 20 minutes, until the crust is golden and bubbly and the fennel is tender.

Pinzimonio ✦ Raw Vegetables and New Olive Oil
November through January

In November and December in Tuscany, the *frantoio*, or olive mill, opens its doors and the freshly harvested olives are pressed. Tuscans take great pride in their green, peppery oil. Unlike in other parts of Italy, where olives are allowed to ripen and fall into nets, here they are handpicked before they ripen. The olives are not bruised from a fall, and since the fruit is not yet ripe, the oil it contains will not have begun to turn rancid. The handpicked fruit is rushed to the olive mill, the time from tree to press being a critical factor in the taste and quality of the oil. The underripe Tuscan olive yields an almost fluorescent green, peppery oil that is so strong when fresh it can make you choke. This is precious stuff—to be eaten "raw" so one can savor its fleeting taste. Tuscan oil is expensive because of the labor involved. Speaking from personal experience, harvesting olives is finger-numbing work. Tuscany at the end of the year can be very cold. At times there is already snow on the ground.

When I first moved here, I found this oil too strong, recalling the mouth-puckering taste of a fresh-picked green olive. Now, of course, I have acquired a taste for it, and like most locals greedily await the end of the year, when this green gold becomes available once again.

The peppery taste of the oil mellows as it ages, so this dish is best appreciated with the new oil that is usually available in the late fall and early new year. A good-quality Tuscan extra virgin olive oil should tell you on the bottle the month and year of the harvest so you know its age. This is not oil for cooking—save it for dressing salad or making *bruschetta* or *pinzimonio*.

Pinzimonio is simply a large platter of raw vegetables that should include some red pepper, celery and fennel. You can add carrot sticks and sliced green cabbage leaves, or whatever else you like. Serve with a bowl of new oil for dipping and a small bowl of sea salt. *Basta!* (That's it!)

Sformato di Cardi ◆ Cardoon Flan
November through December

Shortly after I compost the last pepper, eggplant and tomato plants, around the middle of November, we get our first frost at Petraia, and the frugal season begins. In the house our woodstove is on all the time. The grapes are off, the olives recently harvested. New oil and the *vino novello*, Italy's answer to Beaujolais Nouveau, are available in the market, along with freshly milled chestnut flour and expensive white truffles.

Winter days are usually clear in Tuscany, and from our perch on top of the mountains it feels like you can see forever. Halfway to Rome, at least.

The hunters are out in the forest every morning at dawn, and there is often a gift of boar, pheasant or a few *uccellini* (little birds). Our *agriturismo* has few guests now, as does the town of Radda. This always astounds me. It's a bit cooler than it was a month ago, but the clarity of the light in the cooler months endows the region with an austere and deep beauty. The plethora of game, mushrooms, new olive oil and produce found only at this time of year is astonishing. The glitz and glamor of the tourist season gives way to authenticity and tradition, and I always wonder why at least some of the throngs of summer aren't curious about life here in winter.

In November we need to have our *serra*, a plastic tunnel, installed over the *orto* or we risk losing our winter crop to frost and snow. The garden slows down. Until early spring, when we see the asparagus and rhubarb shoots, we will be relying on a few cabbage, cauliflower, broccoli and root vegetables from our winter garden, along with whatever potatoes, onions, beets and squash are squirreled away in the *cantina*. All of this will augment whatever part of summer's bounty I've managed to put away in jars or freeze.

Fortunately, there are a few hardy plants that can stand up to a Tuscan winter. The cardoon is one of them. A member of the thistle family, it is a big plant. It looks like and is related to the artichoke, but only the stems of the plant are eaten. Cardoons have an intriguing flavor, a hint of bitterness and astringency that is welcome at this time of year, when most seasonal vegetables are either sweet and starchy squash and roots (potatoes, beets, parsnip, carrots *et alia*) or brassicas. The cardoon is a vegetable worth discovering. It is a native Mediterranean plant, but it is grown in North America too. Look for it in specialty or Italian markets in the late fall.

The cardoon stalk can be treated in a similar manner to a celery stalk. The inner hearts are best eaten raw, dipped in extra virgin olive oil and sprinkled with a little sea salt. For the outer stalks you need to peel away the stringy outer skin.

Topped with a little tomato sauce, this flan makes the perfect vegetarian main course or light lunch. As it is a rich dish, it goes nicely with a light main course such as fish or boiled meat. It is reminiscent of macaroni and cheese, with this unusual vegetable in place of the macaroni.

SERVES 4 TO 6

For the cardoons
1 kg (2 ¼ lb) cardoons

For the béchamel
2 cups milk
1 small carrot, roughly chopped
1 small celery stalk, broken in two
¼ onion
1 bay leaf
¼ cup extra virgin olive oil
3 tbsp all-purpose flour
A pinch of freshly grated nutmeg
Salt to taste

To finish
1 cup grated Parmesan cheese

For the cardoons
Bring a large pot of salted water to a boil. Peel the stringy skin away from the outer stalks of the cardoon and chop the stems into 1-inch pieces. Add

the cardoons to the boiling water; when it returns to a rapid boil, reduce the heat and simmer for about 25 minutes. The cardoons should be tender. Drain and cool under cold running water. Dry using a kitchen towel.

In the meantime, preheat the oven to 350°F/175°C. Butter a baking dish large enough to hold all of the cardoons in a single layer.

For the béchamel

Heat the milk with the carrot, celery, onion and bay leaf over low heat. Meanwhile, in another pan, heat the oil over low heat. Add the flour and cook, stirring constantly, for about 10 minutes. Do not let the mixture turn brown.

Strain the hot milk into the flour and use a whisk to incorporate. Continue to cook over low heat, stirring constantly, until the sauce thickens and coats the back of a wooden spoon. Remove from the heat and stir in the nutmeg and the salt.

To finish

Stir ¾ cup of the grated cheese into the béchamel. Place the cardoons in a single layer in the baking dish. Top with the béchamel and then sprinkle with the remaining cheese. Bake until the top begins to brown and starts to bubble, about half an hour.

MAKE-AHEAD NOTE
The béchamel can be made the day before and kept in the fridge. Place a piece of plastic wrap directly on the sauce so it does not form a skin. The cardoon flan can be assembled several hours ahead and kept in the fridge until you plan to bake it, or you can wrap it well and freeze it for up to a month. There is no need to thaw it before baking, but it will require an extra 10 minutes or so in the oven.

Cipolle alla Brace ✦ Roasted Onions

Winter

In winter we grill meat indoors in our hearth. Since our choice of vegetables is limited at this time of year, I usually throw a few onions in the embers of the fire to roast while the meat cooks. The onions steam in their skins, which turn black from the heat of the fire. When they are tender, I remove the charred leaves and halve or quarter what's left. I dress them simply with a little olive oil, a drop of balsamic vinegar, and salt and pepper.

The onions can also be roasted in the oven, but it is best to peel them and wrap them in foil—the dry skins can be a fire hazard. Using a knife, pierce one medium-sized peeled onion per person in two places. Rub the onions with olive oil and wrap them in a large piece of foil along with a sprig of rosemary. Place the package in a baking dish and bake in a 350°F/175°C oven until tender—30 to 45 minutes.

Quartetto di Patate ✦ A Potato Quartet

When we bought Petraia, everyone told me I couldn't grow potatoes. "You have the *terra rossa*," they said, referring to our rich red sienna-colored clay. "Potatoes want a sandy soil. Besides, it's too rocky. Potatoes won't sprout through clay, and if they do they won't grow because of the rocks. If they grow, they'll be small and gnarly. Over there on the other side of the mountain, in the Val d'Arno, you can grow potatoes, but not here."

Their logic, of course, made sense. I had come from a part of Ontario near the Niagara Escarpment where the soil was sandy (and rock free), and there I had grown beautiful potatoes. I would have to get used to the idea of no potatoes. But I love potatoes and was bothered by not being able to grow them with all this land we had. So after a couple of years I decided to throw caution to the wind and plant a few pounds just to see what would happen.

These Tuscans are a no-nonsense, practical lot, and I could tell by the looks I got that skepticism was reigning supreme. Hadn't I been told about the clay? And the rocks? I was a *straniera*—foreigner—indulging a completely unrealistic potato-growing fantasy. What a waste, all this work planting potatoes at La Petraia.

And so we were all quite astonished when I harvested a bumper crop of beautiful spuds that summer. I've been growing potatoes ever since. Now my potato project has grown to include several exotic varieties I've collected from all over Italy. The soil here is rocky. It is made of clay. La Petraia doesn't mean "place of stone" for nothing. Potatoes should not grow here. But, like almost everything else we plant, they thrive. I figure they must love it here as much I do. Here's what I do with them.

Oven-steamed Potatoes

YEAR-ROUND

Better than boiling or baking, this method produces a simple, unadorned, delicious potato that steams in its own skin in the oven. This is my favorite treatment for new potatoes in the spring. It is also a good way to cook potatoes for a salad. In the Italian, French and Swiss Alps, this method is used for cooking the delicious potatoes that accompany famous melted-cheese dishes like *raclette* and *fonduta* (page 273).

These potatoes emerge from their pot intact—the skin is not broken and the inside is cooked to perfection. They are not withered like a baked potato that has lost a lot of its moisture, but plump and fresh-looking. They are good simply dressed with a little olive oil, salt and pepper.

If you own a lidded terra-cotta bean pot, it is the perfect thing to use to steam these potatoes. Special terra-cotta potato cookers can be found in some kitchenware stores. Otherwise, an enameled cast-iron casserole will work. New potatoes or salad or boiling varieties are perfect for this method. *Raclette* potatoes are excellent, if you can find them. Scrub the potatoes but don't peel them. Prick them in one or two places with a knife and place in the casserole. Cover and steam in a 350°F/175°C oven for about 40 minutes, until tender.

Patate al Forno ✦ Oven-roasted Potatoes

YEAR-ROUND

These potatoes are a standard accompaniment to roasted meat in Tuscany. Often the meat is spit-roasted and the pan of potatoes placed under the spit to catch the fat as it drips down.

Count on one medium potato per person. Scrub them clean but leave the skins on. Cut each potato in half and parboil in salted water for 10 minutes. Drain and, when cool enough to handle, cut into bite-sized chunks. Toss them with the fat of your choice—extra virgin olive oil or chicken or duck fat. Finely chop one sprig of rosemary and add along with salt and pepper. Place in a roasting dish and roast in a 350°F/175°C oven for 30 minutes, turning the potatoes once or twice, until they are crispy and golden.

If you make the duck recipe on page 238, you will have rendered fat that you can use for these potatoes.

Patate alla Contadina ✦ Farmer-style Potatoes

SUMMER

Cooking potatoes once on top of the stove in olive oil, then again in tomatoes is a popular Tuscan treatment that recalls a time in the not too distant past when poverty was a fact of life for many people and a simple dish like this would have been all there was to eat. This is the type of meal that was prepared quickly and left to cook slowly while never-ending farm chores were attended to.

The potatoes are washed, peeled and cut into bite-sized chunks. After being tossed in a bowl with olive oil, a minced clove or two of garlic and some salt and pepper, they go into a pan to cook, covered, for about 20 minutes over very low heat. They should be stirred from time to time. You can add a bit of water if they seem too dry. At this point you add 1 tomato, peeled and seeded, for every 2 potatoes. The pan is partially covered and left to cook again over very low heat. Again, you can add a little water from time to time if things look dry. The potatoes will need another 25 to 30 minutes. The tomatoes should have given off all their liquid, which will have evaporated, leaving the potatoes coated in a lush pink sauce. The potatoes will be very soft, some of them starting to fall apart and melt into the sauce. Garnish with finely chopped basil before serving.

To make a feast, crack an egg per person over the potatoes, cover the pan and cook until the egg is done to your liking.

Patate e Verza ✦ Potatoes and Cabbage

WINTER

This is a hearty winter recipe that comes together easily. It is a regular on my menus when there is not much else available in the way of a green vegetable. I use the wrinkly-leaved Savoy cabbage. The deep green leaves, when parboiled, turn even more brilliant, a shade of green not found in nature in these months, giving my table an uplifting respite from winter's dreariness.

SERVES 4 TO 6

6 medium potatoes, scrubbed and cut into bite-sized chunks

12 Savoy cabbage leaves, cut into thick shreds

2 tbsp extra virgin olive oil

2 tbsp butter

1 garlic clove, minced

Salt and pepper to taste

A few leaves of fresh sage, rolled and cut into a fine *chiffonade*

Bring a large pot of water to a rolling boil. Add 1 tbsp salt and the potatoes and cook for 10 to 15 minutes, until they begin to become tender. Add the cabbage and cook for another 5 to 10 minutes, until the leaves are tender and the potatoes are cooked. Drain the potatoes and cabbage well and transfer to a warm serving bowl.

In the meantime, heat the oil and butter in a small skillet over moderate heat. Add the garlic and cook for a few minutes, stirring, until the garlic begins to smell but does not brown.

Drizzle the garlicky oil over the vegetables. Season with the salt and pepper and garnish with the sage.

Chapter 7 *I Dolci* ✣ *The Sweet Course*

My mother, an accomplished cook and baker, used to plan each meal in reverse. Over the years I've come to appreciate the wisdom of beginning at the end. The last impression of a meal is important, so it's worth paying attention to. And many desserts can be prepared in advance. If you start with the sweet course and run into trouble, you've time to fix things.

I don't possess a particularly sweet tooth, but I do like the *idea* of a sweet ending; as a rule I order dessert if I eat out. Experience has taught me the best chef in a restaurant is often the pastry chef. If you don't try dessert, even after hopeless precedents, how will you ever know?

While it is true that Italians often choose a piece of fruit to finish most meals, this is not to say they don't enjoy sweets. Instead, these things are consumed at other times of the day, like breakfast or teatime. The depth of tradition and vast range of the Italian sweet kitchen are at least as rich and diverse as they are in the savory one, and I had trouble limiting the

recipes in this chapter. I had compiled hundreds, but in the end there was simply not enough room.

I have designed this chapter to include a mix of traditional homey Italian sweets, along with a few elegant plated desserts. These more inventive recipes are inspired by the many talented pastry chefs at work today in Italy who are continually finding new ways to showcase the excellent ingredients they have available. To limit things, I've included only recipes that use what we produce here at Petraia—honey, fruit, nuts, berries and even some vegetables.

I use olive oil in place of lard or butter wherever possible and our honey in place of sugar. Honey, after all, is the original sweetener and preservative. It adds not only sweetness but, unlike sugar, flavor. Here at Petraia I get three different kinds of honey as the season progresses. First is the mild acacia-blossom honey—the prize of the Tuscan beekeeper. We get a small amount of this liquid gold, our nearest acacia trees being a mile away, halfway down the mountain. In July our chestnuts are in bloom, and the dark, slightly bitter, complex-tasting honey we harvest then is my favorite. Since the trees are nearby, it's easy work for the bees. If Mother Nature cooperates, we can get quite a lot of it. Another crop comes later in September, a dark forest honey that solidifies almost immediately after it has been taken off the hive.

Choosing the appropriate honey is the key to using it successfully. It is important to select a type that will complement the other ingredients, not overwhelm them. For instance, our chestnut honey competes too heavily with most things chocolate, but it loves dairy products. The beautiful clover honey my brother makes in Canada, on the other hand, will make a chocolate tart sing. The same thing is true with olive oil. Oils from different places have different attributes—Ligurian oil is fruity while Tuscan oil is peppery.

You don't need to get carried away with all of this. I keep two kinds of olive oil on hand—Tuscan and Ligurian. Same thing with honey—two or three kinds, usually our chestnut and acacia and my brother's clover. With these I find I can complement almost anything. The best way to decide what kind of oil or honey to use is to think about the place the dish comes from. The *caprese calda* (page 340), for instance, is inspired by the famous flourless chocolate tart from Capri. There you find light blossom honey and fruity oils. The spice cookies (page 371) from the South Tyrol, on the other hand, are full of pepper, spice and strong flavors. Therefore, chestnut honey and spicy Tuscan oil are my choice.

Finally, I think one of the keys to a successful dessert course is to keep portions small. (You can always offer seconds.) No one really wants to face a huge dessert after a multi-course meal. But a tiny bit of heaven, how can they refuse?

Elegant Plated Desserts

Semifreddo di Miele ✦ Honey Semifreddo

This dessert has a soft, gelato-type consistency. A recent guest at Petraia, a sophisticated gourmand and connoisseur of Italian gelato (arguably the world's best ice cream), told me this was the best "ice cream" he'd ever eaten! Needless to say, I didn't bother correcting him.

This *semifreddo*, with only three ingredients, is simple to make. I usually have some on hand, as it is a wonderful showcase for our chestnut honey and fresh eggs. It loves all things chocolate or chestnut. Serve it alongside the *caprese calda* (page 340) or the apple *frangipane* dessert on page 330.

I don't own an ice cream machine or have a lot of appliances in my kitchen. They take up precious space and require meticulous cleaning and maintenance, not to mention they are expensive and spend much of the time collecting dust. Making things by hand often produces superior results and, contrary to popular belief, can also save time. After all, there is no machine to haul out, put together, take apart, clean and put away. You can easily make numerous frozen desserts without an ice cream machine. The Italians call them *semifreddi*.

SERVES 8 TO 10

4 egg yolks (see page 325 on the use of raw eggs)
150 g (5.3 oz) (scant ½ cup) liquid honey
1 cup heavy cream
Maple syrup or honey (optional) for serving

Line a loaf pan with plastic wrap, leaving enough plastic overhanging the long sides to cover the top. Beat the yolks with the honey until light and frothy. This will take about 10 minutes. Whisk the cream to soft peaks and gently fold it into the yolk-honey mixture. Transfer to the loaf pan and cover the top with the overhanging plastic. Freeze for several hours or overnight, until it firms up. This *semifreddo* will not get really hard, but it will have a soft gelato-type texture. Serve either in slices or scooped out of the container with a spoon.

Variation: Pistachio Praline Semifreddo

Heat ½ cup of sugar with ¼ cup of water until the sugar is completely dissolved and the liquid is clear—it should be around 230°F/110°C if you have a candy thermometer. Add ⅓ cup unsalted pistachio nuts. Stir well and continue to cook over high heat until the syrup starts to turn a dark caramel color or reaches 260°F/125°C.

Turn out onto an oiled surface such as marble or granite, or onto a piece of oiled parchment. Let sit until it cools and hardens, and then break into chunks and briefly process in your food processor—you want something slightly chunkier than a powder. Fold ½ cup of the praline into the *semifreddo* before freezing. Reserve the remainder to sprinkle over the top of the dessert when you serve it.

Variation: Lavender Semifreddo

Add a couple of drops of lavender essence to the cream. Use a mild honey such as clover.

Using Raw Eggs

Some recipes in this book call for the use of raw eggs. In Italy, fresh raw eggs are considered the perfect food and are sold *"da bere,"* or to be drunk, raw. They are given to young children, especially when they are ill. Stirred into a glass with a little sugar or honey, they are considered not just a restorative but a rare treat, loved by young and old alike. As a keeper of free-range, organically fed chickens, I'm frequently asked by friends with youngsters for a fresh egg or two *da bere*.

The Canadian Egg Marketing Agency advises that Canadian eggs are among the safest in the world; however, it is important that eggs be handled properly to avoid food safety concerns. You can find information about egg handling at their website, www.eggs.ca.

If you are concerned about the risk of *Salmonella enteritidis* in raw or lightly cooked eggs, the eggs (whole or yolks only, depending on the recipe) can be mixed with the honey and whisked over a double boiler until they reach a temperature of 140°F/60°C. The mixture should be held at that temperature for 5 minutes. At this point you can transfer the egg-honey mixture to the mixer to beat until cool, thick and frothy before proceeding with the recipe. Cooking the eggs is more of an effort, but it does not significantly alter the texture of the dessert.

Semifreddo di Limone con Salsa ai Frutti di Bosco
◆ Lemon Semifreddo with a Wild Berry Coulis

This is my most popular frozen dessert and is simply made. It keeps well in the freezer for up to a month, so I often have some on hand. It is the best way I know to show off the flavorful lemons from our trees and the wild berries I harvest in our woods each fall.

The *semifreddo* is made by simply folding beaten cream into the honey lemon curd used in the tart on page 332. This mixture is then frozen between layers of Italian *amaretti* cookies.

SERVES 8 TO 10

For the lemon semifreddo

> 1¼ cups heavy cream
> 1 recipe honey lemon curd (page 333)
> 16 *amaretti* cookies (page 369 or use store-bought) or small
>   meringues

For the coulis

> 2 cups mixed berries
> ½ cup liquid honey
> Fresh mint sprigs to garnish

For the lemon semifreddo

Beat the cream to soft peaks and gently fold into the lemon curd. Crush the cookies if they are large. Small cookies can be used whole. Line a loaf pan with plastic wrap, leaving enough plastic overhanging the long sides to cover the top. Spread one-third of the lemon cream on the bottom. Top this with one-third of the cookies. Repeat to make two more layers of cream and cookies, ending with a layer of the cookies. Freeze, tightly covered with the overhanging plastic, for several hours, until the *semifreddo* is hard.

For the coulis

Cook the berries in the honey over moderate heat for 10 to 15 minutes, until the berries are soft. Strain through a fine sieve or pass through the fine disk of a food mill. If the *coulis* seems too thin, return it to the heat and cook it over high heat for a few more minutes to reduce. Let it cool before using. It keeps well for a week in the fridge and can also be frozen.

To serve

Remove the *semifreddo* from the freezer about 10 minutes before you plan to serve it. Cut a slice and put it in the center of a dinner plate. Drizzle some of the *coulis* over the slice and around the outside of the plate. Top with a sprig of mint and serve.

Semifreddo al Panpepato ✦ Semifreddo of Panpepato

Here's a lovely dessert to use leftover *panpepato* (page 373). If you find good-quality orange-flavored (and orange-colored) white chocolate, it is nice to use in this recipe. This is a good frozen dessert for the holiday season. If you don't feel like making the *panpepato*, you can look for it, or its tamer cousin, *panforte*, in specialty Italian grocers.

SERVES 8 TO 10

140 g (5 oz) *panpepato* (page 373 or use store-bought)
280 g (10 oz) white chocolate, broken into small pieces

4 eggs (see page 325 on the use of raw eggs)

3 tbsp liquid honey

2 cups heavy cream

Line a loaf pan with plastic wrap, leaving enough plastic overhanging the long sides to cover the top. Finely grind the *panpepato* in your food processor. Melt the chocolate in the top of a double boiler over low heat. Beat the eggs and honey together until light and frothy, about 10 minutes. Beat the cream to soft peaks.

Mix the melted chocolate a bit at a time into the egg-honey mixture and then fold in the ground *panpepato*, followed by the whipped cream. Transfer to the loaf pan, cover with the overhanging plastic and freeze for several hours or until firm. Let sit at room temperature for about 10 minutes to soften before you serve it, cut in thin slices.

Cesti di Mandorle ✦ Almond Baskets

I make these lacy almond baskets to serve *semifreddo* in. If you don't feel like making baskets, let the lace cool and then break it into large, dramatic pieces to stick into the top of a slice of *semifreddo* or any other dessert.

MAKES 4 6-INCH BASKETS

⅓ cup icing sugar

2 tbsp citrus paste, made using seedless oranges (see page 339)

2 tbsp all-purpose flour

Scant ½ cup sliced almonds

1 tbsp melted butter

1 tsp heavy cream

Preheat the oven to 300°F/150°C. If you own silicone baking mats, they can be used to make these baskets. Otherwise, lightly oil 4 sheets of parchment paper, each one cut to fit a small baking sheet.

In a small saucepan, heat the sugar and the citrus paste together just until the sugar melts. Remove from the heat and stir in the flour, almonds, melted butter and cream.

Spread a scant 2 tbsp batter onto each sheet of parchment or silicone. Have a glass of water at hand. Dip a palette knife in the water and use it to spread the batter as thinly as you can over the liner or parchment. Ideally, you want the basket to be one layer of sliced almonds thick and about 6 inches in diameter. Don't worry if there are small holes or gaps—that is what produces the pretty lacy effect. Since the lace hardens soon after it is removed from the oven, it is best to bake the baskets one at a time.

Transfer to the oven and bake for 15 minutes or until the lace begins to turn a deep caramel color around the edges and a lovely golden color throughout. Have a glass or cup ready. Remove the lace from the oven. It will be very soft, but it will harden quickly as it cools, so it is important to work quickly. Let set for just a few seconds, then begin to carefully loosen the lace with the palette knife. Drape the lace over your chosen mold and apply a bit of pressure with your hands for a few seconds to set the shape. There is your basket. Proceed to bake and mold the remaining baskets. If you find these thin, lacy cookies get too hard before you've had a chance to shape them, simply return them to the oven for a few seconds to soften.

Sfogliata di Mele e Frangipane con la Salsa di Miele al Profumo di Lavanda ✦ Apple and Frangipane Tart with a Lavender-scented Honey Sauce

I serve this glamorous tart with a slice of honey *semifreddo* (page 323). *Frangipane* is easily made, and the puff pastry I keep on hand in the freezer. The honey sauce takes a minute to prepare, and so does the apple filling, so this very sophisticated dessert comes together in no time. Pears can be substituted for the apples. A lavender sprig, placed on each serving, will release its perfume as the hot honey sauce is drizzled over it. This is a great dessert for the late fall and keeps going all winter.

SERVES 4 TO 6

For the pastry

250 g (9 oz) puff pastry (page 390 or use store-bought)

For the frangipane

56 g (2 oz) (scant ⅓ cup) blanched almonds
56 g (2 oz) (3 tbsp) liquid honey
56 g (2 oz) (½ stick) butter
1 egg, beaten
1 tbsp all-purpose flour

For the honey sauce

⅓ cup liquid honey
⅓ cup heavy cream
1 tbsp butter

For the apple filling

3 to 4 Golden Delicious apples, peeled, cored and sliced very thinly
(use a mandoline if you have one)

To finish

½ cup apricot jam heated with 2 tbsp water, strained

Icing sugar

Several sprigs of fresh lavender

For the pastry

Roll the puff pastry out into a fairly thin rectangle about 10 by 12 inches
and transfer to a parchment-lined baking sheet. Cut a ½-inch strip off
each side of the rectangle and place each strip on the edge it was cut from
to form a border. Wrap the dough tightly in plastic and refrigerate it until
you are ready to bake.

For the frangipane

Process all of the *frangipane* ingredients in your food processor until you
have a smooth paste. The *frangipane* can be made ahead and refrigerated
overnight or frozen for up to a month.

For the honey sauce

Place the honey in a small saucepan with a tablespoon of water and bring
to a rolling boil. Remove from the heat and add the cream and butter.
Return to low heat and stir to combine. The honey sauce can be made the
morning of the day you plan to serve the dessert.

The final assembly

Preheat the oven to 350°F/175°C.

Remove the puff pastry from the fridge and spread the *frangipane* evenly over the dough. Lay the apple slices, overlapping them quite thickly, in two or three rows on top of the *frangipane*.

Bake for 40 minutes, until the pastry is golden. Let cool on a rack for 5 to 10 minutes before painting the apples with the strained apricot jam. When completely cool, use a fine sieve to sprinkle icing sugar over the tart.

To serve

Reheat the honey sauce. Cut the tart into thin slices and arrange on your serving plates. Put a lavender sprig on top of each slice and drizzle the hot honey sauce in a zigzag pattern over top. Sieve a light veil of icing sugar over the plate, if desired, and serve.

Torta di Limone con Salsa di Fragole e Basilico
✦ Lemon Tart with Strawberry Sauce and Basil

This luxurious lemon tart is made interesting with the addition of honey rather than sugar in the lemon curd. It is a perfect dessert to serve in early summer, when strawberries are in season and basil leaves are young and tender.

The lemon curd keeps for several days in the fridge if you are not planning on making the tart right away. It is also used in the lemon *semifreddo* on page 326. In fact, I often double the filling and make a lemon *semifreddo* to serve alongside the tart.

SERVES 6 TO 8

For the dough
½ recipe tart dough (page 358)

For the honey lemon curd

    2 eggs

    2 egg yolks

    130 g (4.5 oz) (⅓ cup plus 1 tbsp) mild liquid honey

    56 g (2 oz) (½ stick) butter

    ½ cup freshly squeezed lemon juice

    ¼ cup zest from organic lemons

For the strawberry coulis

    2 cups (1 pint) fresh strawberries

    ¼ cup liquid honey

To garnish

    Fresh basil sprigs

    Whipped cream (optional)

For the dough

Put an 8-inch tart ring (or tart pan with removable bottom) on a parchment-lined baking sheet. Roll the dough out fairly thinly, transfer it to the tart ring and trim the edges (see page 343). Refrigerate for half an hour. In the meantime, preheat the oven to 400°F/200°C.

Prick the bottom of the tart shell in several places with a fork. Place a piece of foil inside the tart shell. Fill the shell with pie weights or dried beans. Bake for 20 minutes. Remove the foil and the weights. Reduce the heat to 350°F/175°C and bake for another 10 minutes or until the shell turns golden. Remove the tart shell from the oven but do not turn off the oven.

For the honey lemon curd

In a heavy-bottomed saucepan, whisk together the whole eggs, yolks and honey. Add the remaining ingredients and cook over moderate heat, stirring constantly until the curd thickens and coats the back of a spoon. Remove from the heat and immediately strain into the warm tart shell. Alternatively, if you do not plan to make the tart immediately or are planning to use the curd to make lemon *semifreddo*, the curd can be strained into a bowl and stored overnight in the fridge; place a piece of plastic wrap directly over the top of the curd so it does not develop a skin.

Bake the tart for 8 to 10 minutes, until the curd just sets.

For the strawberry coulis

Stem and quarter the berries. Cook them with the honey over moderate heat for about 20 minutes. Pass through the fine disk of a food mill or purée in a blender. The sauce will keep for several days in the fridge.

To serve

Cut the tart in thin wedges and arrange on dessert plates. Dip a soup spoon into the berry *coulis* and trail the *coulis* around the rim of the dessert plate to create a red border. Dip the spoon into the *coulis* again and drizzle in graphic patterns over the tart slice. Top the slice with a sprig of fresh basil. If you want, you can pipe rosettes of whipped cream around the outside of each slice of tart.

Mele al Forno con la Crema Zabaione al Miele
✦ Baked Apples with a Honey Cream Zabaione

Simplicity at its best is a baked apple for dessert. The *crema zabaione* adds more than a touch of refinement. Both are easy to make and can be prepared early the day you plan to serve them.

For the crema zabaione

3 egg yolks

2 tbsp mild liquid honey

½ cup sweet wine such as Vin Santo or Marsala

1 cup heavy cream

For the baked apples

4 to 6 Golden Delicious apples

28 g (1 oz) (¼ stick) butter, at room temperature

¼ cup sugar

For the crema zabaione

Beat the yolks and honey together until they are light and frothy, about 10 minutes. Reduce the speed and add the wine. Once the wine has been incorporated, transfer the mixture to a double boiler. Stir constantly over moderate heat until the *zabaione* thickens and feels heavy, resisting your spoon and coating it as you stir. Be careful not to let it boil. Let cool to room temperature and then refrigerate to cool completely.

Whip the cream to soft peaks and fold into the cold *zabaione*. Refrigerate until ready to use.

For the baked apples

Preheat the oven to 350°F/175°C.

Slice the top third off each apple, leaving the stem intact. Remove the core from the apple. Put the apples in a baking dish and rub each one with a little butter, then put another small dab in the hole where the core was. Sprinkle with sugar. Return the lids to the apples and sprinkle more

Crema zabaione is a versatile ingredient in the sweet kitchen. Think of it as an elegant replacement for whipped cream or ice cream, and it will soon become one of your standards.

sugar on top. Bake for 35 to 40 minutes, until the apple is tender. Let cool to room temperature and serve with a dollop of the *crema zabaione*, spread in a thick layer between the lid and base of the apple.

Crema di Cogne ✦ Cooked Cream from Cogne

Cogne is the beautiful alpine town at the entrance to Italy's Gran Paradiso National Park. It is a famous cross-country ski resort, but it is also known for the quality of its food. The small village has several excellent restaurants and boasts exquisite mountain honey and Italy's famous fontina cheese as raw ingredients. Many traditional recipes have made the town a food lover's destination, and this is one of them, made from the sinfully rich cream of the cows whose milk goes to make fontina.

This dessert is normally served with the *tegole* hazelnut wafers on page 364. It is very easy to make, and presents itself in a graceful manner that belies its rustic mountain heritage. Naturally, a little bit goes a long way, as it is very rich. I serve it in a small liqueur glass with a *tegole* wafer dramatically perched on the rim. Most recipes I've seen use sugar as the sweetener, but I think honey works just as well. It adds another layer of flavor and, since Cogne is famous for its mountain honey, I think this transgression is a respectable one.

SERVES 8

2 cups heavy cream
2 cups milk
⅓ cup liquid honey
3 tbsp cocoa

5 fresh organic egg yolks

Zest of ½ orange or lemon

Combine all of the ingredients in a saucepan and whisk to combine. Cook over moderate heat, stirring constantly with the whisk. Remove from the heat when it thickens just enough to coat the back of a spoon—just before it reaches a boil. Pour into glasses (I use champagne flutes or liqueur glasses) and refrigerate, covered with plastic wrap, for several hours or up to 1 day.

To serve

Place the glass on a chilled dessert plate and serve with a *tegole* wafer (page 364) and, if you like, a slice of honey *semifreddo* (page 323).

Traditionally Inspired Cakes and Tarts

Ciambella con Olio di Oliva
✦ Olive Oil and Citrus Ring Cake

This is a recipe I developed after hearing Giovanni Pina talk about his work using olive oil in pastry production. Pina is the president of the Accademia Maestri Pasticceri Italiani and operates a *pasticceria* in the town of Trescore Balneario, near Bergamo.

According to Pina, most of the standard pastry repertoire can be made using olive oil instead of butter. Even puff pastry! He provided samples of his work, and I was immediately sold: a delightful yellow cake, a white chocolate truffle with an intriguing hint of good olive oil, plain and chocolate-flavored choux pastries stuffed with rich pastry creams, several different cookies. I immediately went home and tried to duplicate his irresistible yellow cake.

I make this cake in a *ciambella* ring mold or Bundt pan. I fill the center with fresh strawberries in the summer and serve it with a dollop of *crema zabaione* (page 335). Use the very best and freshest olive oil you can afford. A light, fruity oil works best with this cake, such as that from the Lago di Garda or Liguria regions of Italy.

The cake is a good keeper, and the flavors develop after a day or two, so it is a good one to make ahead. Bergamot essence is available in specialty baking supply stores. Otherwise, inquire at your local health food store, specifying that you require edible-grade oil.

This recipe produces a large cake, but it is easily halved. It is popular with youngsters and makes a perfect birthday cake.

Serves 12

6 eggs, separated, plus 1 egg white
200 g (7 oz) (1 cup) sugar
210 g (7.5 oz) (1½ cups) all-purpose flour
¼ tsp salt
Scant ½ cup extra virgin olive oil
¼ cup citrus paste (see page 339)
A few drops of bergamot essence (optional)

Preheat the oven to 350°F/175°C. Butter and lightly flour a standard-size Bundt pan.

Beat the egg yolks and the sugar together for about 10 minutes or until they are pale, light and frothy. Sift the flour and salt onto a sheet of wax paper, then sift one-third of the flour over the yolks. Gently but thoroughly fold the flour into the yolks, then repeat, using up the remainder of the flour in two more additions. Next, gently fold in the olive oil, citrus paste and bergamot essence, if using. Beat the egg whites until they are stiff, and gently fold them in. Transfer to the prepared pan.

Bake for about 40 minutes, until a cake tester (I use a piece of spaghetti) inserted in the center of the cake comes out clean. Cool for a few minutes in the pan and then invert the cake onto a rack to cool.

A Secret from an Italian Master Pastry Chef —Citrus Paste

So many recipes in the sweet kitchen call for the grated zest of citrus fruit, or citrus juice, or a combination of the two. So often I have gotten involved in a recipe, not quite read all of the ingredients and then discovered too late that there was not a lemon or orange in the house. I was thrilled to learn this secret from *Maestro* Alessandro Inglese, who was my teacher at the Etoile Advanced Institute of Culinary Arts, in Chioggia.

Here is the solution to the problem:

Buy organic citrus at its seasonal peak—here in Italy, that is the winter months. Take a whole piece of fruit and weigh it. Cut it into 4 or 5 pieces and place it in the work bowl of your food processor. (Inglese used the seeds and all, but I like to remove the seeds.) To this, add the equivalent weight of icing sugar. Process until you have a smooth paste. Freeze.

When a recipe calls for zest or juice, or a combination of the two, this paste is an excellent substitute. I always have a container of it on hand in my freezer, and I add it to everything, including pastry dough and all sorts of cakes and cookies.

La Petraia Caprese Calda
◆ La Petraia Hot Chocolate Torte

This is a flourless chocolate torte, similar to a classic *torta caprese,* the famous dense chocolate torte from the Island of Capri. The difference is the addition of hot chili pepper and the use of olive oil rather than butter, and honey rather than refined white sugar. Use the best olive oil you can find, from the most recent harvest. Like most cakes made using honey and olive oil, this one is a good keeper. Serve it in very thin wedges with a dollop of whipped cream.

SERVES 6 TO 8

Several seeds from 1 hot chili pepper (use your personal
    tolerance for heat to define what "several" means)
A demitasse of hot espresso (scant ¼ cup)
112 g (4 oz) dark chocolate containing 70 percent cocoa solids,
    broken into small pieces
1 tbsp *nocino* (see page 411) or coffee-flavored liqueur
85 g (3 oz) (generous ¾ cup loosely packed) ground almonds
⅓ cup fruity extra virgin olive oil
3 tbsp clover or other mild liquid honey
1 tsp ground espresso beans
3 eggs, separated

To decorate (optional)
Icing sugar, cocoa and ground espresso beans
Raspberries or chocolate-covered coffee beans, or edible
    lavender flowers

Crumble the chili pepper seeds into the hot espresso and let steep until cool.

Preheat the oven to 300°F/150°C. Butter and flour an 8-inch round cake pan.

Strain the coffee onto the chocolate in the top of a double boiler. Add the liqueur. Stir over low heat until melted. Add the almonds, olive oil, honey and ground espresso. Stir to combine. Remove from the heat.

Lightly beat the egg yolks and stir them into the chocolate mixture. Beat the egg whites until firm and gently fold them in. Turn the batter into the cake pan. Bake for 35 to 40 minutes or until a cake tester inserted in the center of the cake comes out clean. Let the cake cool completely in the pan before turning it out onto a plate (bottom side up). It will fall quite a bit as it cools.

Decorate, if desired, by sifting the icing sugar and then the cocoa on the top (which was the bottom) of the cake. On top of this, sift a teaspoon of finely ground espresso. Place raspberries or chocolate-covered coffee beans in a circle around the outside, one per slice. Alternatively, you can place a couple of sprigs of fresh lavender or other edible flowers in the middle of the cake.

HOW TO MEASURE LIQUID HONEY
Lightly coat your measuring cup with a little olive oil before you add the honey. The honey will slide out of the cup without sticking. You will have an exact measure, without wasting a drop.

Torta di Grano Saraceno
◆ Buckwheat Torte from the South Tyrol

This lovely torte is found in the province of Trentino–South Tyrol (Alto Adige) of northeastern Italy. Here we are in the Dolomiti, the breathtaking mountains that make up my favorite part of the Alps. Not only is the region one of Italy's most scenic—the food and wine are superb. What more could you ask for? Buckwheat and rye were the principal cereal crops grown in this area before the maize plant was introduced from the Americas.

This is a quick and easy cake using a batter enriched with ground nuts. I have also heard rumors of an apple being added. This stands to reason, coming as it does from one of the largest apple-growing regions in Europe. Oddly enough, I have yet to come across a recipe, or taste a buckwheat torte with apple in it.

Sugar is this *torta's* usual sweetener, but it can also be made using honey. Sugar is easier and cheaper to come by in Italy now, but this was not always the case, especially in this part of the country, where marvelous alpine honey is produced. The addition of honey produces a moister cake with better flavor and a longer shelf life. It usually improves the day after it is made.

I love the monastic simplicity of this rather plain torte, but it can be dressed up for a party with a filling of homemade preserves and a thick dusting of icing sugar.

SERVES 8 TO 10

140 g (5 oz) (1¼ sticks) butter, at room temperature

140 g (5 oz) (¾ cup) sugar, or 112 g (4 oz) (scant ⅓ cup) dark liquid honey, such as buckwheat

4 eggs, separated

1 tsp vanilla

Zest of 1 lemon (or 1 tbsp citrus paste; see page 339)

140 g (5 oz) (¾ cup plus 2 tbsp) buckwheat flour

140 g (5 oz) (1¼ cups) ground hazelnuts

Red or black currant jelly, or blueberry or blackberry preserves for filling (optional)

Icing sugar and cocoa for dusting (optional)

Preheat the oven to 350°F/175°C. Butter and lightly flour an 8- or 9-inch round cake pan.

Cream the butter and sugar (or honey) in a stand mixer fitted with the paddle attachment until light and fluffy. This will take about 10 minutes on medium speed. Add the egg yolks one at a time, beating well after each addition, then beat in the vanilla and lemon zest (or citrus paste). Fold in the flour and the ground hazelnuts, mixing by hand just to combine. Beat the egg whites until soft peaks form and gently but thoroughly fold them in.

Turn the batter into the prepared pan and bake for 45 minutes—until a cake tester inserted in the center of the cake comes out clean. (If you are using honey, check the torte at the halfway point. If it is getting too dark, cover with a piece of foil.) Let cool in the pan for 15 minutes, then turn out onto a rack to cool completely.

The cooled tart can be cut into 2 layers and filled with a thin layer of jam. Sprinkle a fairly thick layer of icing sugar, or a combination of icing sugar and cocoa, over the top before serving.

Tart Rings

Professional bakers use tart rings to make shallow European-style tarts. When the tarts come out of the oven, the rings slip off easily after the tart has cooled for a few minutes. This easy unmolding means less risk of damage to your masterpiece and also means you can roll your pastry dough thinner, producing a professional-looking shell.

To use a tart ring, simply place it on a parchment-lined baking sheet. Roll out the dough in a circle that is a couple of inches larger than the inside diameter of the ring. Place the dough inside the ring, fitting

it snugly inside the edges. Trim the excess dough from the edges by rolling a rolling pin over the ring to make a neat edge. The scraps that fall from the sides can be rolled in sugar to make cookies while you bake the tart. Once the tart is baked, let it cool for 10 to 15 minutes before you lift the ring off. If you need to, run a knife around the edges of the ring to loosen it. Transfer the hot ring to a basin of hot water to soak to ensure easy cleaning.

Tart rings are ideal for the persimmon tart on page 358, the chocolate tart below, the *crostate* on page 350, the *Torta co' Bischeri* on page 346 and the lemon tart on page 332. Naturally, these recipes can also be made using a traditional tart pan with a removable base.

Crostata alla Cioccolata ✦ Chocolate Tart

Elegant and simple, this dessert is a must in the repertoire of any die-hard chocoholic. Versions of *crostata alla cioccolata* are found in pastry shops all over Italy. Sometimes the chocolate filling contains semolina flour, other times it is simply thickened with eggs. In Tuscany, pears are often added for a pear and chocolate tart. I prefer the simplicity of pure chocolate.

Because it is a rich dessert, I roll out the dough quite thinly, spread the filling in a thin layer and bake it in a tart ring. This produces a sophisticated-looking tart, and served in thin wedges does no harm to anyone. Since the main ingredient is the chocolate, go for broke on quality.

As for a sweet wine accompaniment, a glass of Piedmont's famous chocolate flatterer called Brachetto d'Acqui is recommended if you happen to come across a bottle. This fizzy sweet red wine redolent of raspberries and roses comes from the area where Italy's noblest red wines are produced and puts to rest the myth that chocolate and wine can't be friendly.

SERVES 8

For the dough

½ recipe tart dough (page 358)

For the filling

140 g (5 oz) dark chocolate containing 70 percent cocoa solids, finely chopped

½ cup heavy cream

3 eggs

½ cup candied peel

1 tbsp chocolate liqueur (optional)

For the dough

Place an 8-inch tart ring on a parchment-lined baking sheet (or use a tart pan). Roll out the tart dough very thinly, fit it into the tart ring and trim the edges (see page 343). Refrigerate until you make the filling.

For the filling

Preheat the oven to 350°F/175°C.

Melt the chocolate in the top of a double boiler over low heat. In a saucepan, bring the cream just to a boil and remove from the heat. Whisk the eggs together in a medium bowl and whisk in a bit of the hot cream to temper the eggs. Add the remaining cream, whisking constantly. Return the cream mixture to the pan and cook over moderate heat, stirring constantly, until it has thickened—it should coat the back of the spoon. Remove from the heat and fold in the melted chocolate, candied peel and liqueur, if using.

Pour the filling into the tart shell and bake for 40 minutes or until the crust is golden and the filling is firm.

Torta co' Bischeri ✦ Sweet Spinach Tart from Lucca

Versions of sweet and sometimes savory tarts containing spinach, raisins and pine nuts are found along the Italian Riviera and into Provence, where the sweet version is called *tourte de blettes*. People have been enjoying this tart for a long time—its origins date back to the Middle Ages.

Torta con becchi, or *torta co' bischeri* as it is also called, comes from the beautiful walled city of Lucca and the provincial towns surrounding. This area boasts many unique sweets, but this is one of the more unusual ones, a delectable pie containing mounds of Swiss chard or spinach. It recalls the savory tarts made in nearby Liguria (see page 94).

I picked up this recipe one day when I was in Lucca to attend a local fair. Photocopies were being handed out from a small stand I understood to be the equivalent of the women's auxiliary. It was described as a traditional semisweet tart made in Lucca especially on the occasion of the benediction of Luccan homes during Lent or other holy days. I'd never heard of it before and was fascinated by the idea of a sweet containing so much spinach. Later, I asked Melinda McMahon about it. Melinda is from Pittsburgh but now lives in Tuscany with her husband, Tom. She laughed at the name, explaining how a *bischero* in Tuscan slang is an affectionate name for the male genitals, and is also used to describe someone as a bit of a goof! *Becchi*, on the other hand, refers to little beaks, which are what the triangular peaks on the tart are supposed to represent.

Melinda is American, but her family comes from the area around Lucca, and she shared her recipe for *torta con becchi* with me. I was astonished by how similar hers was to the one I'd found at the fair. Later I asked her about *baccalà con la bietola* (page 230), another Luccan specialty I'd found only one recipe for, in a book on Luccan cooking. None of my other Tuscan cookbooks had any mention of it. "Oh yes," she said, "we ate that every year on Christmas Eve." Melinda may have been born and raised in Pittsburgh, but her family, like many others, has preserved the traditional recipes from their region. Often these are specialties that have all but disappeared in their place of origin. Sometimes to track down an authentic Italian recipe it is necessary to travel to the New World!

If North Americans can make delicious pie out of a vegetable many cultures reserve for feeding their livestock (pumpkin), then who is to say that an equally good one can't be made using spinach? And in Lucca it is. Don't be put off by this eclectic mix of sweet and savory ingredients. This tart is sublime.

To confuse things, other tarts with the same name come from this area. A similar one uses rice instead of bread. Others are filled with a variety of ingredients that can include chocolate, cooked rice, pine nuts, ricotta, candied fruit and spices. They are all made with a pastry border of *becchi*.

SERVES 6 TO 8

For the dough
    75 g (2.5 oz) (5 tbsp) butter
    130 g (4.5 oz) (⅔ cup) sugar
    2 eggs
    280 g (10 oz) (2⅓ cups) cake-and-pastry flour
    ¼ tsp baking soda

⅛ tsp baking powder

½ tsp salt

1 tbsp almond liqueur (or 1 tsp almond extract)

1 tbsp olive oil

Zest of 1 lemon

For the filling

½ cup raisins

¼ cup dark rum

140 g (5 oz) day-old sliced white bread

1⅓ cups warm milk

1 tbsp butter

1 tbsp extra virgin olive oil

225 g (½ lb) fresh spinach leaves, washed

Leaves from 1 large bunch parsley, finely chopped (about 56 g/2 oz)

A pinch each of salt and pepper

⅓ cup sugar

1 egg, lightly beaten

¼ tsp cinnamon

Scant ⅛ tsp ground cloves

A pinch of freshly grated nutmeg

⅓ cup grated Parmesan cheese

3 tbsp pine nuts

For the dough

In a stand mixer fitted with the paddle, cream the butter and the sugar until light and fluffy, about 10 minutes, and then add the eggs, one at a time, beating well after each addition. In the meantime, sift together the flour, baking soda, baking powder and salt. Add to the egg mixture along with the almond liqueur, olive oil and lemon zest. Mix briefly, just enough to combine. Form the dough into a ball, cover with plastic wrap and refrigerate at least 1 hour. It can also be frozen for up to a month.

Have ready an 8- or 9-inch tart pan. This dough tends to be a bit sticky, and it is easiest to roll it out between two sheets of wax or parchment paper. Roll it out into a circle, 1 inch in diameter larger than what you need to fill your tart pan. Remove the top sheet of parchment and invert the dough into your tart pan. Remove the second sheet of parchment. Pat the dough securely into place, making sure you have a 1-inch rim above the tart pan. If your dough starts to get soft, put it in the freezer briefly to firm—about 10 minutes.

When you are ready to proceed, using a pair of scissors, cut the 1-inch rim on an angle at 1½-inch intervals around the tart to create a fringe. Fold the outermost point of each fringe down to the opposite bottom corner, pressing the layers together, to form a thick triangle of dough. Your tart shell should now look like a crown. Place the prepared tart shell in the refrigerator until you are ready to fill it and bake.

For the filling

Several hours or the day before you plan to bake the tart, soak the raisins in the rum. When you are ready to make the filling, drain the raisins and pat them dry.

Preheat the oven to 350°F/175°C.

Soak the bread in the warm milk while you prepare the spinach. Heat the butter and olive oil in a frying pan over moderate heat. Add the spinach and parsley leaves, season lightly with salt and pepper, and cook, stirring now and again, until very tender—about 10 minutes. Let cool for 10 to 15 minutes, then transfer to a blender or food processor. Remove the bread from the milk and squeeze it dry. Add to the spinach along with the sugar, egg, spices and half of the cheese. Process briefly, then stir in the drained raisins and half of the pine nuts. Cover and place in the refrigerator for several hours or overnight.

Spoon the filling into the prepared pastry shell. Top with the remaining pine nuts and cheese. Bake for 35 to 40 minutes or until the crust is golden and the tart has set.

Crostate

Crostata is the ubiquitous Italian dessert made from a rich crust spread thinly with a layer of homemade *marmellata* (jam). It is filled with ricotta, pastry cream or other more elaborate fillings. Almost every home cook knows how to make one, and like anything else, when made with good-quality ingredients, these tarts are divine. Watch out, though—the country is filled with cellophane-wrapped, unattractive *crostate* made with margarine and filled with syrupy, industrially made preserves that taste like they contain little real fruit.

These gems are hard to find unless you get invited home for dinner or seek out a high-quality pastry shop. Then you might appreciate the fuss made over such a homely-looking creation. Italians frequently enjoy a wedge of *crostata* for breakfast (standing up in the local bar), and most families boast a living legend, *la mamma, la nonna* or *la zia*—mother, grandmother or aunt—justifiably famous for her *crostate*.

A good *crostata* is as different from a good North American pie (with its thin, flaky crust and a deep, sweet filling) as night is from day. To make an exquisite *crostata*, one must learn the rigor of the minimalist who achieves perfection using two things inherent in all good Italian food: restraint and the very best ingredients.

The *crostata*—the word means "crust" in Italian—is as much about the dough as what it's filled with. The filling is meant to gild the lily, the same way pasta sauce is used sparingly as a condiment for quality pasta and few but high-quality ingredients are used to dress the very best pizza dough. The crust is the star, and what goes inside is not so much a "filling" as a simple, elegant finish. You want to roll out the dough fairly thick and be miserly with the filling.

I've included the recipe for the basic dough used to make *crostate*, called *pasta frolla*, along with two fillings—one using fruit (page 352) and another ricotta (page 353). *Pasta frolla* is more airy and cake-like than the short pastry used to make the other tarts in this chapter, with the exception of the *torta co' bischeri* (page 346), which is made with its own distinctive crust somewhat similar to *pasta frolla*.

Crostate are easy to put together at the last minute. All you need is a jar of good fruit preserves (preferably your own) and a piece of *pasta frolla* in the fridge or freezer. My favorite filling for *crostata* is the apricot compote on page 407.

SERVES 8

For the pasta frolla
   280 g (10 oz) (2 cups) all-purpose flour
   100 g (3.5 oz) (½ cup) superfine sugar
   ½ tsp salt
   ½ tsp baking powder
   140 g (5 oz) (1¼ sticks) cold butter, cut into small pieces
   Zest and juice of ½ lemon or orange (or 1 tbsp citrus paste;
      see page 339)
   1 egg
   1 egg yolk

Place the flour, sugar, salt and baking powder in your food processor and process briefly to blend. Spread the butter pieces evenly over the flour and process briefly again until you have a coarse mixture. Feed the lemon juice and zest (or paste), as well as the egg and egg yolk into the feeding tube and process until the dough comes together. Divide the dough into two pieces, one twice as large as the other. Shape the dough into thick rounds and refrigerate, tightly wrapped in plastic, for at least half an hour before rolling it out and filling it as in the recipes that follow. The dough freezes well for a month.

Crostata di Marmellata ♦ Jam Tart

This *crostata* is the perfect use for the apricot compote on page 407.

Preheat the oven to 350°F/175°C.

You should have enough dough to thickly fill a 9-inch ring or tart pan. This dough is sticky, and I find it easiest and cleanest to roll it out between two sheets of parchment paper rather than on a floured surface. Place the larger piece of dough on a piece of parchment large enough to hold your tart ring. Place another sheet of parchment the same size on top. Roll out the dough between the parchment sheets until it is large enough to fill the tart ring. Slide the dough with the parchment onto a baking sheet and refrigerate for 30 minutes to firm. Alternatively, you can place it in the freezer for a shorter time.

When you are ready to proceed, take the parchment-encased dough off the baking sheet. Remove the top sheet of parchment and transfer it to the baking sheet. Place the tart ring on it. Invert the dough onto the tart ring and peel away the second sheet of parchment. Carefully fit the dough into the tart ring and trim the edges (see page 344).

Spread about 2 cups of preserves over the tart. You want the filling to be thinly spread, about ½ inch. Refrigerate the tart while you prepare the lattice.

Remove the smaller piece of dough from the fridge and roll it into a circle that is thinner than the first one but the same diameter. Cut into 1-inch strips with a pastry cutter, and lay the strips in a criss-cross shape over the tart to form a lattice. Press the edges to seal well.

Bake for 35 minutes or until the crust is golden. This tart seems to improve the day after it is made, and keeps well for several days.

Variation Using Fresh Fruit

Spread 1 cup of apricot jam in a thin layer over the crust. Peel, core and thinly slice (use a mandoline if you own one) 2 Golden Delicious apples or slightly unripe pears. Spread the fruit slices in concentric, overlapping circles over the preserves. Brush the fruit with an additional ¼ cup of apricot jam that has been pushed through a fine sieve and diluted with 1 tbsp of water. You do not need the pastry lattice. Bake as directed above. When cool, sieve a fine dusting of icing sugar over the top.

Crostata di Ricotta ✦ Ricotta Tart

This tart is inspired by Sicily, where the freshest ricotta, sublime candied fruit and chocolate meet up frequently in mouth-watering desserts like this one.

For the dough

1 recipe *pasta frolla* (page 351)

For the filling

    280 g (10 oz) ricotta cheese

    3 eggs, lightly beaten

    ½ cup mild liquid honey, such as clover

    ¼ cup mixed candied fruit

    ¼ cup good-quality miniature chocolate chips

    Zest from 1 orange or lemon (or 1 tbsp citrus paste; see page 339)

Prepare and roll out the dough as described on pages 351 to 352. Preheat the oven to 350°F/175°C.

Beat together the ricotta cheese, the eggs and the honey until well combined. Fold in the remaining ingredients. Fill the tart and top with the lattice as described on page 353.

Bake for 35 minutes or until the crust is golden and the filling is firm. Let cool to room temperature, then refrigerate several hours before serving.

The La Petraia Autumnal Trio

The following three desserts are designed to showcase the wild berries, chestnuts and persimmon that grow on our property. They take us from late summer with the berries through fall with the chestnut harvest and into early December, when our persimmons turn electric orange, lighting up the landscape in the darkest month.

Torta di Frutti di Bosco ✦ Wild Berry Tart

Perhaps my favorite berries to use in this tart are the mulberries that grow on the three-hundred-year-old trees we have next to the house. They were planted by the peasant farmers who originally lived here, to house silkworms. The resultant silk would have been a valuable product sold to their wealthy landlords. These elegant old trees are still producing sweet, plump white-and-black mulberries. More often than not, around sunset, we find a family of wild boar feasting on the day's windfall, even as our guests sit, not fifty feet away, having dinner on the front terrace. The evening's entertainment.

This rustic-looking tart is good served in thin strips alongside a slice of lemon *semifreddo* (page 326). I make it with a mix of our cultivated and wild berries that often includes brambleberries, black currants, mulberries, gooseberries, blueberries and elderberries.

SERVES 4 TO 6

For the pastry
   300 g (10.5 oz) puff pastry (page 390 or use store-bought)

For the filling
   4 cups mixed fresh berries
   ¼ cup mild liquid honey
   2 tbsp all-purpose flour
   1 tbsp lemon juice

You can use commercially grown berries to make this tart, but if you pick your own wild ones be careful to choose only the ripest fruit. Clean them well and remove any stems.

To finish
   Icing sugar to decorate
   Whipped cream to garnish (optional)

For the pastry
Roll the dough out into a rough 10- by 12-inch rectangle. Transfer to a parchment-lined baking sheet and chill for half an hour.

In the meantime, preheat the oven to 425°F/220°C.

For the filling

Combine the berries with the rest of the filling ingredients and let sit for 15 minutes, stirring once or twice.

Spread the filling evenly over the rolled-out pastry to within an inch or so of the edges. Fold the edges of the crust up to form a rustic rim around the tart. Bake for 15 minutes. Lower the heat to 350°F/175°C and bake for another 20 minutes or so, until the crust is golden brown.

When the tart emerges from the oven, it will probably look very messy. Some of the dark berry juices inevitably escape, staining the crust. Don't worry, this is normal and the tart is easily transformed into an elegant masterpiece. Let it cool completely and dust it with icing sugar.

To serve

Cut the tart into strips about 1½ inches wide. Cut each strip in half and place them at odd angles to each other on each serving plate. If you want to add some glamor, you can pipe whipped cream in tiny rosettes along the edges of the tart strips and serve them with a thin slice of lemon *semifreddo* (page 326) drizzled with its berry *coulis*. Dust the whole plate with a thin veil of icing sugar before serving.

Castagnaccio ◆ Chestnut Soufflé

As the owner of a famed grove of ancient chestnut trees bearing the coveted fruit called *marrone*, I am forever on the lookout for chestnut recipes. Never having acquired the taste for *castagnaccio*, the flat chestnut-flour cake studded with raisins and pine nuts that is traditional to Tuscany, I was intrigued when I found a dessert of the same name in Nika Hazelton's

The Swiss Cookbook. According to her, in the Swiss-Italian canton of Ticino, where chestnuts grow in abundance, a *castagnaccio* is a chestnut soufflé.

Inspired by the soufflé of Ticino rather than the pancake of Tuscany, I make this in individual soufflé or pudding molds that hold 1 cup. This recipe makes a sophisticated, light and healthy dessert that is easy to make and packed with flavor.

SERVES 4

100 g (3.5 oz) (approx. ⅔ cup) shelled fresh chestnuts (see page 122)
1 cup milk
½ vanilla bean
1 oz dark chocolate containing 70% cocoa solids, melted
4 eggs, separated
2 tbsp chestnut honey
2 tsp sugar
2 tbsp kirsch*
Butter and sugar for the molds and finishing
If you've made cherries preserved in grappa (see page 411), use some of the cherry-infused grappa the cherries are macerating in instead of kirsch.

Preheat the oven to 400°F/200°C. Butter 4 individual soufflé molds and then sprinkle the inside with sugar, rotating the mold as you go to coat it evenly. Turn it upside down and tap out any excess sugar so only a thin veil remains.

Place the chestnuts in a saucepan with the milk. Cut the vanilla bean lengthwise and scrape the seeds into the milk, stirring to distribute the seeds. Add the bean. Simmer until the chestnuts are tender—about 30 minutes. Remove the vanilla bean. Strain the chestnuts and let cool.

Place them in your blender or food processor with the melted chocolate and add the egg yolks, honey, sugar and kirsch. Process until smooth. Transfer to a large bowl.

Whisk the egg whites to soft peaks and carefully fold them into the chestnut mixture in three additions. Transfer to your molds and sieve a sprinkle of sugar over the top. Put the molds on a baking sheet and bake for 15 minutes or until the soufflés have puffed up generously above the molds. Serve immediately.

Torta di Cachi ✦ Persimmon Tart

Our persimmons usually ripen in December, and as the trees lose their leaves the fruit turns electric orange, looking like it's been lit up for the holidays. Most Italians I know don't do much with persimmons, other than eat them out of hand. But they make lovely tarts, gelato and cakes.

For the persimmons, choose an astringent variety such as the Hachiya. These are the type that cannot be eaten hard but must be allowed to fully ripen until their pulp turns mushy. If you have unripe (hard) persimmons, place them in a bag with an apple to hasten the ripening. If you happen to own a tree and are overwhelmed with the fruit ripening all at once, the pulp freezes beautifully. Or, if you can't be bothered with that, just throw the whole fruit in the freezer. You can remove the pulp later. The frozen pulp is quite lovely on its own, and can be served as a palate-cleansing sorbet.

SERVES 8

For the tart dough
    280 g (10 oz) (2 cups) all-purpose flour
    170 g (6 oz) (1½ sticks) cold butter, cut into 8 pieces

75 g (2.5 (½ cup) icing sugar

30 g (1 oz) (scant ¼ cup loosely packed) ground almonds

Zest of 1 lemon

A pinch of salt

1 egg

For the persimmon filling

2 cups persimmon pulp (from 3 to 4 persimmons)

1 cup heavy cream

½ cup liquid honey

1 egg

A pinch of salt

¼ tsp each cinnamon and allspice

For the dough

Put all the dough ingredients but the egg in the work bowl of your food processor. Pulse until you get a coarse meal, then add the egg and process briefly, just until the dough comes together in a ball. Wrap the dough in plastic. Refrigerate for at least 30 minutes or freeze for up to 1 month.

Place a 10-inch tart ring on a parchment-lined baking sheet (or use a 10-inch tart pan). Roll out the dough between two sheets of parchment paper. Remove the top sheet of parchment and invert the dough onto your tart ring. Remove the second sheet of parchment and fit the dough into your tart ring. Trim the edges (see page 344) and refrigerate until ready to bake.

Preheat the oven to 350°F/175°C.

For the filling

Blend all of the filling ingredients in a blender. Pour the filling into your well-chilled tart shell and bake for 45 to 50 minutes or until the filling is firm and the crust is golden.

This tart can be served as is or can become an element in a more sophisticated plated dessert. To turn it into that, sieve some icing sugar on top of the tart and cut it into thin wedges. Pipe rosettes of whipped cream around the edges of each slice and serve it alongside the honey or *panpepato semifreddi* on pages 323 and 327.

Biscotti

Cavallucci ◆ Anise-flavored Cookies from Siena

Cavallucci is the name given to these cookies found in almost every bakery in the province of Siena. For a reason I have never completely understood, the name means "ponies." Some say it's because they can be so hard you have to have the teeth of a horse to eat them. Another explanation is that they were once on offer in the regional postal stations as refreshment for the workers who stopped there to change horses.

Like many Tuscan sweets, *cavallucci* are rustic and homely and should not be judged by their appearance. They look like rocks, but once you bite into them you will immediately understand their popularity. Their texture has the perfect crisp-to-chew ratio, and their addictive taste is the result of an ingenious combination of walnuts, anise and candied fruit. *Cavallucci* contain no fat other than that found naturally in the nuts. In Siena, they accompany a glass of the local sweet wine or Vin Santo.

450 g (16 oz) (2¼ cups) sugar

170 g (6 oz) (¾ cup) water

550 g (1 lb 3 oz) (4 cups) all-purpose flour, plus more for dusting

170 g (6 oz) (1½ cups) walnuts, chopped

150 g (5.3 oz) (1 cup) candied peel

1½ tbsp anise seed

2 tsp cinnamon

1½ tsp baking powder

56 g (2 oz) (scant 3 tbsp) liquid honey

Preheat the oven to 350°F/175°C.

Combine the sugar and water in a saucepan and bring to a rolling boil. Boil until all of the sugar has dissolved and the temperature on a candy thermometer just reaches 215°F to 220°F (102°C to 105°C). In the meantime, mix together all of the remaining ingredients (except the honey) in the work bowl of a stand mixer fitted with the paddle attachment.

When the syrup is ready, pour it over the dry ingredients and turn the machine to medium speed. Mix until the ingredients are well combined. Add the honey and mix again briefly—you should have a moist, sticky dough. If the dough seems dry and crumbly (which could happen if your sugar syrup was too hot), add a little water, a tablespoon at a time, until the dough feels moist and sticky. Turn the dough out onto a floured surface and cut it into three equal pieces. Form each piece into a ball.

To make the cookies, on a well-floured surface, shape one ball into a rope about 1½ feet long. Cut into 1½-inch pieces, and roll each piece into a ball. Place balls on a parchment-lined baking sheet. Using your thumb, make a slight indent in the middle of each ball. Sieve a very light veil of flour over the cookies.

Bake for about 15 minutes. The cookies are done when their spice aroma starts to fill your kitchen. They will be soft when they come out of the oven and will have colored only slightly. Cool on a rack. The cookies get harder as they cool, retaining a chewy interior thanks to the honey. The cookies keep well for 1 week or more in an airtight container.

Ricciarelli ✦ Sienese Almond Cookies

These pretty almond cookies, another specialty of Siena, are easy to make and even easier to eat. They contain no fat other than that found in the almonds. If you are a marzipan lover, you will appreciate these cookies. A great cookie connoisseur once told me this was the best cookie he'd ever eaten.

This recipe shows off the frugal nature of the Tuscan cook. Because this recipe contains so many almonds, you might think it would be costly to make. Not so for the Italian farm wife, whose property usually boasted at least one almond tree, and who always kept a few hens. The yolks of their eggs might be used to make fresh pasta or thicken a soup, while the whites could be mixed with ground almonds and sugar to make these lovely cookies. And so an effortless, exquisite treat could be made using the freshest, highest-quality ingredients. Like so much that is good about Italian cooking, these cookies, with three principal components of almonds, sugar and egg whites, teach us again of the importance of keeping things simple and seeking out the best-quality ingredients.

In Siena these cookies are baked on sheets of edible rice paper, which can be found in specialty baking supply stores and used instead of parchment paper.

500 g (17.5 oz) (3⅓ cups) blanched almonds

400 g (14 oz) (2 cups) superfine sugar

100 g (3.5 oz) (⅔ cup) icing sugar, plus more for dusting

50 g (1.75 oz) (2.5 tbsp) mild liquid honey

1 tsp baking powder

Zest of 1 orange or lemon

2 large egg whites

Preheat the oven to 300°F/150°C.

Spread the almonds on a baking sheet and place them in the oven for 5 minutes to lightly toast them. They should not take on any color. Remove the almonds and turn off the oven. When the almonds are cool enough to handle, transfer them to the work bowl of your food processor along with half of the superfine sugar. Process to a fine meal.

In a large bowl, combine the almond mixture with the remaining superfine sugar, icing sugar, honey, baking powder and zest. Beat the egg whites until they form soft peaks and knead them into the mixture until you get a stiff dough.

Line two baking sheets with parchment paper. Working with a heaping teaspoon of dough at a time, mold the cookie into a diamond shape by pressing the spoon against your palm. Transfer the dough to a baking sheet and use the bottom of the spoon to slightly extend the dough into a lozenge shape about 2 inches long and ⅓ inch thick. Repeat with the remaining dough, arranging the cookies about 1 inch apart. Sprinkle icing sugar in a thick layer over the cookies. Let the cookies dry at room temperature, uncovered, for 1 hour before baking. Meanwhile, preheat the oven to 300°F/150°C.

Bake the ricciarelli for about 15 minutes. (I prefer to bake one sheet at a time.) They should not have taken on much color and will be soft when you remove them from the oven. Cool on a rack. They will harden as they cool, retaining a soft, chewy interior. Stored in an airtight container, they keep for 1 week.

Variation

I once tasted southern relatives of these cookies that contained bergamot essence. They were made by a Calabrian family that grows bergamot trees and makes natural essences. The cookies I tasted were divine, and I usually add a drop of their exquisite bergamot essence when I make this recipe. Although a citizen of Siena might sneer at the very thought of altering this cookie, I can get away with it and so can you if you can locate edible-grade bergamot essence. Your health food store or herbalist is a good place to start.

Tegole
⋆ Almond and Hazelnut Wafers from the Val d'Aosta

Anyone who has visited Italy's smallest province, the Val d'Aosta, has likely seen or tasted these wafer-thin cookies. Sold everywhere from gas stations to upscale pastry shops, they are one of the many gastronomic specialties of this tiny region. *Tegole* are served in some of the area's finest restaurants as an accompaniment to elegant desserts such as the *crema di Cogne* on page 336. They are also an excellent accompaniment to ice cream or any of the *semifreddi* in this chapter.

The Val d'Aosta is one of Italy's autonomous bilingual regions. Here you are as likely to hear French spoken as you are Italian. The house of Savoy once ruled this area and its influence is still felt today—some houses are still decorated with the Savoy coat of arms. Another distinguishing feature of the Val d'Aosta is its mountain landscape, including the two highest peaks in the Alps, which are shared with neighboring France and Switzerland, Monte Bianco (Mont Blanc) and Monte Rosa.

In Aosta, *tegole* (which means "tiles" in Italian) are cut with intricately carved wooden stamps with traditional designs on them. When still hot from the oven, they are molded over a dowel or rolling pin to take the shape of a curved roof tile.

I roll the dough out and cut it with a pastry cutter to create big, graphic shapes. I store them in an airtight container and use them to add a bit of drama to a dessert course. Perch them on top of a thin slice of *semifreddo* or ice cream. Or go minimalist: pile them up on a plate and serve along with a glass of sweet wine or strong espresso.

Makes about 3 dozen 2-inch-square cookies

112 g (4 oz) (¾ cup) blanched almonds

112 g (4 oz) (scant 1 cup) blanched hazelnuts

112 g (4 oz) (½ cup plus 1 tbsp) sugar

50 g (1.75 oz) (scant ⅓ cup) all-purpose flour

2 egg whites, lightly beaten

Preheat the oven to 350°F/175°C.

Spread the almonds and hazelnuts on a baking sheet and toast in the oven for about 7 minutes. Let your nose tell you when the nuts are ready—the kitchen will fill up with the smell of toasted nuts, and they will have just begun to turn golden.

Let them cool for a few minutes and then process in your food processor with 1 to 2 tbsp of the sugar until you get a fine meal. Be careful

This cookie dough freezes well, and I often freeze half the dough for later. If you live in a humid climate, you may find the cookies do not stay crisp. Simply heat them in a 350°F/175°C oven for a couple of minutes to crisp before serving.

not to over-process the nuts or you will end up with nut butter. Add the remaining sugar, the flour and egg whites and process briefly, until the dough begins to come together. Divide the dough into two pieces. Using wet hands, form each piece into a ball.

Cut two sheets of parchment paper to fit a baking sheet. Place each piece of dough in the middle of a sheet of parchment. Using wet hands, pat out each round into a disk about 4 inches in diameter. Cover one disk with another sheet of parchment and, using a rolling pin, roll it out as thinly as you can. Remove the top sheet of parchment and use it to repeat the process with the other piece of dough.

Slide each parchment sheet onto a baking sheet and, using a pastry cutter, cut the dough into 2-inch squares (or any shape or size you like). Any trimmings can be rerolled and cut to make more cookies.

Bake for about 12 minutes, until golden brown. Cool on a rack. The cookies keep well for 2 weeks in an airtight container.

Cantucci di Prato ✦ Tuscan Almond Biscotti

I first learned how to make *cantucci*, perhaps Tuscany's most famous cookies, from a Neapolitan. That says a lot about how good they are. Italians are notoriously xenophobic and patriotic to their region of origin. Seldom is the cooking from another part of the country as good as that of their own, and rare is the person who has mastered a "foreign" recipe.

Here in Tuscany, these lovely cookies are made by home bakers quickly and simply in the way most Italians I know work in the kitchen: using a recipe retrieved from memory, with no bowls, mixers or wooden spoons. *Cantucci* are whipped up in an instant with the flick of a wrist and a strong arm.

We've all seen the oversized, chocolate-coated, fruit-and-nut-studded cookies called "biscotti" sold coast to coast in trendy coffee shops for a small fortune. The following recipe is the real thing, the authentic and simpler cookie found throughout Tuscany and the original inspiration for the treat that has become so popular in North America. Baked twice (*biscotti* means "twice cooked" in Italian), the cookies are extra hard, and in Tuscany they are eaten for dessert, dipped in a little glass of Vin Santo, the local sweet wine. But a cup of good coffee or tea will also do the trick.

MAKES 4 TO 5 DOZEN COOKIES

500 g (17.5 oz) (3½ cups) all-purpose flour

280 g (10 oz) (1½ cups) sugar

1 tsp baking powder

Zest of 1 lemon and 1 orange*

4 eggs

Juice of ½ orange*

½ tsp vanilla

280 g (10 oz) (2 cups) raw almonds (with skins)

¼ cup of citrus paste (see page 339) can be substituted for the citrus zest and orange juice

Preheat the oven to 400°F/200°C.

To make the dough by hand, make a well with the flour on your work surface and place the sugar, baking powder and lemon and orange zest in the center. Break the eggs into the center of the sugar, and on top of them pour the orange juice and vanilla. Stretch the fingers of your best hand as if they were clutching an imaginary baseball and rapidly move this hand through the egg mixture in a circular motion to stir together the sugar and eggs. Once combined, begin to incorporate the flour from the sides of the well, using your other hand to support the walls of the well as you stir. Once the flour is combined, add the almonds and knead briefly to incorporate. The dough will be fairly sticky, not a stiff cookie dough.

To make the dough in a mixer, stir together the dry ingredients and the zest using the paddle attachment. Lightly beat the eggs and add them along with the orange juice and vanilla. Mix just enough to form the dough. Remove from the work bowl and knead the almonds in by hand.

To shape this sticky dough, it is best to work with lightly floured hands. Turn the dough onto a lightly floured work surface and divide it

into three pieces. Roll each piece out to form a slightly flattened log about 12 inches long. Place on a parchment-lined baking sheet and bake for 20 minutes or until the crust turns golden.

Remove from the oven and, when cool enough to handle, use a sharp knife to slice each log on an angle to form *biscotti* about ½ inch thick. Arrange the *biscotti* on baking sheets and return to the oven for another 10 minutes or until they are dry and just starting to color. Cool on racks. These cookies keep for 6 weeks stored in an airtight container.

Amaretti ✦ Italian Macaroons

Amaretti are the Italian version of the classic French *macaron*, and are a pantry staple. They are made using the same three ingredients—egg whites, almonds and sugar—that the French use to make their beloved *macarons*, but *amaretti* contain a higher ratio of almonds to egg whites, so they are not as delicate or as fussy to make. The *macaron* is the traditional test of a French pastry chef, and years are spent perfecting its execution, just as the savory chef will spend years learning how to perfectly cook a simple egg.

Amaretti are perfect eaten alone, but they are also incorporated into many other sweet and savory dishes, such as the lemon *semifreddo* on page 326. They get their name from the word *amaro*, which means "bitter." Traditionally, bitter almonds (as well as sweet ones) were used in these cookies. Because bitter almonds are toxic if eaten in large enough quantities, they are not used in North America, but these cookies can be made successfully without them.

Amaretti are easy to make and keep for ages in an airtight cookie tin. I keep a yogurt container in my freezer to which I add unused egg whites for the specific purpose of making these lovely cookies. Low in fat and calories, they are a nice guilt-free snack to have around for those days when the sweet tooth demands some attention but a diet calls for restraint. I usually keep a stash of these cookies in my *dispensa*—ready to be used in a *semifreddo* or to serve along with a cup of coffee.

MAKES ABOUT 3 DOZEN COOKIES

225 g (½ lb) (2 cups loosely packed) ground almonds
225 g (½ lb) (1½ cups) icing sugar
3 egg whites

Preheat the oven to 350°F/175°C.

Mix together the ground almonds and half of the sugar. Beat the egg whites to soft peaks and then begin to slowly incorporate the remaining sugar while still beating. Continue to beat until you have stiff, shiny peaks. Gently fold in the nuts and sugar.

To shape the cookies, you can use a piping bag to pipe out small, round cookies onto a parchment-lined baking sheet, or you can use a spoon, dropping the dough by the spoonful onto the parchment. Transfer to the oven and immediately lower the heat to 300°F/150°C.

Bake for 25 minutes or until golden, opening and closing the oven door a couple of times to let some of the steam escape. Turn the oven off. Leave the cookies to dry out in the oven while it cools.

These cookies will keep in an airtight container for 2 to 3 weeks, if not longer.

Variations

Add a couple of drops of edible-grade bergamot or lavender essence to the egg whites.

Biscotti al Miele e Spezie ♦ Honey and Spice Cookies

These cookies are inspired by the Alto Adige, or South Tyrol as the region is known by its German-speaking residents. Peppery cookies made with honey are common in Eastern Europe, and it is strange to think of them as Italian. But this part of Italy not too long ago belonged to the Austro-Hungarian Empire, and here you begin to get a taste of central and Eastern Europe.

I use olive oil rather than butter and whole grain flour, so these spicy cookies become a healthy treat to have on hand.

MAKES ABOUT 30 COOKIES

2 tbsp extra virgin olive oil

2 eggs, lightly beaten

170 g (6 oz) (½ cup) liquid honey

½ cup candied citron

Grated zest of 1 lemon

140 g (5 oz) (1 cup) all-purpose flour

70 g (2.5 oz) (scant ½ cup) whole wheat flour

56 g (2 oz) (½ cup) whole rye flour

1 tsp baking powder

½ tsp ground cloves

½ tsp cinnamon

½ tsp cardamom

⅛ tsp nutmeg

¼ tsp salt

⅛ tsp black or white pepper

1 cup sugar to finish (optional)

Combine the oil, eggs and honey in a large bowl and mix well. Add the candied citron and lemon zest. Sift together the dry ingredients and mix them into the first mixture using a wooden spoon or a stand mixer fitted with the paddle attachment. Transfer this sticky dough to a bowl and cover the surface with plastic wrap. Chill for 1 hour.

Remove the dough from the fridge and roll into walnut-sized balls. Place on parchment-lined baking sheets and use your palm to lightly flatten each cookie. Let the cookies sit for 6 hours or overnight to dry out, then sprinkle the surface with the sugar, if using.

Preheat the oven to 350°F/175°C.

Bake for 15 minutes, until lightly golden. Cool on a rack. Store in an airtight container, where they will keep for 1 week or longer.

CELEBRATORY BREADS

The Christmas holidays in Italy end on January 6 with Epiphany and a visit from the witch, Befana, who arrives on a broomstick and leaves sweets for all the good children. The bad ones are given a piece of coal. Today most children are given a piece of coal made out of sugar as a ritual joke. These are sold in pastry shops all over Italy around Epiphany. After Befana departs, overnight the stores seem to fill with special treats for the *Carnevale* season, and then there is fasting to be done for Lent. Easter brings a final round of indulgence and hopefully the end of winter. Thus, the darkest, coldest corner of the year is turned and made brighter by feasting and fasting. Up and down the peninsula there are special sweets to accompany you almost every day. Here are a few of my favorites.

Panpepato Senese ◆ Peppery Fruit Cake from Siena

This spicy confection makes for a wonderful Christmas gift. It can be made ahead, is not the least bit fragile and doesn't take up a lot of room in a suitcase if you are traveling. *Panpepato* is the spicy cousin of the Senese sweet called *panforte*, which means "strong bread."

This sweet is eaten not only at Christmas but all year round in Siena. It is dense with fruit and nuts and is usually served in small wedges for dessert with a glass of the local sweet wine, Vin Santo. So much do the citizens of Siena love their *panforte*, they have given the cake its own patron saint, San Lorenzo, whose feast day is August 10. Traditionally, these cakes are baked on sheets of edible rice paper, which you can find in some pastry supply shops. Don't worry, however, they're just as good when baked on parchment. It is best to weigh your ingredients for this recipe using kitchen scales.

MAKES ONE 9-INCH CAKE

340 g (12 oz) (2¼ cups) whole unblanched almonds

170 g (6 oz) (½ cup) liquid honey

100 g (3.5 oz) (½ cup) sugar

150 g (5.3 oz) (1 cup) candied fruit, finely chopped (I use orange or citrus peel)

112 g (4 oz) (approx. ¾ cup) dried figs, cut into small pieces

112 g (4 oz) (approx. ¾ cup) dried apricots, cut into small pieces

105 g (3.75oz) (¾ cup) all-purpose flour

28 g (1 oz) (⅓ cup) cocoa

1 tsp freshly ground black pepper

1 tsp cinnamon

1 tsp ground coriander

You can experiment with the dried and candied fruit and nuts. For example, hazelnuts can be used instead of some or all of the almonds and raisins instead of some or all of the figs.

½ tsp ground cloves

½ tsp mace (optional)

Cocoa, cinnamon and ground coriander to finish

Preheat the oven to 350°F/175°C. Place a sheet of rice paper or buttered parchment paper on a baking sheet. Place a 9-inch tart ring (or the rim of a tart pan with a removable bottom) on top. Line the insides of the tart ring (or pan rim) with either rice paper or parchment.

Spread the nuts on a baking sheet and toast them in the oven for 7 minutes or until you start to smell them. Remove the almonds from the oven and, when cool enough to handle, process one-quarter of them in a food processor or chop by hand. You want the nuts to remain in fairly big pieces. Leave the rest of the nuts whole. Turn the oven down to 300°F/150°C.

Stir the honey and sugar together in a heavy-bottomed saucepan. In a large bowl, mix the whole and chopped almonds with of all the remaining ingredients. Heat the honey and sugar until the temperature reaches 240°F/115°C on a candy thermometer. This happens quickly after the syrup reaches a boil, so stay attentive. Pour the thick, hot syrup into the dry ingredients. At this stage you must mix the dough swiftly before things begin to harden. Stir with a wooden spoon until everything is well combined. Better still, if you can stand the heat, wet your hands and knead the ingredients together. The dough will be stiff.

Use wet hands to press the dough firmly into your tart ring. Bake for 40 to 45 minutes. The *panpepato* will be soft and slightly puffed up when you remove it from the oven and will firm up as it cools. Cool on a rack, removing the tart ring and parchment if used.

Dust lightly first with cocoa and then with a little cinnamon and coriander. The cake should be left to ripen for 1 day before cutting and is best stored tightly wrapped in plastic or in a layer of wax paper and then a layer of aluminum foil. It will keep for 2 to 3 weeks.

Schiacciata alla Fiorentina
✦ Florentine Carnival Flat Cake

Once the last feast of the Christmas season is celebrated on January 6 with Befana (Epiphany), families return from holidays, children reluctantly head back to school, and the New Year begins in earnest. But before long comes the Carnival season, with its host of special Carnival sweets along with a variety of masks and costumes for young and old alike. For children, *Carnevale* is like Halloween, a time to dress up in costume and consume an enormous amount of sweets, usually deep-fried fritters that go by a wide variety of names—*fritelle, cenci, bomboloni, chiacchiere, donzinelli,* to list but a few.

In the city of Florence and the provincial towns surrounding it, this brioche-like cake appears for *Carnevale,* dusted with icing sugar and imprinted with the *giglio di Firenze,* the red iris that adorns the city's coat of arms. Sadly, it disappears again almost overnight once the festive period is over. If you want to taste it, you have to come here for *Carnevale*—or make it yourself!

It is an easy cake made with risen bread dough. The long fermentation it undergoes gives it a slightly acidic edge that tames its sweetness and introduces an intriguing flavor. The cake is spartan in its richness, the crumb slightly bread-like and a bit dry. It is one of those unusual sweets to which one can get quite addicted.

I have spent years captivated by this fleeting cake, trying to unearth a good recipe. I talked to bakers, scoured the Internet and plowed through a mountain of Florentine cookbooks in English and Italian. Few and far between were recipes for this seasonal specialty, and those I found were often antiques, not easily transcribed for today's cooks. Traditionally, the dough was enriched with lard and crackling, and most recipes I found still mentioned the use of these two ingredients.

After many failed attempts, I discovered that Tuscan bakers often use risen bread dough to make this specialty, a detail that had escaped me. And so there was a clue to solve the mystery, and this recipe is the result.

Sometimes Florentines split this cake in half and fill it with pastry cream, but I like this more basic version. This is the type of thing you want to eat for breakfast with a cup of strong coffee or serve at an elegant brunch or tea. I make it using our local Tuscan extra virgin olive oil.

SERVES 8 TO 10

1 recipe pizza dough (page 68), mixed and left to rise for 2 to
    3 hours, until doubled
100 g (3.5 oz) (⅔ cup) bread flour
85 g (3 oz) (½ cup less 1 tbsp) sugar
½ tsp instant dry yeast
¼ tsp salt
Zest of 1 lemon or orange (or 1 tbsp citrus paste; see page 339)
3 eggs
⅓ cup plus 1 tbsp extra virgin olive oil
Icing sugar, or icing sugar and cocoa, for sprinkling

Place the pizza dough, flour, sugar, yeast, salt and zest in the work bowl of a stand mixer fitted with the dough hook. Turn the machine on to medium speed and start adding the eggs one at a time, mixing for 2 to 3 minutes after each addition. You will find the dough turning into a batter and will need to switch to the paddle attachment after the first or second egg. Once the eggs are mixed in, slowly begin adding the oil one-third at a time, mixing for 2 to 3 minutes after each addition. Cover the bowl and let the batter rise in a warm place for 2 to 3 hours. The batter will double in bulk, and the surface will be full of bubbles.

Butter and flour a 12- by 9-inch baking sheet. Gently turn the risen dough onto the baking sheet and let sit again for about 40 minutes. Meanwhile, preheat the oven to 350°F/175°C.

Bake for 30 minutes or until the top is golden brown and a tester comes out clean. Cool on a rack for 5 to 10 minutes before removing from the pan.

When completely cool, sprinkle the top with icing sugar, or a mix of icing sugar and cocoa. To be really authentic, cut out a *fleur-de-lys* stencil large enough to cover the cake; keep the surrounding stencil paper. Place the center cutout on the cake and sprinkle icing sugar around it. Remove the cutout and position the stencil paper over the icing sugar on the cake and sprinkle the inside—the *giglio*—with cocoa.

This cake keeps well for several days.

THREE ITALIAN CELEBRATORY BREADS USING NATURAL STARTER

Pandoro, Panettone and Colomba

I couldn't finish this chapter without including a recipe for the celebratory breads made in Italy using natural starter. I will confess at the outset, this is not a recipe for those in need of a quick and easy dessert. *Colomba, panettone* and *pandoro* are for the serious home baker adept at working with natural leavens (sourdough) who wants to discover a fascinating way to use them in the sweet kitchen.

These three sweet breads originated in Italy in different times and places. *Pandoro* comes from Verona around the latter part of the eighteenth century, *panettone* was born in the last half of the seventeenth century in Lombardy, and *colomba* appeared even earlier in Pavia. Today pastry chefs often use the same dough as a base for all three breads, and they are wildly popular all over Italy as the traditional desserts served at countless festive meals during the holidays of Christmas and Easter.

Colomba is the sweet bread shaped like a dove (*colomba* means "dove") that is eaten at Easter. Leavened with a stiff sourdough starter, and usually without commercial yeast, it is a cousin to the Christmastime naturally leavened sweet breads, *panettone* and *pandoro*. The defining feature of this trio is their sophisticated sweet and slightly sour flavor—a result of the acidity in the natural leaven. While recipes abound that simplify the process, calling for the use of commercial yeast instead of natural starters, in Italy this is almost never done. These breads are close to the hearts of all Italians, and shortcuts are not tolerated. Even the industrially produced breads sold in supermarkets at bargain-basement prices during the holidays are made with natural leaven.

These celebratory breads are a passion of mine. Although they are rich with dried fruit, butter and eggs, it is astonishing how light and delicate they taste and to what spectacular heights the natural leaven raises them. I've spent years tracking down authentic recipes for these famous cakes in an attempt to unravel their mystery for the home baker. Finally I attended a special course dedicated to them at the Etoile Institute, one of the country's leading culinary schools, so I could learn from a professional. There, *Maestro* Alessandro Inglese, a very accomplished pastry chef from the Friuli-Venezia Giulia region of northeastern Italy, generously shared the secrets he'd amassed over a career spent making these breads. Not only that—he sent me home with some of his leaven, which he informed me began its life 150 years ago in the Swiss Alps. But no matter; you don't need ancient sourdough to make these breads.

My Italian friends are astonished that I make these breads; they've never heard of anyone who does this at home. These breads were invented by pastry chefs, and their secrets have remained firmly in the realm of the professional. There are good reasons for this, which are worth keeping in mind. First, these breads cannot be rushed. You need time, several days or more if you don't already have an active sourdough. Although there is very little to do each day (just a few minutes are needed), these are not cakes you can just whip up. The starter must be very strong, and this requires time. Second, the mixing time is long, and a heavy-duty stand mixer is essential. Gluten development in the dough is tested by the addition of so many rich ingredients. The egg, sugar and butter must be incorporated very slowly, so as not to challenge the formation of a strong dough. If gluten development is discouraged by the addition of too much fat and sugar too quickly, the dough will not rise. Third, the area where the dough is left to rise must be kept at as constant a temperature as possible and free from drafts. Professional bakers have special climate-controlled rooms called "proofers" for this purpose. The ideal temperature is around 80°F/27°C. Since these are festive breads, made in the cooler months for Christmas and Easter holidays, finding a constant warm area in my drafty stone farmhouse is always my biggest challenge. Finally, kitchen scales are essential.

Having said all that, the actual making of the bread is not that difficult and it is very similar in concept to brioche. If you are captivated with sourdough and interested in a challenge, then give this recipe a try. Once a year I find it a thrill to spend a few days watching the magic happen as these lovely breads take shape.

You will need to buy the proper molds for these breads; they are generally available in specialty Italian grocers or pastry shops around the holidays. *Colomba* molds are made of paper and are shaped like a dove. *Panettone* molds are tall and round, also made of paper. *Pandoro* are baked in special star-shaped fluted baking tins. All these molds are available in several sizes, from 100 grams to 1 kilogram. I find 100-, 250- and 500-gram molds suitable for most home ovens.

The same basic dough can be used to make all three breads. This is a large recipe. It will produce enough dough to make the following amounts:

Pandoro: approximately 1.2 kg (enough for two 500-g molds and two 100-g molds)

or

Panettone: approximately 1.5 kg (enough for three 500-g molds)

or

Colomba: approximately 1.4 kg (enough for two 500-g molds and four 100-g molds)

The natural leaven gives the breads exceptional keeping qualities. Wrapped loosely in plastic wrap, they will keep for two to three weeks. I've heard rumors of *pandoro* made for Christmas still being edible the following August. In Italy, they are kept around for weeks on end, appearing about six weeks before the actual holidays start. Remains go on sale for a good month afterwards, and become the subject of countless jokes. Cookery magazines are full of ways to use them up and, like our fruitcake, they become the hostess gift that keeps on giving, as they move from one house to the next over the season.

You will need to convert your liquid starter to a stiff one, which will take three days. To do this, you refresh the starter three times a day, using half the amount of water you normally use in the liquid levain. You also need to use strong flour (bread flour) with a protein content around 13 percent. Traditionally, Italian bakers wrap their starter in cloth and tie it tightly with rope for the last refreshment to help it gain strength. Alternatively, it is sometimes left in a pail of water, where it is said to gain strength from its pressure, but I have had success without employing either of these techniques. If you do not already have a starter on the go, you will need to create one. See the instructions on pages 40 to 42.

To Convert Your Liquid Starter to a Stiff Starter

This refreshment schedule is based on beginning the first mix on the third evening. This works well for me in the winter, when rising times are longer than they are in the summer. The dough sits overnight, at room temperature, after the first mix, and early the next morning I give it the second mix. It is usually ready for the oven by the early afternoon. In the summer, when rising times can be quite a bit shorter, I find it preferable to extend the refreshment schedule by one feeding, to begin the first mix early on the fourth morning. This avoids the potential problem of getting up in the middle of the night for the second mix and means the bread can be made in one day.

Day 1 Early in the Morning:

85 g (3 oz) active sourdough starter (see page 41)
85 g (3 oz) bread flour
42g (1.5 oz) water

Mix the starter, flour and water together. Knead briefly and shape into a ball. Place in a small bowl, cover with a plate and let sit for 8 hours in a warm spot.

Discard all but 85 g (3 oz) of the starter and repeat the refreshment described above.

Eight hours later:

Repeat the feeding as described above, always beginning with 85 g of the starter. (Discard the rest or use it to make the crackers on page 51.) Cover the starter and let it sit overnight.

Day 2:

Repeat the entire process, giving the starter three more refreshments.

Day 3:

In the morning and at noon, refresh the starter as described above.

Evening:

Reserve 150 g (5.3 oz) of the starter for the first mix. Refresh and refrigerate the remainder for future use (see page 42).

The key to success with this dough is to not overwhelm it by adding too many rich ingredients too quickly, but rather to add the sugar, yolks and butter very slowly. Each mix takes more than an hour. It is a good idea to take several short breaks during both mixes to give the motor of your stand mixer a well-deserved rest.

For the first mix
   340 g (12 oz) bread flour
   150 g (5.3 oz) ripe stiff starter
   250 g (9 oz) tepid water
   140 g (5 oz) sugar

100 g (3.5 oz) (5 to 6) egg yolks (save the whites for the topping if
   you are making colomba)
100 g (3.5 oz) cold butter, cut in 5 pieces

Add the flour to the work bowl of your stand mixer fitted with the dough
hook. Break up the starter and add it to the flour along with the water.
Mix for 7 minutes on low speed before you begin incorporating the sugar.
Add the sugar in three additions, mixing for a further 5 to 7 minutes
between each addition or until the dough appears strong and begins to
clean the sides of the bowl. Next, add the yolks one at a time, mixing
for 5 to 7 minutes after each addition. Finally, start incorporating the
butter one piece at a time, mixing for 5 to 7 minutes after each addition,
and keeping the remaining butter chilled between additions, until the
dough is smooth and glossy, cleans the sides of the bowl and falls from
the dough hook in long, ropey strands when you lift the hook.

Place the dough in a clear plastic container and, using a marker or piece
of tape, indicate the level of the dough on the outside. Cover with a plate
and let sit for several hours in a warm place, ideally around 80°F/27°C,
until it triples in bulk. The time will depend on your starter and the temperature and humidity in your kitchen. In the summer, when my kitchen
is hot and humid, the first rise is usually 4 hours or less. In the winter it
can take 10 to 12 hours. At that time of year my kitchen is also very dry,
so I keep a stock pot of water simmering on the stove to create a humid
environment.

For the second mix
   160 g (5.6 oz) bread flour
   2 tablespoons citrus paste (see page 339)
   1 ½ tsp salt

The seeds scraped from 1 vanilla bean

85 g (3 oz) sugar

56 g (2 oz) (3) egg yolks

56 g (2 oz) cold butter, cut in 3 or 4 pieces

To the first mix add the flour, citrus paste, salt and vanilla seeds. Mix on low speed for 5 minutes. Proceed as described in the instructions for the first mix, adding the sugar in three parts and mixing for 7 minutes between each addition. Add the yolks one at a time and mix for 7 minutes each addition. Finish with the butter, adding each piece separately and mixing for 7 minutes each time, keeping the butter in the refrigerator between additions.

Switch to the paddle attachment and increase the speed to medium. Mix for about 1 minute, until the dough comes together in a tight ball and cleans bottom and sides of the bowl. The final dough should be glossy and very strong. To test for strength, try lifting it from the paddle. It should cling to the paddle in a tight mass before it begins to slowly fall away in one piece. If you take a bit of dough in your hands, you should be able to stretch it out into a thin, shiny film so transparent you can see through it (think of a bubble blown from bubble gum).

To Make *Pandoro*

To finish

Icing sugar for dusting

I find *pandoro* the easiest of these breads to make, so you may want to start with it. It is the same dough used in *colomba* and *panettone* but does not contain any dried fruit. For *pandoro*, you will need special tin molds, which are available in several sizes. The 100-, 250- and 500-gram molds are best for home ovens. The molds need to be very carefully buttered and floured before adding the dough, or the *pandoro* will stick. Brush the molds with a thin layer of melted butter, being careful to reach into every part of the mold. Sift flour evenly over the butter and then tap the mold upside down to remove any excess flour. You are looking for a very thin film of butter and flour.

Turn the final dough out onto a lightly floured surface and cut it into pieces weighed according to the size of your molds. Place the pieces in the molds and put them on a baking sheet. Cover the molds with a clean towel and place them in a warm, draft-free place, ideally around 80°F/27°C. Let the dough rise until it reaches the top of the mold. Assuming the temperature and humidity in your kitchen remain fairly constant, the last rise should take roughly a third less time than the first.

Preheat the oven to 350°F/175°C. Bake for about 30 minutes The *pandoro* is done when a cake tester inserted in the middle of the cake comes out clean. Cool on a rack for 10 minutes, then gently invert the mold and tap the bottom lightly. The cake should slide right out. Let cool completely and then sieve a layer of icing sugar over the top of the cake.

To Make *Panettone*

For *panettone*, you will need special paper molds, which are available in several sizes. The 100- and 500-gram molds are best for home ovens.

To the final dough add 150 g (5.3 oz) each of raisins and mixed candied fruit. Knead these ingredients in by hand briefly to incorporate.

Turn the dough out onto a lightly floured surface and cut it into pieces weighed according to the size of your molds. Place your molds on a baking sheet. Shape each piece of dough into a ball and place a ball in each mold. Cover the molds with a clean kitchen towel. Place in a warm, draft-free place, ideally around 80°F/27°C. Let the dough rise until it reaches the top of the mold. Assuming the temperature and humidity in your kitchen remain fairly constant, the last rise should take roughly a third less time than the first.

Preheat the oven to 350°F/175°C. Bake for about 35 minutes. The *panettone* is done when a cake tester inserted in the middle of the cake comes out clean. Cool on a rack.

Variation
Substitute miniature chocolate chips for half or all of the candied fruit.

To Make *Colomba*

For *colomba*, you will need special paper molds, which are available in several sizes. Molds 500 grams or smaller work best for home ovens.

To the final dough add 200 g (7 oz) candied citrus peel. Mix briefly with your hands just to incorporate.

Turn the dough out onto a lightly floured surface and cut it into pieces weighed according to the size of your *colomba* molds. Shape each piece into a ball. Take one piece of the dough and cut it in two unequal parts, one using about two-thirds of the dough. Working with wet hands, form a tight log (see page 27) with the larger piece. Cut the smaller piece in half and form two tight rounds. Place the log down the center of the mold and place the two balls on each side. Repeat with the remaining pieces of dough.

Transfer the molds to a baking sheet and cover with a clean kitchen towel. Place in a warm, draft-free place, ideally around 80°F/27°C.

Assuming the temperature and humidity in your kitchen remain fairly constant, the last rise should take roughly a third less time than the first. The dough is ready for the oven when it reaches the rim of the mold. In the meantime, prepare the topping.

For the topping
    70 g (2.5 oz) (2 to 3) egg whites
    ½ cup sugar
    ¼ cup cornmeal

Beat the whites until they are frothy. Fold in the sugar and cornmeal.

To finish
    ¾ cup almonds (whole blanched or sliced)
    Large granular white decorating sugar (available in specialty pastry
      stores; optional)
    Metal or wood skewers longer than your *colomba* molds (I use
      shish kabob skewers)

Preheat the oven to 350°F/175°C. When the *colomba* are ready to bake, very gently brush on the topping, and then scatter the whole or sliced almonds over the top, along with some of the decorating sugar. This dough is full of gas and fragile at this stage. It will deflate easily, so you need to be gentle. Transfer the baking sheet to the oven with a steady hand.

Bake for about 35 minutes. The *colomba* is done when a cake tester inserted in the middle of the cake comes out clean. Remove from the oven and immediately pierce the molds horizontally through the center with a skewer and hang the cakes upside down between two chairs to cool. This will prevent the center from falling.

Variation

In Italy one often finds showpiece *pandoro, panettone* and *colomba* iced with white, orange or dark chocolate ganache and decorated like Easter eggs, with colored candy sprinkles, spun sugar, chocolate curls, sugar flowers and other fanciful creations. These masterpieces are sold for a small fortune in the finest pastry shops. The flavor of really good chocolate combined with the taste of these naturally leavened sweet breads is truly extraordinary. For special occasions I make an easy chocolate ganache icing by heating 1 cup of heavy cream until it bubbles and pouring it over 12 ounces of good-quality white, orange-colored white or dark chocolate broken up into very small pieces. I stir it until the chocolate has melted, and then I add 6 table-spoons (¾ stick) of room-temperature butter and stir that in. I refrigerate this icing until it sets to a spreadable consistency, about 20 minutes.

If I am planning to ice a *colomba*, I bake it without the topping or the almond and granular sugar finish called for in the recipe. For *panettone* and *colomba* I peel away the paper molds and ice both the top and the sides of the breads. For *pandoro* I use the icing before it has completely set, icing only the top but generously enough so that some of the ganache dribbles down the sides. I then put the cake in a cool place to set the icing, and dust it with icing sugar before serving.

Chocolate-coated Candied Peel

In November in the markets that I frequent, citrus fruit from southern Italy begins to turn up: beautiful blood oranges, many different kinds of mandarins, clementines, lemons and grapefruit. And sometimes there is even bergamot or citron to be had, large fruits with a thick skin that are grown in Calabria for their peel, which is used to make candied fruit, essential oils and perfume. As a Canadian, when I see these semitropical fruits appearing in the dead of winter, I always marvel at how this sliver of a country that stretches from the highest Alps almost to Africa manages to sustain itself year-round on domestically grown fruits and vegetables. It is rare in Italy, at any time of year, to see imported produce.

As soon as this fruit begins to appear in the late fall, I make my own candied peel to use for Christmas baking. The most beautiful pieces I dip in chocolate and serve with a tiny cup of espresso. It makes a sweet ending to a heavy meal where a more substantial dessert would not be welcome.

Don't worry about all the boiling this recipe involves. The peel may seem overcooked, but this is correct. It will firm up after it has been cooked in the syrup. Look for untreated, organic fruit that has a thick peel.

Organic oranges, lemons or grapefruit
Sugar
Dark chocolate containing 70 percent cocoa solids, finely chopped

Cut the peel off the fruit in thick slices, white pith and all. Place in a saucepan, cover with cold water and bring to a boil. Boil for 7 minutes. Drain, reserving the cooking water. Cool the peel under cold running water. Repeat the process two more times, starting with fresh cold water each time and reserving the water after each use. Drain the peel and dry it gently and thoroughly using a clean kitchen towel. Remove the pith with a knife or a vegetable peeler and cut the peel into thin strips.

Weigh the peel. Weigh the equivalent amount of sugar and the equivalent amount of reserved cooking water. Put the cooking water in a large saucepan and bring to a boil. Stir in the sugar and reduce the heat to low. When the sugar has dissolved and the syrup is clear, add the peel. There should be enough syrup to coat the peel but not cover it completely. Simmer on low heat, stirring occasionally, until the peel has absorbed almost all of the syrup. This could take up to an hour. Drain the peel and roll each strip in more sugar. Place a sheet of paper under a rack and place the peel on the rack to dry. The peel strips should be left for several hours or overnight, until they are no longer sticky.

Melt the chocolate in the top of a double boiler over low heat, and coat one end of each strip of peel in chocolate. Let it harden. Serve with a cup of espresso coffee. The candied peel keeps well in an airtight container for a week.

Pasta Sfoglia ◆ Puff Pastry

While we often assume the French are responsible for the existence of puff pastry (*feuilletage*), it's a much debated topic amongst food scholars. *Larousse Gastronomique* suggests it may have been with us since the Greeks, which makes sense when you consider phyllo. Giuliano Bugialli, in *The Fine Art of Italian Cooking*, mentions a fourteenth-century Tuscan tart made with puff pastry. But one thing is for sure: it has been quite a while now that humans have been folding fat into flour to produce a bit of leaven from heaven. It is astonishing that something so light and delicate is produced from a formula that calls for nothing more than one part flour to one part fat, with a bit of water added for good measure.

Today in Italy, puff pastry, called *pasta sfoglia*, is more often than not produced with margarine as the fat component. It is consumed at breakfast, the meal many Italians eat standing up in a bar. The pastry comes stuffed with a variety of fillings (apples, pastry cream, apricots, etc.) and is eaten dipped into a cup of steaming cappuccino. Most Italians I have met (even some very sophisticated pastry chefs) prefer the taste of *sfoglia* made with margarine. Butter, they say, is what the French use. I prefer to work with butter, if only because it is a natural ingredient.

This versatile dough has a reputation for being difficult to make, and many people have been put off trying it for this reason. Nothing could be further from the truth. The one thing puff pastry does demand is time. Like bread making, it begs patience but demands scarce labor. If you have an afternoon at home, you can make it. Your active time you can count in minutes.

I make *sfoglia* and freeze it in a large quantity on a day when I am not very busy. This recipe produces a little more than a kilogram (2¼ pounds), enough dough for several tarts, and I usually divide it into five or six pieces to store in the freezer. Most of the recipes in this book call for between 200 and 300 grams of puff pastry; 250 grams (9 ounces) will make a tart for four people.

There is nothing like homemade puff pastry—it blows up beautifully in the oven to produce a professional-looking crust for sweet and savory preparations. Use it for the apple *frangipane* tart on page 330, the *timballo* on page 268 or the wild berry tart on page 354. It can also be used in place of flaky pie crust for a lighter, more elegant effect.

Any scrappy bits left over from rolling out your final product can be rolled in chopped toasted almonds and then in cinnamon sugar and baked as a special treat for the younger members of your family.

If you don't feel like making your own puff pastry, it is easy to find ready-made in most supermarkets. If you are concerned about the quality of fats you consume, make sure you check the ingredients list.

If I am making puff pastry to freeze, I usually give it 4 or 5 turns and then roll it out into a long rectangle (roughly 18 by 6 inches) and cut it into 4 or 5 pieces. You can weigh the pieces precisely before freezing according to how you want to use them. I wrap these pieces individually to use as needed, giving the final turns when I roll out the thawed dough. Alternatively, give the dough all 6 turns and roll it out thin and ready to use. Place it on a piece of parchment and roll it up, then wrap well and freeze. In the heat of summer, puff pastry can be hard to make in an un-air-conditioned kitchen like mine. When my kitchen is really hot, I store the dough in the freezer briefly between turns rather than refrigerating it.

For the dough

450 g (1 lb) (3¼ cups) **all-purpose flour**

56 g (2 oz) (½ stick) **melted butter**

225 g (8 oz) (1 cup) **water**

1 tsp **salt**

For the butter filling

350 g (12.5 oz) cold butter

Mix the dough ingredients together on your work surface with a bench scraper just to form a ball—or use your mixer fitted with the paddle attachment and mix for a few seconds just until the dough comes together. Form the dough into a ball, wrap it in plastic and refrigerate for 1 hour.

Place the cold butter on a sheet of wax paper and cover it with another sheet. Using a rolling pin, flatten out the butter to form a thin rectangle about 5 by 7 inches. Wrap it in the wax paper and place it in the fridge while you roll out the dough.

Remove the dough from the fridge and roll it out into a 12-inch square. Place the butter rectangle in the center of the dough and fold the top, bottom and sides of the dough over it to form an envelope.

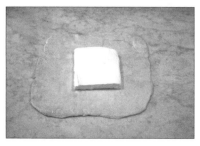

Place the short side of the rectangle in front of you and begin to roll it out into a long rectangle between 18 and 20 inches long and about 6 to 8 inches wide and ½ inch thick. If you find a little butter breaking through the skin of the dough, sieve a little flour over it.

Take the short end of the dough closest to you and fold it up to the middle of the dough sheet. Fold the top of the dough over the bottom as though you were folding a letter. Rotate the dough by 90 degrees so that it is facing you like a book. This is your "first turn," and it is from this position that you begin to roll out the dough again.

Make one fingerprint in the dough (to indicate one turn) on the left-hand side, wrap the dough in plastic and refrigerate it until the butter is hard again, at least half an hour.

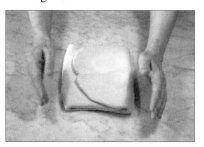  

Remove the dough from the fridge and place it in front of you, with the fingerprinted side to your left. Repeat the above process of rolling out, folding and turning the dough 90 degrees. Mark the dough with 2 fingerprints (your "second turn"), wrap the dough and return it to the refrigerator for half an hour. Repeat this procedure until you have made a total of 6 turns. Don't forget the fingerprints—they keep track of your turns and indicate the position from which you should begin rolling the dough out. The dough will be ready to use after 6 turns.

Depending on the time of year and temperature of your kitchen, you may be able to make more than one turn before the butter gets soft and you have to refrigerate.

Chapter 8 *La Dispensa*
✤ *Preserving the Harvest*

Some of my most enjoyable hours are spent in the old kitchen at Petraia preserving the assorted fruits and vegetables I grow or forage. In summer, my garden, like everything else, is "in season." The rest of the year it slows to a manageable pace, delivering such seasonal vegetables as spring peas, winter leeks, black cabbage, onions, broccoli, fennel, turnips and carrots. Local visitors to Petraia are astounded by the bounty of our *orto*. Our altitude, and the fact that we farm organically, mean we avoid many pests that plague other farms. Water is abundant and uncontaminated; the Pesa River begins its life on our land before winding its way down a long valley through the heart of Chianti and gaining force at Montelupo Fiorentino, where it meets the Arno River and begins the journey to Pisa and the Tyrrhenian Sea. For thousands of years people have worked these fields. But when we found her, farmers had abandoned Petraia for half a century. Her soil

was rich and full of hope. The poverty of postwar Tuscany brought her fortune years later. Having sat out the green revolution, she avoided the years of pesticides and chemical treatments that might otherwise have been her fate.

My summer mornings usually start when the sun comes up, around five-thirty. There is produce to harvest and weeds to deal with. I spend those mornings picking, washing, cutting, bottling. Sometimes my work is interrupted by a neighbor's cows or a couple of local hogs with their dozen tiny piglets who come over to eat in our newly sprouting field of grain. I have to shoo them back to their home on the other side of the mountain. Or an electric fence damaged by hungry wild boar the night before may need attention. There are guests to accommodate. Meals to prepare. Summer is a busy time, and often weeks fly by before I find a minute to leave the property—even just to drive to Radda to pay a bill and get to the bank and post office.

Usually by the middle of September I have my *dispensa* filled with preserves. There are onions, potatoes, squash, pumpkins and green tomatoes we've harvested to store in the *cantina*. Whatever male offspring our flock of chickens has produced that year are likely fat enough to butcher and freeze for the winter. I employ all sorts of preservation methods for the fruits and vegetables—sun drying, lactic acid fermentation, oil (*sott'olio*) and vinegar (*sott'aceto*) and our honey (to make *marmellata*). Chestnuts, figs, olives, berries, herbs, mushrooms, apples, pears, hazelnuts, almonds, plums, grapes, quince and strawberries grow both wild and cultivated on the property. Because we are organic, we also save seeds. Organic seeds are not readily available, especially for many of the heirloom varieties we produce. It's much easier to grow a bit extra and choose the most perfect-looking specimens for next year's crop. This takes time, and involves planting a larger garden. Twenty percent of my potato crop, for instance, is allocated for seed. After harvesting, the seeds must also be dried and properly preserved.

With all methods of preserving, it is important to be sure you are working in a clean environment and using sterilized equipment and storage containers. I refrigerate or freeze anything I don't heat-process. What follow are a few of the staples I put away every year.

Preserving Fresh Olives

Towards the end of November it is time to harvest olives. Because we don't get enough olives from our young trees to take them to the *frantoio*, or olive mill, I preserve them for the table. The idea that Tuscany enjoys year-round sunshine and warm weather is a myth perpetuated by travel writers and holidaymakers who come here "in season," late spring to early fall. Late fall, winter and early spring, a good half of the year at least, can be bitterly cold, and this truth comes from the mouth of a Canadian who knows the definition of that four-letter word very well. Perhaps this is nowhere more deeply felt than in old stone farmhouses. Built centuries before the advent of central heating, they are poorly insulated, full of leaks and cracks that the freezing north wind and rain find easy passage through. We keep fires going all day in our old woodstove and in the fireplace, most years from early October straight through until early May. We turn the heat on in the depth of winter only for an hour at sunrise and again at sunset. Otherwise, the cost of fuel required to properly heat our *casa colonica*, as farmhouses are known, would land us in the poorhouse.

But late fall unveils a deep, ascetic beauty in the hills of Chianti. This is the age-old face of traditional Tuscany not witnessed by the throngs of summer. November days are apt to be clear, summer's haze having disappeared, and while it may be cold, the landscape does not want for splendor. The hills are draped in magnificent fall colors, which the clarity of light brings into sharp focus. Smoke curls out of the chimney, perfuming the cool air with the distinctive musty aroma of burning oak. Hunters wander with their dogs through our meadows and woods, while Siena sits gleaming like a newly polished gem on our southern horizon. When olive-picking time rolls around, I brace myself for a few days of finger-numbing work. The olives must be carefully picked, for they will spoil if they are bruised, and this takes time and patience. We have one old tree on the property that produces large green olives I usually put up *in salamoia* (brine). The other trees yield a smaller variety, which I preserve *in salamoia* or *al forno* (by baking them in a low oven). Although most olives can be preserved in brine, it is my experience that the best olives to use for the *al forno* method are smaller ones such as the *taggiasca, moraiolo* or *niçoise* type. Make sure you start with raw, freshly picked olives. These might be hard to find unless you have your own tree or live in an area where olives grow. They are usually available late in the fall. It is a good idea to seek out untreated or organic olives. In Italy the first olives of the season are from Sicily, and they start to turn up in the markets towards the end of September. As the season progresses, the harvest continues up the peninsula. Both of the recipes that follow give you olives that can be used to make bread or to put on pizza. They can be added to pasta sauces or, perhaps best, just eaten as they are.

Olive in Salamoia ✦ Olives Preserved in Brine

Since I've been harvesting and preserving my own olives, I've found my taste for them has evolved considerably. I suggest you taste your olives at different stages as they mature in the brine so you can become familiar with how their flavor is maturing. The olives we find for sale are often older than they should be, and perhaps too soft. A really good olive preserved in brine should have a bit of a crunch to it and a hint of a bitterness that, like freshly pressed olive oil, mellows over time. For me, that is a sign of purity and freshness, and now that I have acquired the taste it is hard to open a jar of anything less.

Wash the olives and place them in brine that is composed of 1 cup of sea salt for every 4 cups of water. It is best to use a glass or glazed earthenware vat. Cover them with a plate and a weight (I use a clean, sterilized rock) to make sure the olives are submerged in the brine, and leave for one month. After this time, if they are still very bitter, drain and cover with a fresh brine. Check often, changing the brine every few days, until the flavor has mellowed to your taste. Mine usually take at least a couple of months to mature. Drain the olives, rinse them well and weigh them. For every kilogram (2¼ lb) of olives you will need about 56 g (2 oz) of pickling or kosher salt. Layer the olives and salt in jars and then cover with water. They will keep well like this refrigerated for several months, and their flavor will mellow as they age.

Olive al Forno ✦ Oven-dried Olives

I'd been searching for years, asking neighbors, looking in books and scouring the Internet for a method to make these wrinkly black olives, the kind you often see for sale at a great price in gourmet food stores. Previous attempts to make them had failed, so it was lucky for me one November day when some friends happened along as we were picking our olives. Each had their own method for *al forno* olives. The one below is the result of my own subsequent experimentation. You need to have a source of low, steady heat such as that produced near a fireplace or a woodstove. You can also use your oven, with the heat set as low as it will go.

FREEZING OLIVES

One year I was too busy
to preserve our olives
after the harvest, so I froze
them raw. Several months
later I thawed them and
proceeded to bake them
as described at right. They
turned out beautifully.
Now I usually freeze most
of our harvest so I can
make these in small
batches as I need them.

Start with small raw, freshly picked olives. Wash well and dry them with a clean kitchen towel. Spread them out on parchment-lined baking sheets in a single layer and sprinkle with a little salt, just a miserly teaspoon or so per baking sheet—enough to provide each olive with a light sprinkling of a few grains of salt—and transfer to your chosen baking place (woodstove or oven). Turn them several times a day. The olives will shrivel and turn black. Be careful not to let them get too shriveled up and dry, though; they should retain a bit of their plumpness. When you taste them, the flesh should still be soft and slightly bitter tasting. The bitterness mellows over time. The time they take to bake will depend on the size of your olives and the temperature of your "warm place." I put my trays on a shelf above our wood-burning oven, and they usually take two or three days, depending on how hot we are burning it. In a low oven, they will be ready in a few hours.

Once they are done, place them in a jar with a little lemon peel, some flakes of hot chili pepper, a bit of fresh garlic and some fresh or dried oregano. Add enough oil to coat the olives, seal and refrigerate. You will need to turn the jars every few days to make sure that the oil is distributed equally amongst the olives. They can also be completely covered with the oil. They are ready to eat immediately, and keep well for two months or longer, improving somewhat after a few weeks.

Aceto di Vino ◆ Wine Vinegar

I go through gallons of vinegar each year for preserving, cooking and the table. The acetic acid found in vinegar prevents the growth of many organisms in food that cause spoilage, making it a good preservative. Wine vinegar is easy to make and, if you live in an area where good-quality wine is found at a reasonable price, it is a worthwhile effort. Your own vinegar is apt to be of higher quality than anything you can buy. Here in Chianti, I can get a liter of good-quality red or white wine at our local cooperative for the equivalent of a dollar. I keep two vinegar barrels in my kitchen, one for red wine and one for white. The dregs left over from bottles are added to these barrels. I have two more barrels in the *cantina* that I keep going for preserving. Once they are full, I filter the vinegar, bottle and cork it. You can find manually operated corkers in your local winemaking shop for a few dollars. Like wine, vinegar will mellow as it ages.

To make wine vinegar, you need to create a "mother." The mother is a slimy bit of goop that lies on top of the wine in the barrel and is responsible for turning the alcohol in the wine into acetic acid. The beasties in the mother are similar to those found in sourdough culture. They are out there slumming around in the wild; your job is to tame them and put them to work for you.

Glass demijohns or wooden barrels for making wine or vinegar are found in most winemaking shops. Your container should have a tap and a cork lid that allows the barrel to breathe, providing the point of entry for the microorganisms needed to make the mother. Although wooden barrels are more authentic, glass ones are less fiddly, cheaper and easier to clean. The flavor of vinegar that has been aged in a wooden barrel is apt to be richer, so what kind of barrel you choose is a matter of personal taste, budget and the amount of fuss you are willing to put up with.

Start by adding a small amount of wine to the chosen vessel, filling it about a fifth full. Choose an unfiltered wine with a low alcohol content (10 to 12 percent), being careful not to add to your container any sediment at the bottom of the wine bottle. Red and white wine can go in separate barrels or you can mix them to produce rosé-colored vinegar. Keep your barrel at a temperature within the human comfort zone, avoiding extremes of heat and cold. You can kick-start the fermentation process by adding some unfiltered apple cider or wine vinegar (health food stores are good places to look for these) to your barrel. When you see a thin film starting to form on the surface of the wine, your mother is coming to life. This could take a few weeks, or less, depending on where the vinegar is stored and the season.

At this point you need to make another addition of wine—the same amount as the first time. Keep adding wine, a fifth of the vessel at a time, at one-week intervals until the container is full. You will know when your vinegar is ready because it will smell and taste like vinegar, not alcohol. At this point, filter, bottle and cork up to four-fifths of the contents of your container and refill it with wine. The next batch will ferment faster now that you have a working mother. Once a year, empty your barrel (save the mother!) and give it a good clean with unchlorinated water.

If for some reason you go off vinegar making, I have heard that the mother can be dried and frozen. To dry it, squeeze it into a tight ball, removing all the liquid content, and let it harden by leaving it in the sun or on a warm windowsill. I have never tried this, finding it just as easy to start over again by making a new mother. Superstition has it that a bit of dried-up mother worn around the neck offers protection from the evil eye.

Herbal Vinegars

I don't use flavored vinegars or oils very much in my kitchen. If you go to the trouble of making your own vinegar with good-quality wine, you'll have something of high quality best appreciated pure and unadulterated. Having said that, if you have access to good fresh herbs, it can be fun to experiment, and herbal vinegars do make nice gifts.

You will need about a cup of fresh herbs for every 4 cups of vinegar. Wash the herbs and dry them gently. Place them in a jar. Bring the vinegar to a boil and pour over the herbs. Let stand for 2 weeks, covered with a cork or other noncorrosive material. Don't use a metal lid. Keep the jar at room temperature and in the dark. Give it a shake every day or two. When you are ready to bottle the vinegar, remove the herbs and filter it first through a fine sieve and then again through a coffee filter or fine cheesecloth to eliminate the cloudiness. Transfer to clean, sterilized bottles. If you like, you can put a cleaned and dried fresh sprig of whatever herb you used into the bottle.

Chianti Caldo ✦ Hot Chianti Wine Jelly

I make this hot wine jelly to serve with a cheese course. It is particularly good with an aged Tuscan pecorino. I use our red Chianti wine, but it can also be made with white wine or rosé. I buy wine to make this jelly *sfuso*, taking my own jugs to a nearby winery where I can purchase a good-quality table wine inexpensively. You can adjust the amount of hot pepper to suit your own level of heat tolerance. This recipe produces a moderately hot jelly.

MAKES ABOUT 4 CUPS

4 cups wine (red, white or rosé)

⅓ cup lemon juice

The seeds from 1 dried jalapeño or other hot pepper

Powdered pectin*

4 cups sugar

*Follow the manufacturer's instructions regarding the quantity of pectin to use for 4 cups liquid.

Combine the wine, lemon juice, pepper seeds and pectin in a heavy-bottomed saucepan and bring to a boil over high heat. When it boils, add the sugar in a slow stream while stirring constantly. Once all the sugar is added, return to a hard boil until the gel stage is reached. (This is around 220°F/105°C.) Test with a candy thermometer or by spooning a bit onto a cold plate—it should gel immediately.

Skim the jelly if needed, strain into sterilized jars and seal. Process in a boiling-water bath for 15 minutes or, if you intend to use it within a couple of weeks, store it in the refrigerator.

Mostarda di Frutta ✦ Fruit Mustard

Mostarda is a fruit conserve flavored with mustard that is famously made in the Lombard city of Cremona. It is also found in the cuisine of Lombardy and Emilia-Romagna, where it makes a perfect condiment for a wedge of Parmigiano-Reggiano or a boiled-meat dinner. In and around Mantua, an apple *mostarda* is added to cooked pumpkin to make a delicious filling for ravioli. The first mention of *mostarda* made with mustard is said to have been found in a letter written in 1397 by Gian Galeazzo Visconti, the duke of Milan, requesting a tub of it for the Christmas holidays.

Sperlari is a company that has been making *mostarda* in Cremona since 1836, and in one of their brochures they tell an amusing story of how *mostarda* is said to have been discovered. In an apothecary one day, a melon fell into a tub of honey. Having lost his melon, the druggist blamed his errand boy for taking it. Then one day he discovered the lost melon languishing in the depths of the honey pail. Astonished, he washed and sliced the melon to find it still fresh and delicious. He had discovered a valuable secret about the preservative properties of honey. Today Sperlari produces beautiful and elaborately prepared jars of *mostarda* containing whole candied fruit preserved in strong mustard-flavored syrup.

I was surprised when I uncovered a recipe for *mostarda* from the region where I live, in Paolo Petroni's *The Complete Book of Florentine Cooking*. He says its use in Florence was documented as early as the fourteenth century. Artusi, who wrote in the late nineteenth century, also has a recipe for *Mostarda all'uso Toscano*. It's interesting that he qualifies his recipe with "*all'uso Toscano*" (as used in Tuscany) because Artusi was born in Forlimpopoli, a village in Romagna. He moved to Florence as a young man and perhaps found the Tuscans eating a different kind of *mostarda* than the one he'd grown up with.

Although it's not very common anymore in Chianti, it does make sense that something called *mostarda* was made here. The word comes from the Latin *mustum*, which means grape must, or boiled-down grape juice. Chianti, covered in vineyards, would have been a sure source of grape must. Traditionally, the fruit was cooked in this must and then an essence of *senape*, or mustard seed essence, was added. Before the days of refrigeration, the hot and strong-tasting fruit mustard served to mask any off flavors of the meat it was served with.

This recipe produces an easy *mostarda* that makes good friends with cheese and roasted or boiled meats. My favorite use for it is to include it in a cheese course, along with *Chianti Caldo* (see page 403), some of our chestnut honey and a selection of homemade breads. For the cheese, I showcase three or four different kinds of the superb local pecorino.

For the mustard seed essence, ask at your local herbalist or health food store, explaining your culinary use. It is very strong, and should be added a drop a time. The *mostarda* is meant to be fairly hot, so a tiny bit goes a long way, but let your own palate be the judge.

For the mostarda

450 g (1 lb) seedless white grapes

325 g (12 oz) pitted cherries

225 g (½ lb) quartered and pitted apricots

500 g (18 oz) mild liquid honey, such as clover

To finish

6 to 12 drops mustard seed essence *(senape)*

Place all of the ingredients but the mustard seed essence in a glass bowl. Stir well, cover and let sit for 24 hours. Strain the liquid into a saucepan (return the fruit to the glass bowl) and boil it over moderate heat to thicken, about 15 minutes—you are looking for a fairly thick syrup. Pour the hot syrup over the fruit, cover and leave to sit for another 24 hours. The next day, repeat this process, leaving the fruit to sit, covered, for a further 24 hours.

On the last day, place the lot in a heavy-bottomed saucepan and bring to a boil. Boil for 10 minutes. Let cool before adding the mustard essence a drop or two at a time, stirring well after each addition and tasting as you go. Transfer the finished *mostarda* to sterilized jars and seal. It will keep 2 weeks in the refrigerator, or you can process the sealed jars in a boiling-water bath for 15 minutes.

Variation

I also make a *mostarda* of pumpkin and one of green tomatoes in the same way (substitute the fruit called for above with either matchstick-cut pumpkin or seeded and diced green tomatoes). You can experiment with other ingredients; I've seen *mostarda* made from apples, quince, pears, fresh figs, red peppers ...

Marmellata di Albicocche
✦ Apricot and Honey Compote

Apricot preserves are one of the pastry chef's most indispensable ingredients. They are used to fill tarts and to make sauces and glazes for desserts. They are also used to fill breakfast pastries and other confections. I make my own at Petraia using two simple ingredients—the freshest, ripest, most perfect-looking organic apricots I can find and the honey from our bees. Most fruit preserves call for an equal amount of fruit to sugar. You can get away with adding much less sweetener if you start with perfect ripe fruit. The result will be a preserve that retains more of the flavor of the fresh fruit. I prefer to use a mild-flavored honey instead of sugar.

MAKES 4 TO 6 CUPS

1 kg (2¼ lb) ripest organic apricots
450 g (1 lb) mild liquid honey, such as clover

Wash the apricots, cut them in half and stone them, but do not peel. Place them in a glass bowl with the honey, stir it all up and let sit for 24 hours. Place in a saucepan and bring to a boil over moderate heat. Cook for 20 to 30 minutes, until the apricots are tender and the jam is thick. For a smooth jam and to remove the skins, pass through a food mill. Pour into sterilized jars and seal. The compote keeps in the refrigerator for 2 to 3 weeks, or it can be frozen for several months. If you are going to store it at room temperature, process the sealed jars in a boiling-water bath for 15 minutes.

Marmellata di Cipolle e Uva Passa

♦ Onion and Raisin Compote

This compote is perfect served with roast meats, sausages or egg dishes. It also makes a heavenly condiment for fresh pasta with a little fresh cream stirred into it and seasoned with sea salt and freshly ground pepper.

MAKES 3 TO 4 CUPS

½ cup raisins

½ cup grappa

2 tbsp extra virgin olive oil

900 g (2 lb) thinly sliced red onions

½ cup mild liquid honey, such as clover

¼ cup sugar

¼ cup balsamic or red wine vinegar

1 tsp salt

Soak the raisins overnight in the grappa.

Heat the olive oil in a sauté pan large enough to hold the onions. Add the onions and cook them over low heat, partially covered, for an hour. Stir them from time to time, and add a little water if the pan looks too dry. The onions will wilt and become transparent. When they are done, the onions will have shrunk considerably, and it is a good idea to transfer them to a smaller pan for the rest of the cooking.

Add the honey, sugar, vinegar, salt and the raisins and their soaking liquid. Stir well with a wooden spoon. Partially cover and cook for another 30 minutes over moderately low heat. Increase the heat to high, remove the lid and cook for a final 10 minutes, stirring frequently. The onions should appear almost candied and will have turned a beautiful translucent burgundy. The compote is ready to use.

If you don't have an immediate use for it, transfer to a sterilized jar and seal the top with a layer of olive oil. It can be kept in the fridge for 2 weeks if topped up with oil after each use.

Digestivi

A proper dinner in an Italian home is never complete without the offer of a *digestivo*. If you are lucky, which is more often than not, it will be homemade.

To bottle these liqueurs, it is best to cork them. You can purchase a manually operated corker cheaply at most winemaking stores.

Here are three of my most popular preparations. These are quite alcoholic and are best served in very small amounts.

Limoncello ◆ **Lemon Liqueur from Sorrento**

Here is a classic recipe for the famous liqueur of the Amalfi Coast. The region, which boasts some of the best lemons in the world, produces thousands of gallons of this lovely yellow liqueur every year. So do Italians all over Italy. Here in Tuscany, most people I know keep at least one lemon tree for the express purpose of making a bottle or two of *limoncello*. Unfortunately, the trees can't stand the Tuscan winter and have to be kept inside for half the year. Historically, all the grand Tuscan villas had a *limonaia*, a greenhouse specifically to house citrus fruit in the winter. Here at Petraia, as at most farmhouses, the lemon trees are kept in our *capanna*, or barn, in the cooler months.

8 large organic lemons

4 cups 95 percent alcohol (190 proof)

4 cups water

750 g (26 oz) sugar

Using a potato peeler or zester, peel the lemons, being careful to remove the zest only and not the white pith. Place the zest in a jar and cover with the alcohol. Cover and macerate for 7 days, in a dark cupboard.

After 7 days, make a simple syrup by combining the water and the sugar in a saucepan and heating it until the sugar dissolves and the water is clear. Let cool. Strain the lemon-infused liquor into the syrup and bottle. The *limoncello* should sit for a month before you drink it. Once you open it, keep it in the fridge and serve it cold in chilled glasses as an after-dinner drink or digestive. It will keep indefinitely.

Variations

Instead of lemons, use oranges to make orange liqueur. Or you can fill a jar with whole apricots or kumquats, pour in enough liquor to cover, and macerate for 21 days. Pour off the liquor and measure it. Discard the fruit. For every cup of liquor, measure 1 scant cup of sugar and 1 cup of water. Make a simple syrup by dissolving the sugar in the water over moderate heat. Proceed as described above. You can also get creative and try adding spices like whole cloves, allspice berries and a cinnamon stick to the mix, but I prefer to let the fruit speak for itself. Always choose the best-quality organic fruit.

Nocino ♦ Walnut Liqueur

Nocino is frequently made in Tuscany according to a ritual that involves the number 40. Some say the nuts should be left to macerate in the dark, others in the sun. Some add spices such as cloves and cinnamon, others don't. There is no hard-and-fast rule for producing *nocino*, other than the mystery of the number 40. Here's how I do it at Petraia.

Towards the end of June, I pick 40 green, unripe walnuts from a healthy-looking walnut tree that bears large, unblemished fruit. I wash and dry them and place them in a glass container with a lid, filling it with grain alcohol to cover the nuts by about an inch—usually between 1½ and 2 quarts of alcohol, depending on the size of the walnuts. I leave them in the dark for 40 days.

After that I discard the nuts and filter the liquor several times. By now it has turned a dark murky brown color. I measure this heady stuff. For every 225 g (1 cup) of liquor, I measure 225 g (1 cup) of water and half this amount by weight (112 g or ½ cup plus 2 tbsp) of sugar. I make a simple sugar syrup by heating the water and sugar together until the sugar has dissolved. Once the syrup is cool, I add it to the nut-flavored alcohol. I keep the walnut liqueur in a sterilized jar with a tightly fitting lid for 2 weeks, after which I filter it again, bottle and cork it. I put it back in a cool, dark place for another 40 days, after which time the *nocino* should have mellowed and be ready to drink.

Ciliegie nella Grappa ♦ Cherries in Grappa

I preserve cherries in grappa every June, when Italy's famous Vignola cherry hits the local market. I macerate them in my *cantina* until Christmas, when I hand them out as gifts. When I first discovered this method of preserving cherries, I was delighted. They are my favorite fruit, and the idea of preserving them raw in grappa intrigued me. It was also an excuse for a food-motivated road trip in June. First stop I imagined to be the village of Vignola, near Modena in Emilia-Romagna, to buy the cherries. Second stop, Bassano del Grappa, in the northern Veneto, to pick up some of the best grappa made in Italy at wholesale prices. But the reality is, those places are not a day trip for me, and June is a busy time. I've yet to make the pilgrimage. No matter, one of these years I will. In the meantime, grappa is available in the supermarket, and the cherries I find locally.

Choose any firm black cherry variety. If you frequent an Italian grocer, ask for the best variety to put under grappa; they will know. Serve these cherries after dinner, as a digestive you eat rather than drink. One or two per person will be plenty, as they are very strong.

Cherries—as many as you care to preserve
Whole spices such as cinnamon, cloves, allspice, star anise
Grappa—enough to cover the cherries

Put the cherries in sterilized glass jars. For gifts, I like the kind with a rubber ring and a glass lid that snaps shut with a metal closure. Add the spices and cover with the grappa. Seal and store in a cool place for at least 6 months. If you preserve these in June, they will be ready to eat for Christmas.

Further Reading

Cookbooks: Italian and General

Accademia Italiana della Cucina, Touring Club Italiano. *Ricettario della cucina regionale italiana.* Bergamo: Bolis, 2001.

Andrews, Colman. *Flavors of the Riviera: Discovering Real Mediterranean Cooking.* New York: Bantam Books, 1996.

Artusi, Pellegrino. *The Art of Eating Well.* Translated by Kyle M. Phillips III. New York: Random House, 1996. Originally published as *La scienza in cucina e l'arte di mangiar bene: manuale pratico per le famiglie* (1891).

Bianchi, Anne. *From the Tables of Tuscan Women: Recipes and Traditions.* Hopewell, NJ: Ecco Press, 1995.

Bianchi, Anne, and Sandra Lotti. *Dolci Toscani: The Book of Tuscan Desserts.* Hopewell, NJ: Ecco Press, 1998.

Boni, Ada. *The Talisman Italian Cookbook.* Translated and augmented by Matilde La Rosa. 1950; New York: Crown, 1978.

Boscolo, Rossano, and Sergio Mei. *Ne carne ne pesce/Neither Meat nor Fish.* Sottomarina-Venice: Istituto Superiore Arti Culinarie Etoile, 1997.

Bressan, Marina, Giovanna Ludovico Giannattasio and Maurizio Grattoni d'Arcano. *Come mangiavamo: cibi e sapori del passato nel Friuli-Venezia Giulia.* Edited by Giovanna Ludovico Giannattasio. Montefalcone: Edizioni Della Laguna, 1996.

Bugialli, Giuliano. *The Fine Art of Italian Cooking.* 2nd edition. New York: Time Books, 1989.

———. *Foods of Italy.* New York: Stewart, Tabori & Chang, 1984.

Buonassisi, Vincenzo. *Pasta*. Translated by Elisabeth Evans. Wilton, CT: Lyceum Books, 1976. Originally published as *Il codice della pasta* (Milan: Rizzoli, 1973).

Calchera, Bianca Marcoz, Elida Noro Desaymonet, Luciana Faletto Landi, Maria Luisa Di Loreto, and Gemma Ouvrier. *Cucina di tradizione della Valle D'Aosta*. 1997; Pavone Canavese: Priuli & Verlucca, 2003.

Camporesi, Carla Geri. *Cooking with Olive Oil*. Lucca: Maria Pacini Fazzi, 1996.

———. *Siena e il suo Chianti*. Lucca: Maria Pacini Fazzi, 1996.

———. *Traditional Recipes from Florence*. Lucca: Maria Pacini Fazzi, 1999.

David, Elizabeth. *A Book of Mediterranean Food*. 2nd edition. London: Penguin, 1965.

———. *Italian Food*. Revised edition. New York: Penguin Books, 1999.

———. *South Wind through the Kitchen: The Best of Elizabeth David*. Compiled by Jill Norman. London: Penguin, 1998.

De Marinis, Chiara Gatti. *Il lardo di Colonnata*. Lucca: Maria Pacini Fazzi, 2002.

De'Medici, Lorenza. *The Renaissance of Italian Cooking*. London: Pavilion Books, 1989.

———. *The Villa Table*. London: Pavilion Books, 1993.

Dini, Sonia, trans. *Traditional Recipes of Lucchesian Farmers*. Lucca: Maria Pacini Fazzi, 1999.

Famija Albèisa, Ordine dei Cavalieri del Tartufo e dei Vini D'Alba. *Il grande libro della cucina albese*. Alba: Famija Albèisa, 1996.

Gallesi, Adriana. *I mangiari di una volta in Garfagnana*. Lucca: Maria Pacini Fazzi, 1993.

Gho, Paola, and Giovanni Ruffa, eds. *Ricette di osterie e ristoranti del Monferrato*. Bra: Slow Food, 1997.

Gray, Patience. *Honey from a Weed: Fasting and Feasting in Tuscany, Catalonia, the Cyclades and Apulia*. Totnes, UK: Prospect Books, 1986.

Grigson, Jane. *Jane Grigson's Vegetable Book*. London: Michael Joseph, 1978.

Grossi, Francesca. *Cucina tradizionale della Lunigiana*. Lucca: Maria Pacini Fazzi, 1995.

Hazan, Marcella. *Essentials of Classic Italian Cooking*. Revised edition. New York: Knopf, 1992.

Hazelton, Nika Standen. *The Swiss Cookbook*. New York: Atheneum, 1967.

Jenkins, Nancy Harmon. *Flavors of Tuscany: Traditional Recipes from the Tuscan Countryside*. New York: Broadway Books, 1998.

Kasper, Lynne Rossetto. *The Italian Country Table: Home Cooking from Italy's Farmhouse Kitchens*. New York: Scribner, 1999.

———. *The Splendid Table: Recipes from Emilia-Romagna, the Heartland of Northern Italian Food*. New York: William Morrow, 1992.

Kompatscher, Anneliese. *La cucina nelle Dolomiti*. Bolzano-Bozen: Athesia, 2001.

Lodi, Beppe, and Luciano De Giacomi. *Nonna Genia*. Revised edition. Cuneo: Araba Fenice, 1999.

Lotti, Sandra. *Sapori della Maremma*. Lucca: Maria Pacini Fazzi, 1997.

———. *A Taste of Tuscany*. Lucca: Maria Pacini Fazzi, 1998.

Maccioni, Alvaro. *Alvaro's Mamma Toscana*. London: Pavilion Books, 1998.

Marchese, Salvatore. *Cucina di Lunigiana*. Padova: Franco Muzzio, 1989.

Minerdo, Bianca, and Grazia Novellini, eds. *Ricette di osterie d'Italia, l'orto: 720 piatti dall'aglio alla zucca*. Bra: Slow Food, 2005.

Mollo, Claudio. *Cucina tradizionale dell'Isola d'Elba*. Lucca: Maria Pacini Fazzi, 2003.

Morganti, Paolo. *Prodotti veneti in cucina; Food and Wines from the Veneto*. Translated by Patricia Guy. Sommacampagna, Verona: Morganti, 2003.

Novellini, Grazia, ed. *Ricette di osterie d'Italia: 630 piatti di cucina regionale*. 6th edition. Bra: Slow Food, 2005.

———. *Ricette di osterie e ristoranti della Valle d'Aosta*. Bra: Slow Food, 2000.

Pallai, Sonia, with Claudia Buracchini and Laurent Coppini. *Ricettario di Siena: testimonianze di cucina e tradizioni di un popolo*. Siena: Comune di Siena/Headbox, 2002.

Petroni, Paolo. *The Complete Book of Florentine Cooking*. 4th edition. Firenze: Il Centauro, 2002.

Piras, Claudia, and Eugenio Medagliani, eds. *Specialità d'Italia: le regioni in cucina*. Koln: Konemann Verlagsgesellschaft, 2000.

Plotkin, Fred. *Recipes from Paradise: Life and Food on the Italian Riviera*. Boston: Little, Brown, 1997.

———. *La Terra Fortunata: The Splendid Food and Wine of Friuli-Venezia Giulia*. New York: Broadway Books, 2001.

Pontoni, Germano, and Giorgio Busdon, eds. *Frico e …* Udine: Ribis, 1998.

Pradelli, Alessandro Molinari. *La cucina ligure*. Rome: Newton & Compton, 1996.

Raspelli, Edoardo. *L'Italia a tavola con il re dei formaggi*. Reggio Emilia: Consorzio del Formaggio Parmigiano-Reggiano, n.d.

Romanelli, Leonardo, Carlo Macchi and Nanni Ricci. *Ricette di osterie di Firenze e Chianti*. Bra: Slow Food, 1997.

Romer, Elizabeth. *The Tuscan Year: A Life and Food in an Italian Valley*. New York: Atheneum, 1985.

Ross, Janet, and Michael Waterfield. *Leaves from Our Tuscan Kitchen, or How to Cook Vegetables*. 1899; New York: Atheneum, 1974.

Schmuckher, Aidano. *Feste e cucina in Liguria*. Boves: Araba Fenice, 2000.

Simili, Margherita, and Valeria Simili. *Sfida al matterello, sfoglia e dintorni*. Bologna: Gio, 2001.

Stearns, Osborne Putnam. *Italy on a Platter: Recipes for Gourmets*. Los Angeles: Ward Ritchie, 1965.

Turati, Laura. *Ribollita Panzanella e la cucina povera toscana*. Colognola ai Colli: Demetra, 1998.

Vischi, Carlo, and Elisa Zanotti. *Toscana via dei sapori*. Savigliano: Gribaudo, 2004.

Vitali, Benedetta. *Soffritto: Tradition and Innovation in Tuscan Cooking*. Berkeley, CA: Ten Speed Press, 2001.

Cookbooks: Bread and Baking

Bilheux, Roland, Alain Escoffier, Daniel Hervé and Jean-Marie Pouradier. *Special and Decorative Breads*. Translated by Rhona Poritzky-Lauvand and James Peterson. 2 vols. New York: Van Nostrand Reinhold, 1989. Originally published as *Pains spéciaux et décorés*, 2 vols. (Paris: St.-Honoré, 1987–1989).

Calvel, Raymond. *The Taste of Bread*. Translated by James J. MacGuire. Gaithersburg, MD: Aspen, 2001. Originally published as *Le goût du pain: comment le préserver, comment le retrouver* (Paris: J. Villette, 1990).

Field, Carol. *The Italian Baker*. New York: HarperCollins, 1985.

Glezer, Maggie. *Artisan Baking across America*. New York: Workman, 2000.

Hamelman, Jeffrey. *Bread: A Baker's Book of Techniques and Recipes*. Hoboken, NJ: Wiley, 2004.

Romer, Elizabeth. *Italian Pizza and Hearth Breads*. New York: Clarkson N. Potter, 1987.

Rorato, Giampiero. *Dolci e pani del Veneto*. Vicenza: Terra Firma/Regione del Veneto, 2002.

Simili, Margherita, and Valeria Simili. *Pane e roba dolce*. Bologna: Gio, 1997.

Wing, Daniel, and Alan Scott. *The Bread Builders: Hearth Loaves and Masonry Ovens*. White River Junction, VT: Chelsea Green, 1999.

Agriculture, Self-Sufficiency, Preserving

Ashworth, Suzanne. *Seed to Seed: Seed Saving and Growing Techniques for Vegetable Gardeners.* Decorah, IA: Seed Savers Exchange, 2002.

Aubert, Claude, ed. *Keeping Food Fresh: Old World Techniques and Recipes: The Gardeners & Farmers of Terra Vivante.* White River Junction, VT: Chelsea Green, 1999. Originally published as *Les conserves naturelles des quatre saisons* (Paris: Terre Vivante, 1989).

Bailey, Janet. *Keeping Food Fresh.* Revised edition. New York: Harper & Row, 1989.

Berry, Wendell. *The Art of the Commonplace: The Agrarian Essays of Wendell Berry.* Washington, DC: Counterpoint, 2002.

Cato. *On Farming/De Agricultura: A Modern Translation with Commentary by Andrew Dalby.* Totnes, UK: Prospect Books, 1998.

Coleman, Eliot. *The Four-Season Harvest: Organic Vegetables from Your Home Garden All Year Long.* White River Junction, VT: Chelsea Green, 1999. Revised edition of *The New Organic Grower's Four-Season Harvest* (1992).

Eck, Joe, and Wayne Winterrowd. *Living Seasonally: The Kitchen Garden and the Table at North Hill.* New York: Holt, 1999.

Emery, Carla. *The Encyclopedia of Country Living.* 9th edition. Seattle, WA: Sasquatch Books, 2003.

Graham, Joe M., ed. *The Hive and the Honey Bee: A New Book on Beekeeping Which Continues the Tradition of "Langstroth on the Hive and the Honeybee."* Revised edition. Hamilton, IL: Dadant, 1992.

Seymour, John. *The Complete Book of Self-Sufficiency.* 1976; London: Dorling Kindersley, 1996.

Thorez, Jean-Paul. *Le guide du jardinage biologique.* Mens: Terre Vivante, 2004.

Tudge, Colin. *Neanderthals, Bandits and Farmers: How Agriculture Really Began.* London: Weidenfeld & Nicolson, 1998.

———. *So Shall We Reap: How Everyone Who Is Liable to Be Born in the Next Ten Thousand Years Could Eat Very Well Indeed; and Why, in Practice, Our Immediate Descendants Are Likely to Be in Serious Trouble.* London: Allen Lane, 2003.

Guides and Reference

Bazzanti, Natale, and Carla Lazzarotto. *La qualità certificata: i prodotti DOP e IGP in Toscana.* Firenze: Agenzia Regionale per lo Sviluppo e l'Innovazione nel Settore Agricolo-Forestale/Regione Toscana, 2004.

Bordo, Valter, and Angelo Surrusca, eds. *L'Italia dei dolci.* Bra: Slow Food, 2003.

———. *L'Italia del pane.* Bra: Slow Food, 2002.

Bordo, Valter, Giacomo Mojoli, and Angelo Surrusca, eds. *Salumi d'Italia.* Bra: Slow Food, 2001.

Bufalari, Vieri, Andrea Semplici and Massimo Ricciolini. *Journey through Tuscany to Discover Typical Products.* Firenze: Giunti Gruppo Editoriale/Regione Toscana, 2001.

Chamberlain, Samuel. *Italian Bouquet: An Epicurean Tour of Italy.* New York: Gourmet, 1958.

Counihan, Carole M. *Around the Tuscan Table: Food, Family and Gender in Twentieth-Century Florence.* New York: Routledge, 2004.

Davidson, Alan. *Mediterranean Seafood.* 3rd edition. 1972; Totnes, UK: Prospect Books, 2002.

Gho, Paola, ed. *Osterie d'Italia 2004.* Bra: Slow Food, 2003.

Giavedone, Fabio, and Maurizio Gily, eds. *Guida ai vitigni d'Italia.* Bra: Slow Food, 2005.

Istituto Nazionale di Sociologia Rurale. *Atlante dei prodotti tipici: il pane.* Roma: RAI/AGRA, 2000.

Lappé, Frances Moore, and Anna Lappé. *Hope's Edge: The Next Diet for a Small Planet*. New York: Jeremy P. Tarcher/Putnam, 2003.

Lazzarotto, Carla, Walter Giorgi and Cecilia Piacenti, eds. *Toscana, la tradizione del gusto*. Firenze: Agenzia Regionale per lo Sviluppo e l'Innovazione nel Settore Agricolo-Forestale/Regione Toscana, 2004.

Manganelli, Vittorio, and Pierluigi Piumatti, eds. *Guida al vino quotidiano*. Bra: Slow Food, 2001.

McGee, Harold. *On Food and Cooking: The Science and Lore of the Kitchen*. Revised edition. New York: Scribner, 2004.

Milano, Serena, Raffaella Ponzio and Piero Sardo, eds. *L'Italia dei Presìdi*. Bra: Slow Food, 2004.

Montagné, Prosper. *The Larousse Gastronomique: The New American Edition of the World's Greatest Culinary Encyclopedia*. Edited by Jenifer Harvey Lang. New York: Crown, 1988.

Piumatti, Gigi, Piero Sardo and Cinzia Scaffidi, eds. *Il buon paese*. Bra: Slow Food, 2000.

Plotkin, Fred. *Italy for the Gourmet Traveler*. Boston: Little, Brown, 1996.

Root, Waverley. *The Food of Italy*. New York: Atheneum, 1971.

Rubino, Roberto, Piero Sardo and Angelo Surrusca, eds. *Formaggi d'Italia*. 4th edition. Bra: Slow Food, 2005.

Tempestini, Marzia. *Sapori e tradizioni di Toscana*. Firenze: Toscana Promozione Agenzia di Promozione Economica della Toscana, 2003.

History, Folklore, Culture, Environment

Allport, Susan. *The Primal Feast: Food, Sex, Foraging and Love*. New York: Harmony Books, 2000.

Bainbridge, John. *Another Way of Living: A Gallery of Americans Who Choose to Live in Europe*. New York: Holt, Rinehart and Winston, 1968.

Barzini, Luigi. *The Italians*. New York: Atheneum, 1964.

Bellonzi, Fortunato. *Proverbi toscani*. Firenze: Giunti Gruppo, 2000.

Cornelisen, Ann. *Women of the Shadows: Wives and Mothers of Southern Italy*. 1976; South Royalton, VT: Steerforth, 2001.

Falassi, Alessandro. *Folklore by the Fireside: Text and Context of the Tuscan Veglia*. Austin: Universtiy of Texas Press, 1980.

Fazio, Venera, and Delia De Santis, eds. *Sweet Lemons: Writings with a Sicilian Accent*. Mineola, NY: Legas, 2004.

Ginsborg, Paul. *Italy and Its Discontents, 1980–2001*. London: Penguin, 2001.

Honoré, Carl. *In Praise of Slow: How a Worldwide Movement Is Challenging the Cult of Speed*. Toronto: Knopf, 2004.

Jones, Tobias. *The Dark Heart of Italy*. London: Faber and Faber, 2003.

Nabhan, Gary Paul. *Coming Home to Eat: The Pleasures and Politics of Local Foods*. New York: Norton, 2002.

Richards, Charles. *The New Italians*. London: Penguin, 1995.

Periodicals

Behr, Edward. *The Art of Eating Quarterly*. Peacham, VT.

The Bread Bakers Guild of America. *Bread Lines*. Newsletter. North Versailles, PA: The Bread Bakers Guild of America.

Casamia cucina. Milan: Edizioni Idea Donna. Previously published as *La cucina di casa mia*.

Acknowledgments

A solitary endeavor like writing a cookbook only becomes a worthwhile and realizable project if a great many people lend it their collaboration and support. I was fortunate to have my first book enthusiastically embraced by many creative and talented people.

Andrea Luria was the first person to see what has now become this book—a small collection of recipes I had written for friends, relatives and guests who asked for them. She felt there was a possibility for a cookbook and encouraged me to write one. Andrea is a painter and, like many fine artists, is also a good and instinctive cook. On her frequent trips to Italy, she tasted many of the recipes in this book. The rest she took home with her to cook for her family and friends, making them her own in the process—something I wish for every one of my readers. She continues to be this book's most ardent supporter.

When I first met Karen Cossar, she was taking leave from a busy career in publishing and working in the language school in Siena where

I was enrolled. She eventually returned to Toronto and her career. It was a happy coincidence when she came back to Tuscany to visit. I hadn't heard she'd gone back to the world of publishing, nor did she know I was at work on a cookbook. It was Karen's enthusiasm that turned my dream into a reality, and it is because of her that I have not only a book but one that has found a great home at HarperCollins Canada.

The team at HarperCollins has been wonderful. Kirsten Hanson believed in the project from the get-go, and has done nothing but encourage me to stay true to my vision. I never dreamed a publisher would want to keep my working title, *Piano, Piano, Pieno.* It was Kirsten who felt this was the right title for the book, and for that I will always be grateful. Noelle Zitzer has been extraordinary, as have the rest of the team, including Iris Tupholme, Felicia Quon, Steve Osgoode and Eric Jensen. Sharon Kish designed the cover and interior of the book and has made it look like *my* book in a way I never imagined. I also had the good fortune of working with freelance editor Shaun Oakey. His rigorous attention to detail and countless useful suggestions have been particularly appreciated.

In Italy I owe a great debt to a long list of people. First of all is Alessandro Mini, a.k.a. "Stioppo," who helps us manage the restoration of Petraia to a working farm after more than fifty years of abandonment. He keeps me furnished with a constant supply of wild boar, pheasant, venison, his exceptional olive oil, wine and his father's famous *amaro.* His friendship and generosity have helped make our life here richer than we ever imagined, so warmly has he adopted us into his large family of friends and relatives, including his parents, Elda and Bruno, and his brother, Andrea Mini; the Gambelli family, including Roberta, Giuseppe and Ersilia; Franco Notturni; Adriano Pagni; Luciano Pierazzi and his son Alessandro; and Daniele and Carlo Cantalici, Marco Panichi, Ivano and Christian Fineschi. Instrumental to our endeavors here have been

Franco Tanzini, Remigio Bordini, Paolo Semplici, Monica Coletta, Elisa Ianni, David Mattasini and Brutto and Bella Senese. Along the way, they have tasted many of the dishes in this book, and shared with me recipes, stories, seedlings, saplings, food and wine. Marcello Regoli gave me his recipe for *spaghetti ai cinque sapori*.

Tom and Melinda McMahon invited me to their home in San Gimignano both to bake bread and to break bread. More than twelve years ago Tom founded the Bread Bakers Guild of America, the organization that deserves most of the credit for the emergence of the ever-growing industry of artisanal bakers in North America. I have learned an enormous amount from watching Tom bake and listening to him talk about bread. Mostly what I learned from him is how much I have left to learn. Melinda's fine palate has been the judge of several of my loaves, and she has shared with me some of the stories of the great Tuscan food she was lucky enough to grow up eating. I am especially indebted to her for the recipe for her family's *torta con becchi*.

Robin Young braved being snowed in at Petraia one particularly brutal Tuscan winter to test the bread chapter as well as several other recipes in the book. Didier Rosada generously allowed me to pick his brain as I wrote and refined the bread chapter. He reviewed some of the more technical parts for me and answered many questions I had. Alicia Peres helped me to track down some of the quotes in the introduction. Naomi Duguid lent us her ear early on, when we were looking for a publisher, and generously provided us with much good advice. Patricia Van Der Leun was one of the people who believed in the book at a very early stage, and who tried to find a home for it in the United States. Deborah Verginella reviewed the Italian text.

The guests who have come to our *agriturismo* have all been gracious and have eaten most of the dishes in this book. They brought welcome company with them and have generously given our project their best word of mouth. Thanks to them, our dining room never seems to want for appreciative visitors.

I am grateful for the love and support of my siblings and their families: Thomas McKenna, Patricia Poland, Denis McKenna and Catherine Lawless and all my *nipoti*. My parents died before we moved to Petraia, but I know they would have loved it here as much I do. From both of them I inherited a fondness for life on the farm. My mother had a reputation for both her cooking and her baking, and it was from her that I gained early on an appreciation for good food. My father was a hunter-gatherer and *bon vivant extraordinaire* who taught his family to find not only beauty but a delicious food source in the wild.

Lastly, there are not words to thank my husband, Michael, whose gorgeous photographs grace the pages of this book. He has labored tirelessly on the project, working hundreds of hours, not just taking pictures but also editing many revisions of the text. He spent countless months over the past decade traveling with me in our camper van to some of Italy's lesser-known corners for my research, and he tasted, time and again, every recipe in the book. I don't know how he managed it amidst the pressure of starting a business in Canada and a winery in Italy, but he always had time to help me when I needed him and, thank goodness, he never seems to run out of patience with my endless culinary obsessions.

Index